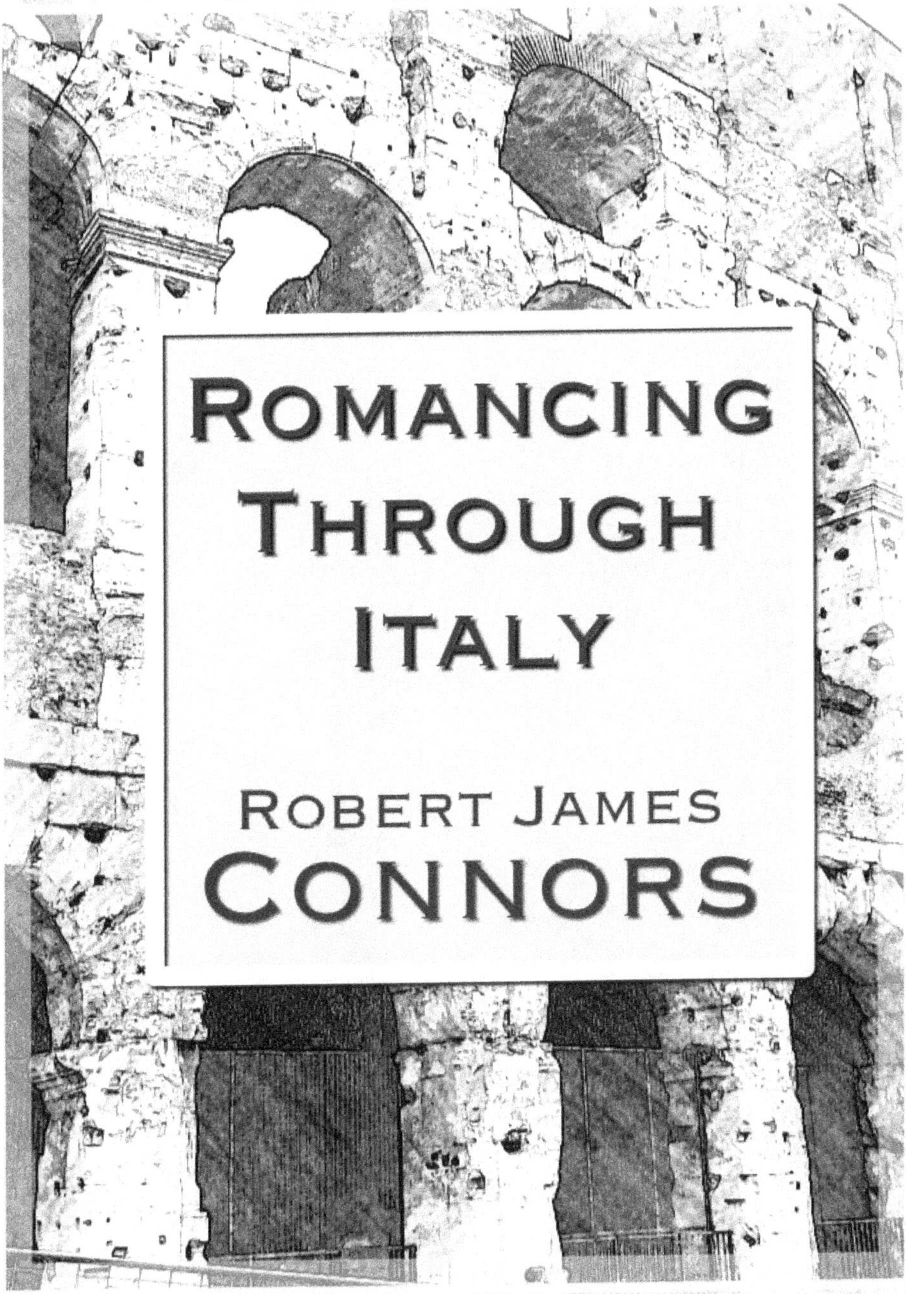

Romancing Through Italy

Robert James Connors

Romancing Through Italy - Second Edition

© 2017 Robert James Connors

Inquiries may be directed to Plumeria Publishing
3311 Harbor Beach Drive, Lake Wales, Florida, 33859-8082.
www.plumeriapublishing.net

Publisher's Cataloging-in-Publication data

Names: Connors, Robert James, author.
Title: Romancing through Italy / Robert James Connors.
Description: Lake Wales, FL: Plumeria Publishing, 2017.
Identifiers: ISBN 978-0-9991904-8-7 | LCCN 2017947939
Subjects: LCSH Italy--Description and travel. | World War, 1939-1945--Personal narratives, American. | BISAC TRAVEL / Europe / Italy
Classification: LCC DG430.2 .C66 2017 | DDC 914.504--dc23

Connors, R. J. -1951-
        Romancing Through Italy – 2nd Ed.

Printed on Acid-free paper

Credits
Susan C. Connors, Sr. Editor
Cover: Curchy Design Studios
Photos:
Florence Duomo: George Cihocki
Goatherd: Susan C. Connors
Interior images by author

The Italian Peninsula, and some of our stops along the way

Special thanks to:

Susan Connors,
Claudio Albertazzi and Silvana AF Conversano,
Maria Pia Balboni, Pierpaolo Bonarelli,
Pina Carpentieri and Gino Scarpato, Pasquale Ciacco,
Susan and George Cihocki, Paul Comkowycz,
Rossella Contiero and Renzo Bortoli,
Grace Engholm, Daniela and Alessandro Ronny Ferretti,
Umberto Magnani, Sante Massini, Arrigo Montanari,
Stefania Saccani and Paolo Schianchi, Antonella Sinopoli,
our treasured traveling companions,
dozens of other friends we've made along the way,
and
**The Veterans of the armed forces of the world
who stood against tyranny and Fascism**

<u>In Memoriam</u>

George Fortunato DeLuca
Giovanni Gitti
Arnaldo Naldi
Fran Updike
Mary Updike

Dedicated to all who create art and beauty,

or have served, in order to oppose wrongs,

seek justice and freedom,

and create a better world.

Table of Contents

A Propitious Introduction

It was the proverbial example of the square peg and the round hole. The low, arcing shape of the narrow two-lane tunnel that loomed ahead was obviously impassable for our tall, and very rectangular, inter-city passenger coach, which slowed to a crawl as it approached its dark maw. It was clear that the tunnel wasn't built with our bus in mind, and now, wedged between a looming mountain and a sheer drop to the sea, we wondered what sort of solution Italian ingenuity would produce.

My wife Susan and I had confidently left nearby Sorrento en route to the famed Amalfi coast, sightseeing as our bus climbed up the steeply sloping mountains that offered glimpses of Mount Vesuvio looming over the sparkling waters of the Gulf of Napoli. Atop the narrow ridge we had suddenly caught our first view of the open sea to the south. The peninsula rises to more than 1,100 meters, or more than 3,700 feet, at its highest. We had chosen the front

1

right seat hoping for a good view of the Latteri Mountains and Italy's rocky Amalfi coast, but perhaps had received more than expected. The view that appeared before us seemed to be, terrifyingly, straight down, without even a low guardrail between our bus and a drop of perhaps two thousand feet.

Our camera had come out to capture the image of a fishing boat leaving a curving wake through the deep blue of the water, pulling a clearly-visible seine net. It was as if seen from an airplane. To our left, sheer walls of rock rose nearly a thousand feet above our heads, defying even trees to gain a treacherous foothold. To our right was the sheer precipice. An expanse of blue sky arced over sparkling Mediterranean waters where, impossibly far below, waves dashed against the face of the cliff, rebounding in powerful surges back toward distant Sicily.

We tensed as we passed around heart-stopping curves, goggle-eyed at the scenery. As our bus snaked along the narrow, twisting roadway, few intrepid drivers had taken the rare opportunities to pass us. No doubt we were leading an entourage as we approached the small tunnel ahead. Before us was the storied challenge. There was no possibility of turning around. Our knuckles were whitened by our grips on the metal bar that seemed our only defense against a sudden and terrifying plunge.

No doubt cut through the solid rock of the mountain many years earlier, when motorized traffic was uncommon, the narrow arc ahead could accommodate the square shape of our bus only if we took to the center, straddling the double stripe. That's exactly what our driver proceeded to do, clearly comfortable with this often-repeated maneuver accompanied by the loud blaring of the buses' distinctive two-note horn. "OoookAnnnnng" reverberated through the very seats, only to be echoed by a returning two-note sound. No, it wasn't an echo, but another bus approaching from the opposite direction, using the same center-of-the-road technique. The on-coming headlights gave us another moment of angst.

Both buses came to a stop near the center of the tunnel, with warning flashers on. In response, no doubt, to some unwritten rule, our driver promptly put our bus into reverse. Our trailing entourage of vehicles seemed familiar with the drill as well, and passengers dutifully leaped from their cars, waving their arms and shouting to stop the approach of yet more cars.

True to form, Italy was introducing us to its enchanting ways. Glimpsed through our rear-view mirror, the entire line of traffic began snaking backwards like a giant inch-worm, a couple of meters at a time, in a scene evocative of Italy of imagination. We eventually found ourselves out of the tunnel, where the opposing bus, trailed by its own entourage, quickly squeezed past us, allowing us to resume our journey with the horn blaring as before.

The year was 1995, and it was our first trip to Italy together. Even though it's a place known as the heart of romance, we found plenty of other sorts of experiences, including some sad, some that brought tears of laughter, and others that left us feeling haunted. We had embarked on a voyage of discovery of new places, experiences, and adventures.

During multiple visits over two decades, we wandered through ghost towns, were stopped by military police, delighted in charming hilltop towns and brooding Etruscan ruins, watched artists create spectacular treasures, and visited a park of monsters. But most importantly, we made friends, creating bonds that endure for lifetimes. The stories and adventures related here are all true (although a few names have been changed to protect the innocence of bystanders and friends).

Despite the legendary beauty of the Italian landscape, the famous landmarks, and the wealth of art, architecture, and history that permeates the nation, it was the Italian people themselves who made the deepest impression upon us. Their openness to strangers, the joy of living that they exhibit every day, even the peculiarities of their lifestyle seemed to elevate the commonplace to become special. These are a few of the stories we gathered, the insights we gained, and the people we came to love.

An Un-Guided Tour

It was apparent to me even in my childhood that life is not meant to be spent in one place. I was quick to succumb to the wanderlusts that frequently walk in step with us in our youth. Before I reached my twentieth year I had stuck out my thumb and traveled, upon the kindness of strangers and the fifty dollars in my pocket, to pass the Gateway Arch in St. Louis, across the high plains to Colorado, Idaho, Oregon, and Washington. The Rocky Mountains, capped with summer snow, surpassed any wonder I had ever imagined I would see in my lifetime, and then the Cascades exceeded them. I thus learned early the benefits, and the challenges, of travel. It was a seminal part of my education, as it should be for each of us.

I was still a young man when I'd had the good fortune to be spotted across a crowded room by a beautiful woman, who decided, however improbably, that I was worth an investment of her time. Having just moved to Fort Lauderdale, Florida for work, and rather lost and friendless in the city, my early-evening exploration of the neighborhood had led me into a new restaurant where I ordered a beer at the bar. Unbeknownst to me, as I sat busily calculating my new living expenses on a napkin, my quiet presence had been noted. A feminine voice at my shoulder suggested that, with her degree in mathematics, she could probably solve my problem. I quickly wadded the napkin, and turned to stare into a pair of sea-green eyes set over a mischievous grin.

Behind her smile I detected a hint of sadness, and was determined to find out why. I eventually learned that she had survived both a painful divorce, and a head-on collision with a drunk driver only three months earlier. She was enjoying her first night out after weeks of hospitalization. The courses of our existence are full of unpredictable twists, and that near-tragedy somehow led us to the same place in time. In retrospect, it seemed fated.

She showed me a recent photograph of herself with the largest of her collection of stuffed-toy pandas, most gifts from friends who had learned of her delight in the antics of the improbable black-eyed bears. She and the bear made a close match, each with their eyes set in black rings, Susan smiling through her recovery, the three-foot bear clutched in her arms. It would be weeks before I realized that her degree was not in mathematics, but adventure. She was a flight attendant.

Her career had been remarkable, most notably for the tragedy she had narrowly avoided being a part of only five months before our meeting. She had swapped a flight on her work rotation to attend a class reunion. It was a fateful decision. Caught in a violent thunderstorm while attempting to land, the plane had crashed. Her parents and classmates withheld the news for the long weekend, hiding newspapers and keeping the television off. She was devastated to learn that some of her friends, including the young woman who had taken her seat, were among those lost in the disaster. Her auto accident had followed only two months after that first brush with death. She was a survivor, a cat with nine lives.

Susan and I had had different life experiences, philosophies, and even musical tastes. She was four years older, and at a time when I was just discovering Jefferson Airplane, she was already exploring the world, taking her parents on trips to Europe, or wandering around Australia and Polynesia. Her job had allowed her to visit such destinations as Fiji, Tahiti, New Zealand, and

Japan. She was the real thing, a 'jet-setter.'

Susan was certainly not my Grace Slick, and I was not her Perry Como, but somehow our relationship was very comfortable. We loved finding the things we both enjoyed, each learning to share the others' passions. I took up golf, and she hiked with me to the top of Arizona's Mount Wrightson. We quickly became best friends. Neither of us were seeking new entanglements, but we somehow began to see each other on a regular basis. We 'clicked' on a level that was immensely rewarding, talking for hours about the world, and things we wanted from life.

I was enchanted by this determined woman. We shared a love of adventure, and she insisted that we take advantage of travel opportunities. She wanted to share many of the places she had already seen, as well as make new discoveries together. We were destined to do both. Perhaps because neither of us expected to find new love, we were surprised by the intensity of our relationship. Our wedding was followed by a trip to explore the mountains and canyons of Kauai.

Before our first, fateful visit to Italy together, we were fortunate enough to receive the advice of a friend. We had met Fortunato George DeLuca as a retiree in our small Florida town of Lake Wales. He modestly mentioned that he had been a teacher of both art and Italian language in New York schools, and he seemed to have one foot in each of these very different worlds. His experiences and the bonds they forged became a significant part of our own experiences in Italy, and gave us a deeper insight into the people of that land. I met him when he was already grizzled with age, although still quite sharp of wit, and full of wisdom. His modest way of describing his own life, typical of many veterans of the war, left out details that would only later come to light.

"You lived in Italy?" I asked one day when he mentioned his home there as we worked on an art project. He smiled. He had gone back, he told me, to reclaim a heritage, but admitted that his first return was more difficult. He had fought on the front lines in some of the toughest battles of the Second World War as part of the U.S. Army's 88th Infantry, the famed 'Blue Devils.'

He was an unlikely warrior, standing only a rumor taller than five feet, and we questioned him about his experiences there. Like many veterans, he didn't like to talk much about the war, but upon gentle prodding began to share some stories.

Much of the war in Italy had been fought in terrible conditions on steep terrain far from field hospitals. Some of the combat was face-to-face with the enemy. George's hands, skilled in many creative things, had no doubt performed darker deeds than his lively expression disclosed. He and his friends had done what the times had demanded of them. They had become, as Tom Brokaw later said, "The Greatest Generation."

George explained that for time immemorial his ancestors had owned a villa on Capri, but had lost it in the 1930's. He left the reason for that loss unspoken, but my thoughts went to the events of the war and Fascist rule, which had disrupted so many families, created so many refugees, and sustained years of evil and subterfuge. George had been able to re-purchase it, an investment no doubt in emotional triumph. He had lived there seasonally for many years and knew the island well. After so much turmoil, it had come down to his roots, represented by stone and *terracotta*.

George also revealed that he would be traveling to Italy with mutual friends at the same time as us, and invited us to join them for a 'festival.' It was serendipity. Our plans were soon coordinated, and we arranged to rendezvous with George and his party, first in Rome, and then again in Bologna.

George taught me to pronounce a few important phrases in Italian, and gave me a few social suggestions, but ultimately, we would be on our own. The language barrier in the 'touristy' areas wasn't a worry, as we knew that many hotel and transit clerks spoke English, but I wanted to be prepared. Susan had shared with me her earlier cautionary experience with crossed communications in Italy. Invited to attend a wedding in Italy, she had traveled with a girlfriend. Familiar with her sketchy navigational skills, her tale of getting lost during a short afternoon drive the day of the rehearsal dinner was not surprising to me.

They had wandered the unlighted roads after sunset in a long and almost futile hunt for the landmarks that had been so apparent during the daylight hours. That prominent church bell tower had completely disappeared in the darkness. The entire pre-wedding dinner was delayed as the guests organized search parties to hunt for their missing American friends. At last they walked in, defended by apologies and sheepish grins. Their embarrassment was temporary at least, they thought, as the rest of the guests settled down to their delayed dinner.

At the end of the typical Italian feast of multiple courses of appetizers, pastas, salads, meats and fish, cheeses and wine, it came time for *i dulci*, the sweets. As everyone ordered desserts, Susan eyed a large bowl of fruit, then surprised the hosts and the chef by requesting *una pesce*. Her own surprise arrived on a platter in the form of a whole grilled fish. She had expected a peach, *una pesca*. Although fish for dessert may not have been funny at the time, we laughed at the story until we had tears in our eyes, and promised ourselves we wouldn't repeat the mistake. The pronunciations of "pesh-e" and "pes-ca" were firmly lodged in our brains.

Fast Trains, Fast Friends

Travel by bus and train led us to many memorable encounters, but the first was the most significant, and resulted from our complete ignorance of how to travel by train in the 1990's. We arrived in Milano after a breath-taking descent over the snow-covered Alps, and were soon immersed in the strange ways of Italy. We had missed a connecting flight to Naples, and had been forced into a fateful change of travel plans. We found a hotel, relaxed and showered, receiving a reminder in the process that the 'C' on an Italian water faucet does not stand for cold, but rather *calda*, as in scalding!

The next morning, a brief taxi ride brought us to the *Stazione Centrale*, where we waded through the complexities of the Italian train system, and its several classes of trains. We were thoroughly unaware of the wisdom of reserving seats only because we were unable to understand the busy ticket agent.

Wandering through the nearly-full train with our luggage we spied an empty compartment, opened the glass door and settled in. Just as the train was preparing to depart we were joined by a family of four, who entered without a word. We smiled at the classic nuclear family of parents, son and daughter as they stowed their luggage and chose their seats. They smiled back, and we began to make clumsy attempts to speak with them.

The natural hospitality of most Italians became our ally as we pulled out our dictionary to attempt to ease into some basic communication. Introductions were eventually exchanged, and we learned that the adults were Pina and Gino, and their children Rosalba, perhaps nine years of age, and her younger brother Jonathan, about seven. "*Americani,*" we told them, and they nodded enthusiastically.

"*Dové habita?*" we asked, "where do you live?"

"*Lago di Como,*" we were told, and marveled at the idea that they resided near the legendary beauty of that alpine lake, surrounded by snow-capped peaks. We could never imagine the wonderful twist which life was about to offer us, and the many wonderful days we were to spend beside that deep stronghold within the embrace of the Alps. They were equally impressed with the idea of Florida.

Our camera came out, and we quickly learned through their explanations and our dictionary that it wasn't a 'camera' in Italy, for that is the word for a room, as in a '*camera di letto,*" a bedroom. Ours was a '*macchina fotografica,*" a photograph machine. I realized then the reason we took our word from Leonardo da Vinci's famous invention, which was called a *camera obscura.* It was, after all, an entire room darkened except for a pinhole, which allowed light to enter and, without the use of a lens, project an image of the exterior on the opposite wall, albeit upside-down.

While we tried to use the Italian versions of our American names, Susana and Roberto, Pina insisted on using our American pronunciations. Mine came out as 'Raa-bairt,' but it was nevertheless pleasing to hear her say it. Everyone smiled enough that there was no need to pose for the photos we snapped.

As we sped along on the train at speeds of 160 kilometers per hour, the daughter, Rosalba, drew out a tiny yellow notepad, her delicate fingers clutching a pencil as she made sketches of things she had seen on their trip. One sketch was of a beautiful facade of a small church, which I admired greatly. Rosalba refers to the first pink blush of dawn, a fitting name for a beautiful child. Her eyes sparkled as she patiently explained that the church in her drawing was in her hometown of Lierna. "It's very beautiful," we told her, "and some day we will see it." We didn't imagine that "someday" would be only weeks away.

Our dictionary became quite well-thumbed during the remainder of our all-day trip, and Pina's ready smile, quick laugh, and relentless efforts to communicate made the time fly. Gino watched it all with male reserve, chiming

10

in when he thought we might be having difficulty.

We gradually learned that they were returning to visit family in Napoli for Easter, having moved from the *regione* of Campagna to the north some years before for Gino's job. His work, he explained, was for the railroad, but it was very important for them to 'go home' for important holidays.

Families lie at the heart of Italian culture, and the importance of blood relations is held high, for these relationships were the very keys to survival for generations untold. Defense against brigands, or even hostile neighbors, began with family. The strength of family and the local community were the solid bedrock that served to shelter them from the frequent waves of invaders that swept over this land, many of whom gradually became integrated into the communities they had sought to dominate or plunder.

Saracens, Phoenicians, and Greeks subsumed previous cultures in turn. Senone Gauls, a Celtic tribe, had defeated the Etruscans and sacked early Rome itself. Rival cities and tribes of Italy had made war upon the Romans before being conquered. Arabs, Normans, and Spaniards each had their days of influence, triumph and disaster. Those lessons run deep in the Italian psyche. Always family was the cement, the mortar that bound people to each other, and gave them the ability to survive.

In the modern world of job-related mobility, holidays are peak travel times. Nothing is more important to the Italians than opportunities to reunite family, no less true when the family has been scattered.

Our travel by train was an enjoyable experience as Bologna, Firenze, and Roma were reached, each brief stop sliding by as we noted the peculiar landmarks that symbolized them. The Apennine mountains and their dark tunnels, the churches and towns, the tractors and mules, horses, sheep and chickens, each took a starring role in sequence as this most magical of train trips unfolded.

We struggled to identify the fabulous yellow rapeseed flowers filling field after Tuscan field we passed, basking in fresh glory under the growing warmth of the spring sun. Wild poppies bobbed their red crowns along roads and railways. "*Bella, bella, bellissimo!*" we said at each new wonder, and our new friends smiled and nodded their agreement.

We marveled at the impressive number of construction cranes, known as *gru*, that dominated the skylines of even small villages. The name *gru* also applies to the avian species of crane. When stone is the principal material of construction, even a small remodeling job requires heavy lifting. We created smiles when we suggested that the *gru* must be the national bird of Italy.

Before we reached Napoli, Pina began to repeat the phrase "*vieni a nostra casa*," and we came to understand that she was inviting us to come to visit them at their home! These people, whom we had only just met, without a mutual acquaintance or proper introduction, were insisting that we should take advantage of their hospitality. Into my hand she pressed a scrap of paper with their phone number and address scratched upon it, and explained that they would be at home when we planned to return to nearby Milano before our departure. "*Sì, sì,*" we agreed, "*grazie mille!*" We would make an effort, give them a call to thank them again, but little expected that we would actually visit. Such are most often the results of good intentions and casual encounters.

Disembarking at the Napoli terminal just before dusk, we walked behind as they ran to meet their family, with parents, aunts, and cousins apparently turning out in force to escort them to their special holiday gathering. They made certain that their family met their new American friends. These were indeed very special people, and we promised to stay in touch. Our introduction to the amazing warmth of Italy had begun.

It was only years later that we came to realize that, in our unfamiliarity with the train system, we had invaded their reserved private compartment, and in a perfect display of Italian hospitality, had been accepted without a word. Today's system of reserved seating would have prevented our chance meeting. It was a friendship that would last through the years.

The Heart of the South

We were shuttled from the Napoli train to our hotel by an exuberant and animated taxi-driver, who seemed delighted to be carrying guests to a waterfront hotel, Susan's splurge for the night. We were met by a formally-dressed doorman, and ushered through the check-in procedure. Used to doing the heavy lifting of travel, I was enjoying the luxury. If I was a bit spoiled, the coming days would cure that.

Our room offered a private balcony overlooking the boulevard of Via Partenope, the waterfront marina, and a large castle. We lingered there for a few minutes attempting to memorize the distinctly Neapolitan view. That day small boats bobbed in rows on the gentle waves that washed their berths, and white clouds floated serenely above the blue of the sea. Streams of pedestrians moved to and fro along the sidewalks below, and shorebirds darted above the waters in search of stray cast-off fish.

Dominating our view was the castle. The fact that we were really in historic Italy sank in. We realized that in the two prior days, most of the things we had seen were modern. Here was the symbol of the city, the *Castel dell'Ovo*, or Castle of the Egg. Time to investigate.

We learned that Ruggiero the Norman had constructed it in 1140 as his private residence on the small island of Megaride, and became only another in a long series of foreign rulers to dominate the southern peninsula. It was built upon the site and foundations of an opulent First Century BC villa known as the "*Castrum Lucullanum*," which had been built by a Roman patrician with a fun, tongue-twisting name: Lucius Licinius Lucullus. Our ears began to tune more closely to the entertaining syllables of the Italian language.

Legend tells of a magic egg hidden deep within the foundations of the *Castel dell'Ovo* by the Roman poet, Virgil, who was also known as a powerful sorcerer. The egg, or *ovo*, was believed to hold the key to the future of the castle and the city of Napoli. Like Napoli itself, it had survived the eruption of Pompeii.

Our experience meeting Pina and Gino had left us very open to meeting more Italians, and we began to observe them, communicating when we could. We were fortunate that we had started our exploration of Italy in what is undoubtedly the most intensely Italian city. Situated well to the south, it is removed from the continental influences that have given Milano its cosmopolitan, trans-European flavor. There the proximity of Switzerland, France, even Germany and northern European cultures, has somewhat diluted and moderated the traditional Italian lifestyles and traditions. In Napoli we found the flavor of a large city that was still closely tied to the life of rural farms and villages.

Napoli makes an impression. Wandering through narrow streets, one passes a compact blend of busy shops surmounted by aging, post-war apartment blocks. Festoons of laundry drape overhead, a sky full of sheets, towels, skirts, jeans and overalls that dangle between the buildings. Narrow balconies lend a foothold to pots burgeoning with herbs, especially fresh basil, that make ideal pairings with the freshly-made buffalo-milk mozzarella that is the pride of the region.

The scenery was great. The islands and mountainous coasts of the Bay of Naples have always been an attraction, and in Roman times the bay was popular as a summer resort away from the heat of the city. Bracketed by the rocky arms of the *Sorrentina* Peninsula to the south and those of the *Marrechiaro* to the north, the waters Italians call the *Golfo di Napoli* are crossed by numerous vessels, large and small. Above that landscape looms the foreshortened remains of *Vesuvio*, which hasn't erupted since 1945.

A fresh and breezy day in Napoli is a delight, and invites a wandering walk while absorbing the smells of this new world. Aromas of fresh-baked bread and diesel fumes, flowers and wood smoke took turns making their impressions. Scattered clouds slid across the sky like a fleet of swift sailing ships, their regalia flung before them.

Sounds, too, are distinctive in the city. The noisy roar of the traffic, which seems invariably to fashions five lanes out of three, echoes through canyon-like streets. Drivers jockey for position at every stop as though the starting flag of the Gran Prix was only moments away. Windshield washers with soapy sponges and squeegees ply their sometimes-unwelcome trade at intersections, and delivery boys on *motorini*, especially Vespas, spar with rumbling city buses for pavement space, sometimes dashing onto sidewalks for shortcuts through the sea of parked cars.

Three-wheeled *Ape* trucks laden with bags of mortar and ceramic tile whine along in the flow, mustachioed workman-drivers often reminding us of video game characters. (Interestingly, *Ape* is pronounced with two syllables, "ah-pay," meaning 'bee,' so-called because of the insistent buzzing of their tiny engines. *Vespa* means 'wasp.') Pigeons dart deftly away from the myriad motorbikes and scooters, while pedestrians scurry to cross boulevards that find traffic barely delayed by the inconvenience of changing traffic signals.

Wandering away from the busier quarters into the quiet areas, we passed through the shaded streets into a district of banks and retail stores fronting graceful four and five-story buildings. Every third door appeared to be a *pizzeria or trattoria*, a *gelateria* featuring the frozen, creamy delight of Italians everywhere, or a *'bar'* offering *espresso, cappuccino*, liqueurs and pastries. The smells of food overwhelmed. Italians are obviously also fond of not only Italian *panini*, but even Chinese noodles, Indian curried rice, and other ethnic foods.

Eventually our explorations led us back to upscale shopping areas, where we followed a stream of tourists, and perhaps a few pilgrims, to the broad *Piazza del Duomo* and the remarkable cathedral, known as the Duomo, that lends its name. A fantasy of Gothic architecture, it features hundreds of arches, spires, and statues that dazzle the eye. Just across the street we found the *Galleria Umberto I*, which we had seen touted at the hotel. We paused to gaze upward at the mammoth archway that beckoned us to enter this pedestrian refuge, and were awed by the twenty-meter high arc of glass roof, constructed in hundreds or perhaps thousands of panels. They enclosed four long blocks of buildings that meet at a roofed-over crossroads.

The sounds of traffic died away in the Galleria, and we strolled slowly, admiring the rich displays of fashion and jewelry that filled dozens of windows. More than a shopping mall, this was a veritable community of shops, apartments and a variety of offices and businesses within a once-futuristic glass dome. Constructed between 1887 and 1891, it was part of the renewal of Napoli's urban center, and named after the first king of unified Italy.

We bought *gelato* at a shop inside the Galleria, and stopped to attempt translations of bronze memorial plaques. The floors were paved with tiny mosaic tiles in ornate patterns featuring zodiacal signs and whimsy. Wafts of fresh-baked pastry aromas tempted us, and displays of fashion eye wear at the *ottica* made us gasp at the prices Italians paid for style.

On the opposite side of the Galleria we passed the famous statue of Leonardo, the brilliant artist from the tiny village of Vinci, which dominates a small park. Across the street the plain facade of La Scala, the city's premier opera house, hid the extravagant décor of the interior, designed to impress royalty. We gawked openly at the tiers of golden balconies.

Climbing to the Capo di Monte district of the city to explore, we found shops filled with ceramic fantasies, brightly-colored flowers, human figures, ships and animals shining with glaze, all created by craftsmen using skills refined over many generations.

Sated at last by the opulent displays, and longing for the earthier side of the city, we wandered back to the working-class districts and found our dinner at an authentic and inviting *pizzeria*, where our order was perfectly crisped and slightly charred on the bottom in under two minutes over the flames of a 1,200° F wood-fired oven. We quietly shared a bottle of wine and our impressions of the first stages of our Italian journey.

To Rome and Tragedy

We arrived in *Roma* by train in late afternoon. Rome, with its busy expressways, multiple train stations, and threads of underground 'Metro' lines, is a daunting challenge for first-time visitors. We managed to find a phone at the *stazione*, and after a couple of attempts, eventually connected with a friend of George's, who managed to give us basic directions. Our travels would again depend upon the assistance of Italian strangers.

We rode the Metro, changed trains as instructed, called again, and were given an address that we scribbled down for an accommodating *tassista*, or taxi driver. The windows of his taxi were filled with passing scenes of the bustling city, the streets an incomprehensible maze as we attempted to follow our progress on a folded map. *"Ecco!"* he announced with a smile as we stopped on a well-groomed residential street, only to realize that he had already passed the address in the previous block. He carefully backed up through the sparse traffic to find our destination.

We stood looking up at a row of six-story apartment buildings, balconies trimmed with balustrades and dentil-work. Our luggage stood on the sidewalk as we studied the tiny names adjacent to the buzzer-buttons on a building directory, but could not find the name we had been given on the phone. Several minutes of frustrating reading, checking adjacent building directories, and wondering what to do followed. We tried pushing a button with a similar name. No reply. We tried another, and repeated the name we were given to an understandably-confused resident, but got nowhere.

Finally, at another wrong button, someone pressed the buzzer, and we were at least admitted to the lobby. Susan was holding the door as I began moving our suitcases, when suddenly a man excitedly approached us. To our surprise it was our taxi driver, waving my wallet! He had been several kilometers away when he glanced into his back seat and saw it there, where I had set it while counting out our fare. We realized that if we hadn't been delayed at the door, he would never have found us. Repeatedly refusing a tip, he dashed away with a smile. Our faith in both human nature and the twists of fate had just taken a turn for the better. From that time on I stopped carrying my cash in my critically-essential wallet.

Just as the taxi driver was off again to find his next fare, the elevator door opened to reveal a well-dressed young man, who smiled and addressed Susan. "Signora Connors? I am Luciano. Here, let me help!" Grabbing a pair of suitcases, he began loading our bags into the lift, and we were whisked into a luxurious apartment, marble floors reflecting crystal chandeliers, already occupied by this young man's family, as well as George's sister Emily, and our friends, Mary and Fran, sisters and art patrons whom we knew from Lake Wales. They had arrived the previous day from the United States. Our friend George, we were assured, would join the group momentarily. It was a reassuring reunion for uncertain, first-time wanderers in a strange land.

George arrived looking pleased with himself. We later learned that he had been making further arrangements for our group. He spent most of the evening chatting in Italian with our hosts. Unable to follow their conversation, we listened as the other Americans with us spoke about their travel experiences, and we shared our own stories.

Our travels that day had prevented us from keeping to any semblance of a meal schedule, and by the time dinner was served that evening, we were famished. We tried not to embarrass ourselves as we partook of a traditional Italian multiple-course dinner. Successive courses of *prosciutto*, cheese, fish, fruit, bowls of green salads, pasta, and the lightest pastries were passed around the large table.

When dinner was over, Luciano drove us and our luggage to another apartment nearby, where arrangements had been made to house us. We were introduced to an elderly Italian couple, led into a luxurious bedroom, and told to make ourselves at home. Our hosts, we were told, were friends of George, and were happy to host important American visitors.

Left without an interpreter, and exhausted from our travels, we soon retired. We awoke the following morning to find a silent apartment. We peeked around looking for our hosts, but the place was empty. Our explorations, however, led us to the surprise conclusion that we had been given the master bedroom, while the owners of the apartment had slept in a smaller bed in a side room. We next discovered a table set with a pitcher of fruit juice, and a plate of pastries. Italian hospitality was only beginning to make its extraordinary impression.

Incommunicado, and completely unfamiliar with the neighborhood, we had no choice but to remain in the apartment and partake of a breakfast, although both of us craved our normal kick-start jolt of coffee in one form or another. Happily, a short while later a young man arrived who spoke a modicum of English, introduced himself as the grandson, Vittorio, and told us he was a student in the university, and hoped to become an engineer. His grandfather, he told us, was a *un dottore*, an honorary term that doesn't necessarily mean *un medico*, a medical doctor, but could also be applied to a college professor, or anyone who had achieved recognition in his or her field.

After our brief chat, Vittorio turned on the television, giving us a somber look, and announced that there had been a great tragedy. We looked at the screen and saw a large, bomb-blasted building.

"Where is that," we asked, expecting to hear a response of Beirut or the Balkans.

"America," he told us. "Oklahoma City."

My heart leaped to my throat as I thought of my sister and her extended family living in and near the city. It was only after an hour of patient interpretation that we learned that the Murrah Federal Building had been destroyed in an act of terrorism, and that more than a hundred persons, including many children, had died in the blast.

We stared at the screen, gleaning only shreds, as a news commentator condemned those who caused the blast, which all then assumed to have been orchestrated by foreigners. "*Perche?*" 'Why?' I remember him asking repeatedly, as he spoke about the "*bambini, innocenti*", the babies, the innocents. Italy, so intimately familiar with the destruction of Fascism, was shocked. It was only later that we learned that the massacre had been conducted by America's own home-grown, neo-Fascist extremists. As it would be again several years later, Italy's sympathies were with America.

The tragedy set a somber cloud over our first visit to Roma, but we were treated to a brief driving tour of the city, passing bustling business streets, the Roman Forum and the curve of the Coliseum, and ending up at the botanical gardens, which offered a splendid overview of the famed seven hills from Monte Gianicolo, in the *Trastevere*, or 'across the Tevere' on the west side of the river.

Roma, we knew, had many more treasures and wonders to be seen, but our plans had been made, and time was growing short. The rest, we resolved, would wait for our return, as would so many other places in this vast and fascinating country. An even greater adventure lay ahead, one that would change the way we viewed both our friends and our lives in ways we had not imagined.

After confirming our plans to rendezvous with our friends once again in Bologna, we said our goodbyes, and thanked our Roman hosts with a small gift that said much more than we could given our limited vocabulary, which we resolved to improve.

George then introduced us to another friend, Alfredo, who spoke good English and had volunteered to drive us to the airport, where we could pick up a one-way rental car. Alfredo, like many Italian men, was a garrulous and friendly chap who envisioned himself as a serious rival to driving legend Mario Andretti.

Although his Fiat sedan would never be mistaken for a Ferrari in passing, he maneuvered it through crowded streets while keeping up a non-stop narrative about the traffic, the confusing traffic laws, the terrible pattern of streets, population growth, Roman customs, the Italian passion for soccer, known as *calcio*, as well as food, women, and favorite wines. He had traveled in America, and hoped to return to New York in the next year or two for a long visit. We should call him when we return to Rome, he insisted, and he would show us some of the best, least-known, places in the city.

Once out of the city's congested streets and onto the expressway, he made up for lost time, and swiftly deposited us and our bags directly in front of the terminal in a no-stopping zone.

"Thanks so much!" We told him, pressing a few lire into his hands for his troubles.

"Any time, I enjoyed it!" he replied, and we could tell that he really did.

We stepped into the terminal, and followed the *autonoleggio* signs on a long, looping walk to a distant wing that housed the rental agencies. Susan had called from the city to reserve a car, but when we finally found the right desk, she stopped in her tracks, and turned to me with a gasp, her hand clamping my arm like a vise.

"Oh, my...she gasped." She was speechless for a second, and I hoped she was not falling ill. Finally she found her voice. "It's true what they say about Italian men," she said.

I glanced toward the counter where a tall, particularly striking young man was helping another customer. I felt a pang of jealousy, but then quickly recognized the validity of her observation. This guy should have been on film. His chiseled good looks were apparent, no doubt, to everyone in the room. He could have been type-cast for an Italian James Bond, built to break hearts on several continents, and in multiple languages.

Susan struggled to collect herself, and when her turn to be served arrived, and the clerk switched deftly to passable English, she managed to keep her cool, despite being offered a higher rate than what she had negotiated over the phone. She stuck to her guns, smiling, and eventually won the agreed rate, with no penalty for our planned drop in Bologna. A backward glance over her shoulder as we left made it clear that she wished she had taken photographs.

"I am loving Italy! The scenery here is awesome," she added, grinning.

I stifled my jealousy and grinned as we loaded our luggage into an efficient, European-sized compact. We were quickly on the expressway, taking a quick exit towards Rome's port city of *Civitavecchia*, leaving the distraction behind, and striking out north into the rolling countryside of the region of *Lazio*.

Can We Just Wander?

Susan and I loved finding the things we both enjoyed, and learning to share the others' passions. We had traveled together, but Italy was a magnet for both of us, and now we were soaking it up.

The road north from Roma's Leonardo DaVinci Airport is a broad and modern four-lane affair that runs through mostly level countryside, making for easy driving. Two hours carried us well into the verdant hills of northern Lazio, and we passed only scattered villages and small towns among the broad expanses of agriculture and forests. We were close to the coast, but away from the larger towns that hugged them.

The countryside of Lazio offers a shady respite from the crush of the city of Rome, and we were enticed to explore its now-peaceful corners. Several ancient volcanic craters hold beautiful lakes, their shores strung with scenic villages. Fishermen ply the waters, bringing their flopping catches to local markets that offer the freshest and best of local produce. Along the shores of the *Mare Tyrrhenia*, nice beaches attract tourists and locals alike to bathe in the clear and normally placid waters. At some points, surfers rush to take advantage of waves generated by occasional storms.

Ready for rest and dinner, we paused one evening near Montalto di Castro and drove up to a modern hotel with an adjacent restaurant. The restaurant contained a comforting number of 'locals,' but we found that our knowledge of 'restaurant Italian' was suddenly inadequate. The names of the dishes were unlike anything we had seen in the States.

I asked questions about several items, but our young server was uncharacteristically shy and tight-lipped, perhaps not used to serving foreigners, or very new to her position. She recommended, and I accepted. Italy is famous for its delicious food, what could go wrong? Susan kindly shared bits of her own dinner after my own guesswork brought forth a generous portion of cuttlefish cooked in a serious black broth of its own ink. I gave it an attempt, but decided it was an 'acquired taste.' On to new adventures!

Our first trip allowed us only two days to wander the back roads of Tuscany, taking in the evocative landscapes that have inspired painters for centuries. Tall cypresses lined quiet lanes and driveways just as we imagined. Vineyards, many times interspersed with grey-green olive trees, decorated hillsides. Green pastures were ornamented by white sheep, and over it all the sun poured a unique light that seemed to create a dream-like quality.

Central Italy is full of artistic attractions, but its important not to overlook the natural ones. One of the more beautiful sights in Tuscany is the shore of the *Lago di Bolsena*, an ancient volcanic crater filled with crystalline waters. Fishing boats ply its surface to bring the catch to local markets in the few towns that cling to its shores. During the summer it bustles with activity. In the winter months, many of the residents seek warmer climes.

We drove through beautifully-forested hills high above the lake to take in the view, before climbing a steep ridge to descend toward Orvieto, just inside neighboring Umbria. The weather had been cloudy with drizzle, but the cloud-wrapped, peek-a-boo ridges above made for a fascinating scenery.

Eventually we achieved the pass and began to descend into a cloud-filled valley. Without warning we saw it, and the sight caused us to immediately brake and pull off the road, wedging our car onto a narrow shoulder above a steep mountainside. There below us, seeming to float in the clouds, was the old city of Orvieto, bristling with its *campanili* and the prominent dome of the city's cathedral. The fog and clouds that filled the valley beneath it concealed the lower part of the steep mesa that bears the town, and had provided its defense from invaders throughout the Middle Ages. It was as memorable a sight as I had ever seen. Orvieto was added to an ever-growing list of 'must return to explore' cities in Tuscany.

Following the advice of the guidebook, we decided to seek the warm waters of *Saturnia Terme*, a thermal spring located at the southern foot of the extinct volcanic cone of Monte Amiata. After a delightful drive through vineyards and stone farmhouses, we spotted a prominent sign pointing to a large spa-hotel built directly over the springs, from where waters rush in a steaming torrent for a kilometer across the flat plain before tumbling over their famous waterfall. We chose the latter.

We parked in a stony lot under scattered *quercie*, or oak trees, and scrambled down a steep path toward the sound of splashing water. At the bottom we found cascading pools, their stony rims spilling the sulfurous warm waters in a series of terraces. Nature had built, with geothermal energy, an ideal outdoor hot-tub, the minerals in the water depositing themselves to constantly build the basins. A crumbling old mill stood beside the falls like an aging sentinel.

The *termi* are reminders of the active clash of tectonic plates that have pushed Italy's peninsula from the sea, and the hundreds of volcanoes that have laid their cooling basalt over her frame. They attract hundreds of thousands of visitors, many from colder climates to the north seeking winter relief.

The spring's waters are widely believed to have medicinal and healing properties. We only knew that we enjoyed great peace of mind bathing in them, while any concerns of the world faded to insignificance. We basked in warm sunshine, and doused ourselves in their sunny soak. Later visits found the old mill reconstructed and secured, and the waters of the spring somewhat diminished.

Churches, Wine, and Walls

Our earlier glimpses from the train hadn't fully prepared us for the remote areas we traversed. We wandered through a beautiful countryside that matched, and soon exceeded, our expectations of Tuscany. Walled towns ornamented steep hilltops, always topped by a tall *campanile*, the bell tower of the town church. Narrow twisting roads wound their way through groves of olive trees and vineyards flush with spring growth.

Catching the first glimpses of the improbable hill-top towns that are emblematic of Italy left us breathless. These walled fortresses once provided the advantage offered by their heights against any approaching enemy, and neighbors clustered closely within defensive walls that grew over time. Today, despite the lack of need for mutual defense, the hill-towns continue to grow, spilling modern apartments buildings and suburbs into the lower slopes like so many overflowing *amphorae*.

We followed a beautiful, broad route that led from Grossetto to Sienna, passing romantic views of the verdant countryside of forests and farms on a drive around the slopes of Monte Amiata, Tuscany's highest peak. We were aiming at the charming Medieval town of San Gimignano, famed as "the Manhattan of the Middle Ages." Located only about thirty minutes from either Firenze or Sienna, it would provide a good central base for exploring the heart of Tuscany.

We arrived in San Gimignano (pronounced Gee-men-YA-no) on the winding, hill-climbing road that threads through the green, camel-back hills from the town of Poggibonsi just to the east. That road passes through a mile-long *zona industriale* full of wine warehouses and *fabbriche* looking every bit like something one would see in Atlanta, Los Angeles, or Cleveland. It's a reminder of the business side of agriculture. Amidst the rural beauty one comes to expect of *Toscana*, it shocks the senses, but restores a comparative sense of value to the other sights.

The road out of Poggibonsi passes over several hills covered with pastures and vineyards, before one is suddenly struck by the unexpected silhouette of distant skyscrapers juxtaposed behind the landscape of stone walls and farmhouses. As the perspective changes with the light and distance, the scene more clearly becomes a Medieval town topped by spindly towers.

During the Middle Ages San Gimignano was one of many small towns caught up in the rivalries of the larger cities that surrounded them. Pisa, Firenze, and Sienna often fought for dominance over each other, and the surrounding lands. Political intrigues ran thick, and allegiances shifted with the rise and fall of wealth, or success in battle. In this small town, those outside rivalries were reflected and amplified by the wealthy town leaders, who began to fortify their homes by building private towers from which they could observe the happenings around and be forewarned of approaching dangers.

Neighbors loathe to be looked down upon, competed by building their own towers, often edging a bit higher. Soon the rivalries were out of control, and more than sixty towers rose to improbable heights within the impressive defenses, casting much of the village into permanent shadow.

The fortified walls surround an area only a few narrow blocks in length. It was easy to see how daunting it would be for attackers to approach the city while arrows rained upon them from above.

We walked from the shady maze of parking lots under an overarching canopy of leaves, up the hill and through the looming walls by way of an imposing gate. An alley-like main street paved with cobblestone and busy with passers-by. A window full of the latest shoe styles was framed by ancient-looking stones. Buildings with eight or nine hundred years of history obvious on their facades housed modern shops offering wines, coffee, bread and pastries of every description. The wafting aromas mingled into a distinctive and tantalizing signature of the town before being swept up by the breezes that swayed the colorful canvas awnings.

People hurried about their business bearing white paper bags of half-concealed loaves of crusty brown bread or leafy vegetables. Some examined the deep redness of the tomatoes and apples and bright orange carrots piled in front of the *fruttivendolo*, the green grocer. The proprietor alone handled what the customers pointed at to select, adamant that his produce was ready to eat, never shop-worn by handling. We munched on luscious pears as we threaded our way through the growing crowd of locals sprinkled liberally with tourists.

Today the remaining fourteen towers of San Gimignano create a unique fantasy atmosphere and draw thousands of tourists, many of whom climb to the top of the tallest tower. Now part of a city museum, from *Torre Grosso*, literally the 'fat tower,' we looked down 154 meters at the *Piazza della Cisterna*, the piazza of the well. On a rainy-day return visit the view was of passers-by strolling with their umbrellas like a colorful waltz of flowers.

At the top of the museum tower hangs an enormous bell, protected by a cage of bars and wire. On one visit a young girl discovered her small hand could fit through the openings, and gave the bell a shove. As it swung toward me I cooperated by pushing it back with a finger. She grinned and pushed again. As the bell gathered momentum, it suddenly pealed with a thunderous 'blang' that echoed back from the street below. We both gasped and fled, grinning. As I hurried back down the hundreds of steps, I happened to glance at my watch. It was noon.

We paused before a shop window displaying the head of a wild boar, proof to shoppers that the rest of the unfortunate creature being offered for sale was the freshest imaginable. For unknown reasons we also wandered into the town's most bizarre feature, a museum of torture, which documents the many ways, some hopefully only ugly imaginings, in which cruel leaders once punished recalcitrant criminals, rogues, and rebels. Half the tour was more than enough to satisfy our curiosities.

•

Hoping to make the area our base of explorations during our first visit, we began seeking lodgings, but without success. Every place we enquired, both within the town walls and along the row of modern hotels below, was already reserved for the night.

We stopped at the handy *ufficio turistico* to see if the tourist office folks could offer any help. "No," we were told, "every hotel is full. But perhaps... there may be room at an *agriturismo* just a short drive from town... No, we don't have the number, but it is close, just down that way..."

An *agriturismo* is a class of lodging in Italy separate from hotels. The word combines agriculture and tourism, and indicates a class of farms licensed to let rooms. We had never considered one, but were game for anything at that point.

We followed their directions, but found no evidence on the right, as indicated. However, at the foot of a gravel road ascending a hill we spotted another of the now-familiar brown-and-yellow signs with a depiction of a bed, so we took a chance.

The road passed through broad pastures and meadows affording an excellent view of the town behind us before passing beneath a substantial church building, which seemed to have been built directly over the road. There was a small sign at the roadside bearing the name 'Pancole.'

We continued another few hundred meters or so, and found a surprisingly modern-looking hotel-sized *agriturismo*, but again, it was fully booked. Our desperation growing, and dusk gathering, the clerk there suggested we try at the next place, only another hundred meters or so. Perhaps they had a room.

We navigated tentatively into the unpaved drive of the *Agriturismo Vagnoni*, and were met by a pleasant middle-aged woman who told us that they also had no rooms.

"*Per piacere*," we begged, "we need a room for the night, can you help us?"

Seeing our desperation, and perhaps doubtful of the arrival of others who had ahead, she relented, and said she had a place that might be acceptable. It was. In fact, it was delightful. The room in a newly-restored farmhouse building featured a beautiful brick-vaulted ceiling, cloud-soft down pillows and comforters, a high-tech modern bathroom, and windows that opened toward a view of the vast vineyards beyond. Best of all, the price was only 81,000 Lire. At the exchange rate of that time, it worked out to about US$45.

Our friendly hostess, the Signora Vagnoni, soon reappeared with her husband. Luigi Vagnoni tended several acres of grape vines, and proudly showed me his new stainless-steel grape press and vinifying tanks built into a cellar beneath their home. Large doors opened directly to the vineyards, where a tractor sat parked next to the well-tended vines in the shade of gnarled olive trees.

A picnic table under the cypress trees at dusk was beckoning us to spread our array of Italian goodies out for a light dinner. Fresh mozzarella and aged Parmesan cheeses, vine-ripened tomatoes, olives, fresh basil, crusty breads, fruit, chocolate, and more began to emerge from our small cooler. Our hostess reappeared and presented us with a chilled bottle of white wine. *"Facciamo lo proprio qui,"* she said, indicating that they had made and bottled the wine 'right there' on their farm. *Vernaccia di San Gimignano,* the label read, and we were delighted that it was crisp, dry, and flavorful, a surprising new variety we had never tasted. Our unplanned wandering had once again rewarded us with happy new discoveries.

While we enjoyed the setting, another couple emerged from an adjacent room and struck up a conversation. They were on a holiday from their home in Germany, but spoke English well enough that we had no trouble relating our different adventures, and hearing some advice on things to see and do.

After dark we snagged chairs from the courtyard, walked across the gravel road, and settled in among the vineyards, just bearing their early growth. There, with a commanding view over the entire Val di Pesa, we sat holding hands and watched the twinkling lights of the traffic far below, and the yet-more distant lights on the mountains, some twenty kilometers away. The silence was almost total.

We sipped the remainder of our wine, and listened to the hoot of an owl, and a dog that barked faintly somewhere in the valley. The distant sound of tires crunching on gravel came with the passing of a lone car along a driveway in a village. Pancole was perfect for us! This was the Italy of our imaginations, and we were content to have found it.

After a good night's sleep we arose to continue our journey, and found that our new German friends had already departed after leaving a note on the windshield of our car, along with a single small branch from an olive tree, several of the small green fruits still clinging amid the leathery leaves. It left us both smiling.

Did We Break the Law, Officer?

We had a direct experience with the police one evening in Tuscany. Traveling in Italy you soon learn that *la polizia* come in a confusing array of 'colors and flavors' that can baffle outsiders. Municipal police alone can go under such names as *Polizia Municipiale, Locale, Communale, Urbana,* or even *Vigili Urbana*, although the term *'vigili'* is normally reserved for firefighters. *Polizia Provenciale* are responsible for environmental laws and wildlife. Traffic laws are the particular responsibility of the *Polizia dello Stato*, who are also responsible for most criminal investigations. The *Guardia di Finanza* is actually part of the Italian Army given charge of blue-collar crimes ranging from tax fraud and counterfeiting to drug trafficking and border security.

Perhaps the most distinctive in their flashy uniforms, the *Carabinieri*, are intimidating quasi-military police who have been a fixture in Italy for more than two hundred years. The service predates the Italian Republic itself by almost fifty years, having been established by the king in 1814. They were separated from the Army to become an independent branch of military police. The name derives from the officers' original weapons, the advanced carbine rifles they carried in those early days. Working in pairs, one now normally toting a modern and fearsome-looking automatic weapon, they turn up everywhere from street corners to airports.

One particular evening our after-dinner drive was interrupted as we returned to our *agriturismo*. Rounding a dark curve just outside San Gimignano, the glare of our headlights suddenly illuminated a pair of *Carabinieri*. One held the ubiquitous Uzi, while the other extended the familiar circular stop sign on a stick, which Susan always insisted on referring to as a lollipop. I quickly braked our rental car and pulled over to stop, and the sharply-uniformed young duo approached us cautiously, their brass buttons gleaming and red sashes smartly accenting their black uniforms. I rolled down the window.

"*I suoi documenti*," the obvious leader said gruffly, while his partner stood ready with the enforcer.

"*Buona sera*," I said cheerfully, and handed him the requested documents, including the auto-rental papers and my passport and U.S. driver's license. He glanced through them quickly.

"American?" he asked.

"Si," I replied, only a bit nervously.

"Do you speak English?" he asked in English, stern and unsmiling.

"Si." I replied, momentarily flummoxed. "Yes, certainly," I corrected, still hoping to disarm him with my smile.

"Where are you coming from?"

We struggled, but under pressure failed to come up with the name of the town of Colle di Val d'Elsa. "Um, a restaurant, down there in the valley," I told him. He glanced at the lights far below.

"When you were there, was it raining?"

"No," I replied, puzzled.

"Or perhaps foggy?" he asked.

My brain did an immediate back-flip. There were bright stars above, a crescent moon... He had stopped me to ask for a weather report? No, there had to be more to this...

"No, no fog."

"Then why are your fog lights on?"

Uh-oh. Apparently, unlike the United States, where rude drivers seem to thrive upon blinding others with arrays of lights, in Italy this practice is, 'ahem,' strongly discouraged.

"Are they on?" I asked innocently and honestly, trying all the array of switches, which sent the headlights angling up and down, and made them even brighter. "I don't know how they work. It's a French car!"

At that hint at the obvious superiority of Italian cars, the commanding officer calmly reached in through my window and began to fiddle with the controls, while the second officer, still hefting his Uzi, repeatedly shook his head as the headlights swiveled up and down, got brighter and dimmer. He fumbled with the switches. After a minute or so his partner nodded that the fog lights were off, perhaps a bit disappointed that he didn't get the order to shoot them out.

Apparently satisfied that we were indeed innocent of intentional felonious fog-light-shining, the commander returned our documents, gave us an abrupt dismissal, and waved us on our way. We laughed over the experience for the rest of the evening. I was just relieved that Susan hadn't used her 'lollipop cop' line.

Years later we began to invite friends to join us on our wandering trips through Italy. Together we shared many of the favorite places and unique sights that have made Tuscany a famous destination, and that led us to another interesting encounter.

Just off the main route between Firenze and Siena we found the unique circular walls of Monteriggione, built as a defensive outpost during the frequent battles between the two powerful neighbors. It was a small hamlet with impressively over-sized fortifications, more fortress than village. On our first visit we were able to drive directly into the quiet town. On later visits, we found that parking had been established beneath the walls, and visitors were required to walk up the low hill.

Returning to share the discovery with friends, we visited the town, then circled to the north side of the hill and parked on a dirt road to take in a different view. The crenelated walls, designed to be defended by a small army, are so evocative of the Renaissance as to be symbolic of that period. We walked below them, making photos of their bulk silhouetted against the sky.

After only five minutes we drove away with a new appreciation of the strategic value of the hilltop, but had only gone a few kilometers before our friend Rick realized that he had lost his wallet. Certain that he had dropped it where we had parked, we quickly returned to the narrow gravel drive between rows of olive trees and were surprised to see a pair of *Carabinieri* with their distinctive blue car.

We pulled cautiously into our former parking space, and stepped from the car. The *Carabinieri* quickly approached us, and asked what we were doing there.

"Our friend dropped his wallet," I explained. "We think it may be here."

"What is your friend's name?" they asked.

We answered, and they asked for our identity papers. Satisfied at last, they removed a wallet from their black leather pouch. "This may be yours, then," they said, handing it back to a very relieved Rick.

We never learned how it was that, in the scant five minutes between our departure and return, they had managed to visit our isolated stopping point and recover the wallet. We were convinced that they knew everything that went on in Italy.

Where Heroes Walked

It was on our first trip that we learned much of why the bonds between Italy and the United States, as well as other allied nations, are so strong. It was thanks to our friend George and many others that they exist at all.

The city of Bologna stands like a Medieval sentry within its walls, its back secured by fortifications atop the rugged Appenine mountains, its face turned toward the north, where enemies once flourished. It was there that we had arranged to rendezvous with George and head to the 'festival' he had mentioned. We found the city hunched under a bank of low, threatening clouds, but met our friends in a dry railroad station, and were swiftly directed into a large van for the trip south to Monghidoro.

As the light disappeared from the sky, rain set in, and soon it became a deluge. We attempted to relax as the van climbed, swerved, and swayed, following the narrow mountain road. There were no guardrails, and few lights to be seen. Only lightning illuminated the deepening valley below through gaps in the clouds. I half-expected that, at any moment, we would slide from the rain-slick asphalt and plunge over a nameless cliff, never to be found. Fate had kinder plans for us, however, and after perhaps an hour we found ourselves in the still-dripping town of Monghidoro, standing outside a large

36

furniture store.

"This is where you'll stay," George said, and we eyed the huge array of comfortable-looking beds through the store windows. "We'll be scattered around town with friends, but we'll come get you in the morning," George assured us.

At that moment a light came on, and a young man came out to meet us. Introducing himself as Simon, he told us that the store belonged to his family, and we would be their guests. He showed us to a comfortable apartment at the back of the store, and we quickly settled in. Our adventure was, for the time being, out of our control.

We arose to chilly sunshine through parting clouds, our windows overlooking a deep valley and adjacent mountains. We were soon met by George and our Italian hosts, this time led by the patriarch of the family, Arrigo Montanari. We were ushered into the heart of pleasant village, where we enjoyed cappuccino and sweet pastries with our friends, including George's sister Emily, and sisters Fran and Mary Updike, friends from our hometown arts council. George, we were assured, would join us shortly.

We were high in the mountains and a brisk north wind chilled us, but the growing sunshine brightened streets already decked with Italian flags and bunting, making the town a pretty scene.

As we watched a crowd began to gather. A few men were sporting distinctively-peaked alpine hats with feathers protruding jauntily. Musicians began to appear, horns and drums emerging from cases as the group assembled to form the beginnings of a band. Soon there was a group of more than a score, and the random rat-a-tat tapping of drumsticks and tuning toots of clarinets began to draw a bigger crowd.

George then surprised us by appearing in a complete WWII U.S. Army uniform, only his familiar lined face and white hair giving him away. He seemed transformed. His dress shoes gleamed, and even his belt was polished. At age 80, George was suddenly, once again, an American soldier. On his shoulder he wore blue *quadrifoglio* shoulder patches. We asked, and learned that it was the symbol his 88th Division, known as the 'Blue Devils.' Because of the shape of the patches they were also sometimes referred to as the Clover Leaf Division. Those were names that would echo through our experiences.

George had barely arrived before he was surrounded by a small cluster of men, some of whom hugged and kissed him enthusiastically on both cheeks in the Italian manner. Most wore the distinctive peaked cap of the Alpini troops, marked by their plumes, and many had dressed in remnants of their old uniforms as well. These Alpine mountain forces had served alongside the U.S. Army during the war. With so many well-wishers surrounding him and speaking excitedly in Italian, we had no further opportunity to get close. The crowd began to swell and the band struck up a lively tune.

Our visit to Italy was about to come to an emotional crescendo. We slowly came to realize from the uniforms and posters that the day was an observance of the 'Liberation,' and was apparently being held to mark the anniversary of the end of the war. We did the math and realized that it had been exactly fifty years. This was to be a reunion of heroes, a gathering of those who had survived the terrible conditions and bloody fighting.

Like many Americans of the post-war generations, what we knew of the war had come mostly from television and movies. Films like "The Longest Day" and "Midway" had taught us some of the heroism of Americans fighting for global liberty. We were both familiar with the Normandy landings, the Battle of the Bulge, and the terrible fighting that had taken place on tiny Pacific islands, yet we knew little of the war that had taken place in these high mountains in Italy.

We were then naive about the reality of the war, and the terrible and vivid memories that were being silently shared among not only those veterans, but the gathered townspeople who surrounded them. In that cold winter of 1944-45, the American Army had grown immensely since the start of the war. They had drafted every available and suitable man. Most had been very young. They had been through training, but were late-comers to the military arts, facing an experienced German Army. Yet they had beaten them repeatedly in a series of bloody battles during a sixteen-month drive up the mountainous peninsula.

We stood at the rear of the large crowd as about sixty men of the Alpini forces stood at attention during the playing of the Italian national anthem with its dramatic orchestral opening. A large number of those men were the Alpini of Sulmona, far to the south, who had returned for the observance. They, too, had fought, shed blood, and lost friends in Monghidoro.

Two mayors, Paolo Gamberini of Monghidoro and Arnaldo Naldi of the neighboring town of Loiano, each bedecked in their broad sashes in the red, white and green *tricolore* of Italy, addressed the crowd. An Alpini veteran gave an address that brought tears to the eyes of many, particularly those citizens who had lived through the tragedy of the war, and the veterans who had served in it. Although we could understand only a little of what was said, the emotions of the moment could be easily read, and they affected us as well.

Mayor Naldi then called upon the name of George Fortunato DeLuca, with an emphatic introduction. We looked at each other, surprised that George would be speaking. The familiar figure of our friend, looking every bit the veteran, took command of the microphone and the ears of the crowd. His Italian was obviously fluent, and they listened intently to him as he reflected upon the horrors of the war, the demands placed upon those he knew, and the terrible price paid by many. He told tales that once brought laughter from the crowd, and other times tears. Unfamiliar with the language then, we understood only scattered words, but the reaction of his audience made clear the notes of humor and pathos that he shared.

George was an icon that day. He was interrupted by applause, and received a ringing expression of gratitude for his words, and no doubt, his service, at the end. We initially thought it was because he was the only representative of the massive U.S. forces that had help liberate Italy.

Still a bit in awe of George's status in this place, we fell into line as the marching band followed the priest and a small knot of VIP's, including George, and the entire crowd trailed along, out of the piazza and down a sloping street through the town.

After marching proudly for several short blocks, the group halted before a wall for a moment of prayer. There, we learned, four men had been murdered by the Nazis on the night before the Americans had liberated the town, part of an ongoing effort to maintain control through terror. Accused of being Partisans, part of the anti-fascist underground, they were arrested and tortured. Afterwards they were led to a nearby pigsty and shot. The moment was no doubt still fresh in the memories of some present. Mayors Naldo and Gamberini joined in placing a *corona*, a large wreath of flowers, at the foot of the monument. The parade then wound its way past other significant points in town in the same fashion before we returned to the piazza, where most of the crowd slowly dispersed.

We had been to observances in the United States that drew little attention beyond a few veterans, family members, and an honor guard. In Italy, it seemed, they paid much closer attention to their history. We only later began to fully understand the terrible sacrifices that had been endured, and how indelibly those events were burned into the communal memory.

We asked about what had happened in Monghidoro during the war. It seemed like a peaceful and insignificant small town, not the sort of place that world powers would spend much time fighting over. This, George explained, was where the Germans had made their second winter defensive line and was the scene of bloody fighting. His story was gripping.

"I was the only one in my division who could speak Italian, so I did a lot of translating, even though I wasn't an official translator. People would approach the troops with an issue, or we would need to tell them something, and I would get the call. I guess I helped a few people out that way," he told us in his understated manner.

"These mountains were strategic, because if we could get through them, there was nothing else to hold back our armor, and we would take all of northern Italy. We called this their Gothic Line, and it had taken us all summer to battle our way here after we finally cracked their old Gustav Line north of Napoli in May. The Alpini fought their way up the mountains with us. We needed them, especially because they knew the mountains better than we ever could, even with good maps. They were our eyes and ears. They knew the roads, and the attack routes."

"To drive the Germans out of Monghidoro we had to use our artillery. We blasted the town to pieces," he told us. "There was probably not an undamaged building in town. Most had their roofs destroyed, some were just a wall or two. Some buildings had burned. The trees along the main street, and even on the hills and mountainsides, were just shreds and stumps. We felt bad about it, but we hadn't had a choice. Everything was devastated, and most of the people were hiding in the mountains or in cellars, but when we reached the rubble, they poured out to greet us, cheering. We passed out food and blankets, and even chocolates for the children, which some of them had never seen."

"When we had first arrived in Monghidoro in October it was all mud, but soon it began to freeze up. Then winter set in hard. At first the jeeps would freeze into the mud overnight, and we had to crack them out in the mornings. Then the snow started, and everything was frozen solid. It was almost impossible to move, and the roads were slick with ice, but we were still trying to push the Germans. We lived in tents, and pretty much without heat."

"Christmas was coming. The church in town had been destroyed when we drove the Germans out. It was just a hollowed-out shell, and most of the roof was missing. We sort of fixed it up, used some of our field tents to put a roof over it so they could have a Christmas mass. Lots of people came, even though it was very dangerous, and we made a bit of a feast for them. People brought what they could. It was a moment of brightness. Those people had been through so much..."

Glancing around the alpine setting and the deep valley below, it was easy to imagine the town in the dead of winter, with slick, icy roads and footpaths through the rough terrain. George continued his story, quietly relating the long-ago events. "A man approached our troops, begging for help, and they sent him to me, because I could understand him. He told me his son was sick, dying in an unheated cave. I went with him, and found the child, half-starved and freezing, maybe with pneumonia. Regulations said we were supposed to keep our supplies for ourselves, but none of us could turn our backs on the suffering. We shared. I brought him food and medicine, and eventually got him transported to a field hospital near Firenze..."

As George spoke we began to understand the outpouring we had witnessed. For the people of Monghidoro, it was Liberation Day once again. The war was over at last for them and their families. I tried to imagine the emotions that the day must have evoked. Tears of joy and sorrow flowed as people rejoiced at their own survival, but remembered those who hadn't.

People, by circumstance, are often placed in situations they could not have imagined, and called upon to perform acts of heroism. Hundreds of thousands respond, and act in heroic ways as though it is the everyday expectation.

The memories and experiences of a human lifetime often include moments of both deep sorrow and great joy, fear and triumph, heroism and failure. It is easy to look at the surface of another person and imagine that what you see is all there is: those features, that voice, and of course some family, parents, probably school friends... The reality is that our fellows have often been shaped by experiences that we will never be able to understand. My respect for George grew immeasurably.

A few moments passed before George asked me to accompany him, and we slipped away from the crowd into a nearby house. We were met at the door by a lean, elderly man who stood a head taller than George, yet obviously looked up to him. They spoke quietly in Italian for several minutes, and I listened reverently. Although they spoke openly, I could understand only a little of what they said to one another, but all of what they felt. Here were two veterans and survivors, improbably reunited fifty years later, both grateful for what they had shared then, and knowing that this would likely be their last meeting. Hands squeezed shoulders, and eyes moistened, the tears clinging tightly as they shared a funny story from the distant past.

They spoke of fallen friends, and those who couldn't join them due to failing health. They marveled at their own lives, and their improbable survival after all they had endured. It was at that moment that I came to fully appreciate the deep bonds that connect Italy with the United States but also much of the world. Comrades in arms, these two frail men, with their long memories, embodied that solid affinity.

At length George indicated that we should walk, and as we did so, he began again to speak of the events of the war.

"These men," he told me, "Suffered more than anyone can imagine. They froze in the snow and ice, most of the time without enough food, without heat, all the while being shelled by the German troops. They endured it because to them, their freedom was worth their lives. They did it for family, for their town, and for everyone they cared about.

"These other men, the *Alpini di Sulmona*, came here and fought even though their town was already liberated. They did it for Italian liberation, and out of loyalty to the *Alpini* here. They were brothers, and they couldn't let them down."

George spoke matter-of-factly, without sign of the emotion I knew he felt. Yet at that moment he was a soldier again, and despite his 80 years, he was strong.

There is no doubt that the years of the war were terrible for many, and that we, as so-called moderns, enjoy the fruits of their sacrifices. Yet during those terrible years they learned to treasure life, and saw more clearly the beauty and splendor that surrounds us. It is no doubt only the darkness of night that allows us to see the stars.

•

Within the hour we had gathered our American delegation and joined a thin stream of people walking up the steep street to a large and modern building on a hill above the center of town. This, George explained as we approached, was the *baita*, the lodge of the Alpini, the rough equivalent of the American Legion or VFW halls that dot American towns.

We entered a foyer that led past a photo gallery of Alpini memories, many of the war years. Images of ruined remains of buildings, American Army jeeps parked along a row of houses reduced to rubble, a burned-out German tank, and alpine troops leading a train of mules laden with heavy packs covered the walls. In one photo a Sherman tank was parked in the tiny space in front of a shoe-maker's shop, barely out of the street, its guns trained on the road. It was a different perspective of the neat, ordered town.

Mayor Naldi appeared, and invited us to join him in the museum of the Alpini, which was in the lower level of the building. There we stood before a shrine dedicated 'ai caduti,' to the fallen Alpini, who, as they said, had *andata in avanti*, 'gone ahead.' It was easy to imagine the phrase, born in the heat of battle, the grinding years of war. "Where's Ronaldo?" one might have asked as a patrol returned from a skirmish. "He's gone ahead," would come the somber reply.

Too many of their fellows had *andata in avanti*.

We stood for a few moments before the shrine, no doubt each of us deep in our own private thoughts and devotions.

An adjacent room was filled with memorabilia. There we found an original mule saddle, old radios, ammunition boxes, ragged uniforms, shattered helmets. These objects spoke of the magnitude of what they had been through.

We passed at length into the large hall upstairs. To the left, long tables laden with food were fussed over by scores of wives, daughters, and a couple of stereotypical smiling Italian uncles. More food appeared in a stream from a kitchen on the lower level. It was a feast fit for twice the crowd that had assembled.

The band that had led the parade assembled once again, and struck up a celebratory note, and were soon accompanied by a chorus of Alpini singers. We were introduced to a couple of young Alpini who spoke some English, and got a bit of a tour of the facilities, and some explanation of who some of the VIP's were.

A handsome young man in an Alpini uniform pressed a rolled commemorative poster into Susan's hands, and posed for pictures with her, Fran, Mary, and Emily. The Alpini of Sulmona presented me one of their distinctive bandanas. Dozens of people approached us, smiling, to meet the friends of the hero, George. A bit embarrassed, we thanked them in turn, grateful for the warm reception as best we could. Our smiles and theirs, no doubt, spoke words neither could command.

Dinner was a time of laughter and celebratory reunions, as friends who had not seen each other in years came together. Jokes and reminiscences became the order of the afternoon. A slide show of old photographs, showing the terrible conditions of the town during the war, augmented the large collection of tributes and memories that filled the walls, but failed to dampen the mood.

Wine flowed all around, and the years fell away, until all that remained was the spirit of warmth and fellowship. We felt as though had been absorbed into the community.

At length the dinner wound down, and the inevitable time for speech-making began. The mayor and Alpini officers stood at the front of the room as a few of the men shared their memories of the war. One of those called to offer a couple of comments was our host Signor Montanari. Well over six feet in height, George stood next to him as he spoke, and they made a strange contrast. Montanari towered over George as he spoke clearly and deliberately of the purpose of the gathering, the solemn memories that the elderly carried of the war years, and the hope that such terrors would never again be visited upon their descendants.

Then he finished his speech, and handed the microphone to George, who began to describe the actions of the American Army during that terrible winter, and the heroic actions that had led to the liberation we were gathered to mark. An honor guard brought forth a beautiful plate, inscribed to George, and presented it with warm remarks and intense applause. Then the most remarkable thing happened. Mayor Naldo stepped behind George, wrapped him in arms and hoisted him in the air.

Everyone laughed, and then someone shouted: "There is our hero!" and the entire room broke into cheers. "*Grazie, Fortunato! Grazie per gli Americani!*" 'Thank you, Fortunato! Thanks for the Americans!' A woman shouted that he had saved her family. The room was a tumult. Some wept. We were awestruck. It was a moment that would echo for a generation.

Hospitality Redefined

Although on that first trip we had seen only a small portion of her wonders, there was no doubt that we had fallen in love with Italy. Yet our time for touring was growing short. We promised ourselves that we would return soon, and bid our warm goodbyes to our hosts, and friends both old and new.

We arose early the next morning, our luggage packed with the collected treasures of our trip, and walked the short blocks to the piazza, where we bought our *biglietti* at the bar and climbed aboard a comfortable intercity bus. Weaving our way along twisting mountain roads on a sunny, chilly morning, we absorbed the sights of the high passes of the *Appenini* mountains, and the isolated, rust-colored villages that clung to the heights. After an hour of winding two-lane asphalt, we joined the speeding stream of the *autostrada*, and we were swiftly out of the mountains and back at the *stazione* in Bologna. Although only two days had passed, it seemed the world had changed since last we were there.

Tickets again in hand, we boarded a fast train that brought us to Milano by early afternoon. The vast, noisy cavern of the station was vaguely familiar now, but just as confusing. The sound of announcements from scattered speakers echoed unintelligibly from the walls and ceiling, mixing with the hubbub of a thousand voices and the noise of trains arriving and departing.

Remembering our promise, I searched in my passport and found the slip of paper bearing the telephone number of Pina and Gino, the wonderful couple we had met on the train only two weeks before. Dialing the number, Pina's bright chirp was a welcome sound. "Raaahberrrt!" she drew my name out excitedly. "*Finalmente! Vieni, vieni!*" "Finally! Come, come!" she insisted, instructing us to purchase tickets to Lierna.

We hadn't yet found a hotel, but knew that Pina would be a good resource in that regard. We agreed, and were soon aboard the train rumbling northbound out of the vastness of Milano, across the countryside of Lombardia, toward the Alps we knew were not far away. In reality they were closer than we expected, for in only thirty minutes we were passing through tunnels under rising hills, and soon emerged above a river with the peaks of the lower mountains already looming high above us. The famous Alps were living up to their reputation for beauty.

We changed trains in Lecco to board a *diretto*, a local train that stops at each village. It began to follow the broad expanse of Lago di Como, its waters reflecting the deeper blue of the sky, and the impossibly steep mountains opposite. Towns clung to impossibly-steep mountainsides, and we wondered how it was possible that roads could reach them. Along the lake shore below us, palm trees grew, while on the mountaintops, winter snows still clung. It was a fairy-tale scene as the lowering sun played hide-and-seek behind the mountains as they passed in turn.

The rumbling of the wheels and the leading blast of a whistle at the crossings were the only sounds from the electric train. After only fifteen minutes it pulled into its fourth stop, and the sign at the approach clearly said 'Lierna.' We scrambled out with our luggage, a bit bewildered as to which way to walk as the train began to glide away.

Suddenly a voice from the heavens was shouting: "*Ciao, Susan, ciao Robert! Benvenuti!*" Looking around, we spied Pina, not on the ground across the tracks as expected, but leaning from an upstairs window in the station. She pointed to our right, and we turned to see a set of stairs descending to a walkway beneath the tracks, the normal arrangement in Italian *stazioni*.

Before we could mount the opposite stairs, Pina was there, giving us both warm hugs and the traditional kisses on each cheek, acting as if we were long-lost children of hers. She led us up two flights of stairs to their lofty apartment, directly above the train station.

Ospitalità isn't just a word in Italian. Rather, the concept of hospitality permeates everything they do. They scoffed when we mentioned a hotel: we would stay with them! Ushered to a comfortable bedroom, offered use of the shower, and treated to a wonderful home-cooked meal with the gathered family, we felt almost as though we had once again somehow been mistaken for others. We had no way of knowing what we had done to deserve all this, but in reality, we needed to have done nothing but be ourselves, for that is all that these wonderful people were expecting.

In the morning, we explained, we would have to take the earliest train, because we had to pass back through Milano to get to Malpensa airport, which we had learned would also require a taxi or Metro transfer for the half-mile between the *Stazione Centrale* and the *Stazione Garibaldi*, two of the several stations which serve the sprawling city from where we would take a bus. (Today the problem doesn't exist, because of better connections, and a direct train from the airport terminal.)

No, Gino insisted. He would drive us to the airport. It would be much faster. He could take time from work in the morning, and that way we wouldn't be as pressed for our morning departure, which required us to be there by 9:30 a.m. We objected that it would be too difficult, but his insistence won out. Sensing our fatigue and theirs, we bid each other goodnight and headed for the sack.

Early next morning, as we hurriedly sucked down Pina's excellent cups of *espresso*, we got to peek around their modern apartment in the light of day, only to be surprised to discover that we had, once again, been housed in the master bedroom. Our hosts had inflated an air mattress while allowing us the best bed in the house. In Italy, hospitality reigned supreme.

Our departure from Italy was as much an adventure as our arrival had been. Gino had apparently never actually driven to Malpensa airport, which serves primarily international flights, and the trip stretched as even he had trouble with the confusing Italian road-sign system. No, that's too kind, because it's more of a lack of a system. Signs appear, pointing this way and that, and when the direction is followed, the signs seemingly disappear.

Twice while navigating the confusing roads around Como, Gino

48

stopped to ask directions. Then, sure of his route, he pressed on through the early-morning crush of traffic. We arrived at Malpensa airport with only a few minutes to spare, and thanked Gino repeatedly for his wonderful and unexpected service, but once again, simply repeating *Grazie!* didn't seem to be enough.

As we departed on our flight, I gazed back at the Alps that defined their northern edge and wondered at the experiences that could be found within her borders. Like a gigantic mosaic, I realized, each fragment of Italy has its own colors and textures, and it can be broken down into infinitely smaller pieces without losing its charm.

We had arrived in Italy knowing only the dozen or two 'critical' words and phrases that wise travelers practice before they arrive in a strange land. With those and the familiar lexicon of the Italian restaurant, I thought I could get by, as I had before in France, Mexico, and Germany. I was wrong. *Italia* demanded more of me.

It was not enough to be able to ask *"dové un buon albergo"* and be satisfied that a hotel was what one sought. When confronted with a lover that takes one's breath away, it is important to be able to ask more important questions. The ones that will unveil the secrets, the wonders, the beauties and magic that were known only to those who lived within her embrace.

Questi erano gli Alpini di Sulmona

50 ANNI DOPO

24 • 25 APRILE 1995

Saranno di nuovo qui
con noi per ricordare
la Liberazione
del nostro paese.

Never Enough of Italy

We returned home from our first visit tired but enthused, and feeling somehow different in our own skins. I was left with the distinct notion that the time I had spent in Italy was not subtracted from my days on earth, but rather added to them.

We unwrapped the rolled package we had been given in Monghidoro, and found that it was a poster printed by the *commune* to announce the visit of the *Alpini di Sulmona* for the events commemorating the liberation. A large photo depicted an Alpini pack-mule train passing GI's gathered around flaming barrels in the snow. The burned-out rubble of the town formed the grim backdrop to the scene. We brought out the dictionary to translate it. "Fifty Years After," it proclaimed in bold print. "These were the Alpini of Sulmona. They will be here again with us to remember the liberation of our country."

We had it framed and hung it in our home.

50

Browsing through our photos and transparencies we found many from the events in Monghidoro. We reunited our entire travel party for a dinner at George and Emily's home several weeks later, and brought a slide projector to share the images. The delight on George's face as we shared the photos of him being honored, then hoisted in the air by his friend, was priceless. We soon realized that we were completely hooked and within months were talking of our return to Italy.

It was apparent that our most memorable experiences had revolved around people, not places. The people of Italy had touched our hearts. We wanted to know them better, and learn more about what it's like to live a life in that unique land, to share in the powerful forces that both unite and divide them. We decided then that we would become 'cultural visitors,' intent upon understanding Italy through the eyes of her people, rather than just seeing famous places.

Getting to know the people of Italy would certainly help us understand the stunning beauty in context. That would require understanding their language, since we couldn't expect all of them to suddenly learn ours! We began with a variety of audio lessons and books, and began picking up phrases rapidly.

I often asked George about different places he went during the war, trying to pull more details from his memory. We had read some history of the Italian campaign, and knew that about 60,000 Allied troops and 50,000 defenders had died there. It was a bitter killing zone. George had a far-away look in his eyes as he recalled, and perhaps re-lived, some of those dark winter days.

"The Alpini troops were the elite mountain forces of the Italian Army," he told me "They had fought for Italy for years, even before America got into the war. Mussolini had sent thousands of them to the Eastern Front to support Germany's invasion of Russia, and only a few ever came back after the war. The Alpini were furious. They hated Mussolini and the Fascists.

"Because the Germans had heavier guns, they could out-shoot us. The only way to even the score was to get our artillery higher up the mountains, so we could get more range. Places where a jeep couldn't go, Alpini mules could. Together we could get a chance to hit them back. We dragged our guns as high as we could. Sometimes we used a block and tackle we rigged up and winched them, using trees to support the weight. The Alpini used their mules to haul up ammunition and food.

George's dark eyes, set under his active, bushy eyebrows, lent an intensity to his words as he recalled the problems they had faced. "It was extremely bitter cold, deep snows, no heat except small fires. The troops, the civilians, everyone suffered..."

Italy had made an indelible mark upon him, and us. All the things we did in our daily routines seemed slightly modified, as if we had suddenly donned eyeglasses for the first time, and now saw the world clearer. Everything was filtered, and slightly clarified by comparison. Creative juices were flowing. It seemed that the days we had spent in Italy were not deducted from our lives, but had somehow been added to them. We had been enriched, and were eager for more.

George had certainly been changed by what he, a school-teacher from New York, experienced under fire in the mountains. Yet he had survived, and prospered. His efforts helped create the bonds that tie Italy to the English-speaking world of the United States, Great Britain, Australia, New Zealand and Canada.

Waves of immigration had brought the blood of Italy to all of those places, but few ties are stronger than those created by the terrible conflict of the Second World War. There in Italy hundreds of thousands of soldiers served, and many died, to liberate the mountainous peninsula. Scattered across the landscape are cemeteries for the soldiers of New Zealand, Australia, Poland, India, Britain, Canada, and others who participated in the fight against Fascism.

Italians have never forgotten, and as we were to learn, the gratitude still resonate through the generations. Italian towns and villages saw first-hand the horrors of war, and most observe the anniversaries of events in a way that the people of the United States, in particular, can scarcely appreciate. Every small village, it seems, has a monument, a memorial *ai caduti*, "to the fallen," who had given their lives to liberate them. Many are engraved with long lists of names: local men who had died in war, or even women who had been executed. High in the Apennine Mountains we came into close contact with the power of those vivid memories, and the way they can still shape the events of today.

Sadly, it was not long after that our friend George passed away. We felt honored to have been a part of his reunion trip, and vowed to tend the friendship we had formed, and do what we could to honor the memories of what he and his companions had done.

Wandering Through Wine Country

We returned to Italia as conventional tourists, and set out to learn more about her. Tuscany had much more to show us, so we eventually returned to San Gimignano and the pleasant *agriturismo* in Pancole. There we enjoyed relaxing drives through the evocative countryside, well-ornamented with olive groves, rows of tall cypress trees, and thousands of hectares of vineyards. *Cabernet, Merlot,* and *Pinot Nero,* which the French call *Pinot Noir,* joined the vast acreages of *Sangiovese,* the dominant grape. A dozen other varieties commanded their own plots.

The art of wine-making was established well before the rise of the Roman Republic, based upon knowledge spread throughout the Mediterranean by Phoenician sailors, and shared by Greeks and Etruscans. In Italy it achieved perhaps its highest form. Traveling back-roads it's not difficult to find signs pointing to *vendemmia*, and visitors will find them typically welcoming, and intensely authentic. There, farmers sell their own products. Olive oil and honey may be offered, but especially one will find wines in a handful of the hundred varieties made there. Almost invariably they are good, and occasionally outstanding.

On one fine Spring day we made our way to the village of Tavernelle in the *Val di Pesa*, home of its own *Chianti Colle Sinesi* wines, and then eastward over the rugged hills that divided them from the roots of the Chianti tradition. Here amid the lush greenery in the heart of Tuscany lay the region of the *Chianti Classico*.

Each of the various districts of Chianti, eight in total, offers their own tasty bouquet of the grapes approved for blending under strict Italian wine laws. The most famous of these is the original, or *Chianti Classico*, district, marked by the black rooster, or *Gallo Nero*, found on each bottle. Its mystique seemed to generate demand that evaded even superior wines from adjoining districts. There are today seventy-four regions that bear the honorific DOCG classification.

Italian wine law sets strict standards of content and place of origin, so that in thousands of places throughout the nation, a simple line on the map determines which winemakers may use a traditional name. The wines are ranked, many times by fame and history, into a set of classifications that are only marginally reflective of the true quality of the product. The common labels of DOC and DOCG are shorthand for *Denominazione di Origine Controllata*, with the 'G' adding a further *Garantita*. That translates as "name of origin controlled and guaranteed." They mean it. Wine-makers are subject to government inspections, and even the hint of improper, or off-label blending, generates arrests and headlines. Each DOC is restricted to particular grapes, percentages, vinification and aging standards.

We drove almost empty roads across the Tuscan countryside through the vineyards, stopping to sample the products of attractive places along the way. On several occasions we followed the north-south path of the famed SP222 through the heart of the *Classico* region. The two-lane road that follows the valley belies the great wealth that has been accumulated in this narrow valley just south of the city of Firenze. It winds its way south through the towns of

Strada in Chianti, Greve, and Panzano.

Along the way we passed numerous well-known wine estates, prosperous farms, and expansive houses with tasting salons boasting uniformed employees. In the less-famous areas, however, one can often find an authentic experience, where the wine-maker might appear in person to pour samples. The area is perhaps the model for California's famed Napa Valley, but is a bit more rugged and wooded. Unfortunately, some of the wine makers have begun to adopt California's abominable practice of charging visitors just to walk into their sanctums and sample the wines. We made it a point to avoid those places and their wines, finding many equal or superior choices that refused to join the non-traditional parade.

In recent years some wine-makers have chosen to forego the traditions and lofty ratings and produce non-compliant wines, which earned the sobriquet of "Super Tuscans." By experimentation they have been able to produce wine capable of standing on its own merits on a world stage.

As much as wine-making is both an art and a science, it remains highly dependent upon the weather. Ideal soils, exposures, and micro-climates can all be undone by an ill-timed, late season rain. Once that happens no amount of perfect blending, vinifying, and cellaring can undo the damage.

Many proud owners would pour tastings of their *extra-virgine* olive oils in much the same way as their wines, the sweet and pungent flavors hitting all the right notes in their soft sonatas. The term *extra-virgine* refers to the fact that the oil is produced in the first, or virgin, cold extraction. This oil is of the highest quality. Afterward the resultant mash is heated and additional oil is extracted and sold as simple olive oil, much used for commercial purposes in prepared products.

Whether of wine or oil, we rewarded each tasting with the purchase of at least a bottle, or a few bottles of wine if it was worthy. Even a case to be shipped was in the cards if the products were outstanding.

On one trip we had the good fortune to be present at the end of the wine harvest. We arose one morning only to encounter an unusually large tractor-trailer truck, a rig the Italians call an *autoarticolato*. It had driven carefully onto the flatter ground of the vineyard outside our agriturismo, and was backing slowly toward the farms' barns. Once jacked up and leveled into place, the sides of the long trailer were folded down to become walkways, exposing an impressive array of machinery inside. Intrigued, we waited to see what was happening.

The crew aboard the truck moved with a practiced rhythm, and uncoiled a long hose which they snaked into the barn and connected to one of the several large stainless-steel tanks that stood inside. Then they began unpacking boxes full of empty bottles, and filling racks on the trailer. Soon a pump was put into action, and the entire mechanism came to life as wine began flowing, and bottles were filled, corked, foiled, and labeled while moving along the efficient lines of the conveyor. At the opposite end, several men completed their tasks by boxing the newly-filled bottles.

We were fortunate enough to be witnessing the issuance of the *Vino Novello*, the new wine, which would be opened in little more than a week. It's the counterpart of France's Beaujolais Nouveau, the first quick fermentation of a wine meant to be consumed immediately without aging. It was the winemakers' way of testing the new vintage, the better to estimate the value of the mature product two or three years later. The event has taken on a celebrity-event cachet, with crowds gathering to taste the new year's wine at the stroke of midnight on the 30th of October.

We drove slowly in the wine regions, watching for the small signs bearing the single word '*vendemmia*,' indicating that wine is made and sold there. We followed several single-lane gravel drives in search of the perfect wines that have been Italy's pride for centuries.

Many times we have arrived at a seemingly empty farm, the owners busy working the vineyards out of sight. A sound of a car engine is normally enough to bring a response. The delicious elixirs were poured for our appraisals, held to the light, sniffed deeply, and finally, sipped and swirled about the mouth, drawing out the complexities the fruit had inherited from weather and soils, enhanced by aging and the skills of the winemakers.

Near Castellina in Chianti, just off the narrow SR222 we spotted a hand-painted sign pointing toward a steep, rocky driveway that crossed a narrow culvert over a brook and ascended through a forest. We crossed and began to climb, tires slipping slightly on the loose gravel. After a hundred meters we emerged into vineyards and olive trees, then passed a row of slender

Italian cypresses, so emblematic of the central region. There beside spreading oaks stood a substantial, upright house, and a couple of outbuildings.

A stone building labeled *Cantina* had a venerable arched doorway with a thick oaken door. Heavy iron hinges looked as though they had been beaten out by a local blacksmith, a hundred years earlier. It was locked tight. Being new to the country at that time, we didn't realize that it was siesta hour, after 1:00 p.m., and the family was likely enjoying a meal or napping. We were turning to leave when a woman of about sixty years strode quickly toward us, smiling and jingling skeleton keys on a huge iron ring. We were soon gathered around an impressive stout oak tasting-table where our hostess Giuseppina produced samples of wine and olive oil called *produzione propria*, meaning all were produced from their own land. Her face beamed with pride. After an informative tasting, we made our selections. I watched Giuseppina as she quickly rolled each purchase in a wrapper, and tied the bottles into a bound package. She had done it thousand times; no, a thousand times a thousand. Her hands were as the hands of generations.

Fun and Games in Firenze

We couldn't contemplate the thought of leaving Tuscany again without finally exploring her most famous destination, the city which long ruled her. We had made our *prenotazione* in a venerable hotel near the *Piazza di Santa Croce*, named after yet another gorgeous church with a facade of black and white stone.

The *piazza* itself was the scene of vibrant nightlife and a day-time market. Children chased soccer balls across the broad flagstone-paved expanse while mothers shopped for flowers and vegetables. Bars and restaurants made for a lively scene.

Nearby was the famed 16th century covered market known as the *Mercato del Porcellino*. The name means 'piglet' but in fact the object is an enormous bronze hog. We touched the nose of the *porcellino* for luck, just as tens of thousands of others have done.

The heart of any Italian city is its market, and Firenze is no exception. Scores of stalls spilled into the walkways, offering a wealth of delicious temptations. We bought crusty bread and local cheeses, fresh fruit and more, and watched *i Fiorentini* dash to their favorite stalls to buy the freshest products before the waves of tourists arrived to poke and prod, to the irritation of the shop-keepers.

On another walk we explored the delightfully-ornate *Duomo*, and of course, the museum with its famous statue of David, by Michelangelo. The original, now housed in its protected space, once stood in the the large *Piazza della Signoria*, where today a replica defies both the weather and the pigeons.

One early morning we strolled across the shady *Ponte Vecchio*, or old bridge, just as the gold-smiths and jewelers were opening their shops, large metal overhead doors making a distinctive rattle as they coiled into their boxes. The three arches of the old stone structure span the river while bearing the weight of a double row of three-story buildings housing the expensive jewelry shops that have occupied the bridge for centuries, following the eviction of the butchers who once dominated. Early environmental laws had ended their habit of throwing offal into the river.

Above the shops is the little-known *Corrodio Vasariano*, or Vasari Corridor. It provides a private passageway from the *Palazzo Pitti* to the *Palazzo Vecchio*. Built in 1564 at the order of the Grand Duke Cosimo I dei Medici, it was a way for justifiably-paranoid 'royalty' to pass between the official and residential palaces without mingling with the conquered population of the former Republic of Florence. Today the corridor is filled with precious art, and a short length is available for tours.

Much of the vast wealth of art, rare illuminated books, frescoes, and other treasures of Florence were lost or damaged in the historic flood of 1966. In a scenario repeated several times over the last millennia, freak storms upstream poured their bounty into the basin of the Arno River. That year, however, was nothing like what Florentines might have expected. In a matter of only a few hours the river filled its deep channel and rose to the top of the high walls that normally usher it through the city. Continuing to rise, the waters put the population in a panic. A hundred were drowned attempting to escape.

During that cataclysmic event, water rose in the quiet *Piazza di Santa Croce* by our hotel to an astounding 6.7 meters in depth, reaching the ceilings of upstairs apartments. The torrent burst through the shops of the gold-smiths on the Ponte Vecchio, tearing them away and dashing them to pieces. The very structure of the bridge shook and trembled as the flood waters tore through it. Yet in the Vasari Corridor, a few brave souls ran into the darkened hall to snatch irreplaceable art works from the walls and dash back to safety, repeating the hazardous journey dozens of times, never knowing when the entire structure might suddenly collapse from the weight of the raging torrent tearing at its foundations.

When the flood waters finally receded, the city lay covered with an estimated 600,000 tons of mud, in places several feet thick. More than three million books lay in the ugly mix of water, mud, and fuel oil. Some 14,000 other works of art were likewise damaged or destroyed. Yet in that hour of dark despair, around the world there were people mobilizing, packing their bags and coming to help. They became known as the *angeli di fango*, the mud angels.

Today Firenze still feels the loss created by that flood, both economically and artistically. Despite the horrific impact, it remains a center for the conservation of Italy's art, culture, and history for the benefit of the world.

We strolled along the bridge in the cool of early morning, mindful of the history represented in the venerable structure. While Susan browsed, distracted, I ducked into a shop and chose a pair of beautiful gold earrings, promising to return when they were wrapped. Keeping a secret from her was never easy, but I managed to dash back down the length of the bridge a few minutes later to retrieve the package and return undetected. The reward of her pleased smile at dinner made my efforts worthwhile.

We climbed the broad slope of the Via de Giucciardini to visit the Palazzo Pitti, where Cosimo I and his descendants ruled as the Dukes of Toscana. There we found the royal residences replete with so much art it was overwhelming. Paintings on easels hid others hanging on walls, and sculptures, which themselves hid the elaborate friezes and plaster-work trim. Ceilings were elaborate enough to please any lover of Rococo detail.

One of the more amazing features of the palace is the exterior, which utilizes a sort of visual trickery to disguise its enormity. A succession of architects brought the entire facade down to human scale by enlarging the windows and doors to mythic proportions, which in turn shrinks the buildings' perspective. A casual glance from the streets below fail to disclose just how large the structure really is. As one walks toward the building it seems to grow in scope.

Behind the palace are the famed Boboli Gardens. There in one corner the architect Bernardo Buontalenti, a Mannerist, had created a bizarre *grotto* where figures, both human and otherwise, seem to emerge from the stone of the walls.

Firenze is a popular destination, but it is one perhaps best reached through public transportation. On that particular visit to Firenze we made the mistake of arriving by rental car. We had booked our hotel in the old city, where traffic is restricted, but knew that hotel guests received a pass. We drove through the old city gate and wandered a maze of narrow one-way streets, but missed our hotel, and ended up back outside the walls. It was a maneuver we repeated several times before finally finding the narrow alleyway that concealed our intended residence.

We unloaded luggage for five people before parking the car, at considerable expense, and walking back a half-dozen blocks to the hotel. The rental car had remained parked for the rest of our visit.

Our pleasant memories of the trip were somewhat spoiled when, upon returning home, we received notice that our credit card had been debited no less than a dozen times for violating the *centro storico,* the historic center, in our search for our hotel. Happily, American Express dealt with the confusion over our hotel exemption, and the problem disappeared.

While we vowed to never again enter Firenze by car, we eventually found a delightful solution during a driving tour with friends. We booked our hotel at a tiny village called *Passo dei Pecorai,* or the pass of the shepherds. Lying south of Firenze in the direction of Greve, it offers direct inter-city bus service. Our hotel was clean, offered an excellent restaurant, and from the bus stop at the front we were whisked directly to the heart of Florence in minutes in clean and comfortable motor-coaches.

The Ghosts of Craco

Our explorations of Italy often led us to wonderful encounters with the people, but one place was memorable simply because of the lack of them. In the southern land of Basilicata lies an ancient culture, with traditions and superstitions that date far back into the dusty pages of history. Here, long before the arrival of Christianity, people were aware of the close connection of both men and animals to the land. The stories of terrible beasts and dragons were passed down from generations long ago.

People carry much of the animal world in themselves, and in the beliefs of these remote people, animals also know much of humans, and have abilities that they keep hidden. In this shadowy land of imagination, creatures may live partly in each of these worlds, perhaps inhabiting the world of humans in daylight, and the world of animals at night. They may manifest strange abilities, or simply shift their shape to become something else entirely. Men became bears, or boars, manifesting their deepest characters.

For the people of the hill towns and isolated villages of Basilicata and neighboring parts of Italy, those beliefs still have force. The legends and stories of the shape-shifters are held close, and are not normally shared with outsiders, with those who might mock them, or disbelieve. For the people that have inhabited these rugged and isolated places, though, the stories have power to affect their worlds, and their lives.

We drove north from Basilicata's *Jonica* coast with a special mission in mind: today we would see if such ghosts still haunted the crumbling ruins of isolated, half-forgotten Craco. In that exceptional spot we found all that we hoped for.

It is an appropriate setting for connections to the otherworldly phantoms that many believe still haunt these hills. Even the name Craco has a haunted feel, rhyming as it does with Draco, the constellation of the dragon that spins in the night sky above.

There, among the abandoned ruins, the stories of the past might seem especially tangible. There one may still grasp the pith of the force, the power that remains potent despite the advent of science. Folk-legend says that there may remain in the town a man-boar, who stalks the streets at night, defending against human interlopers. Yet people had ultimately fled because it was the town itself that was the danger.

We arrived instead on a sunny afternoon, winding through the dramatic and changing landscapes of Basilicata. The light, broken only by scattered clouds, played upon the rolling golden wheat fields and rocky crags, the deep-green of the pine forests, and the walls of the high city of Pisticci.

Our well-maintained road climbed and dipped, and the beautiful views caused many a pause as they manifested the varied land-forms in turn. Then, as we rounded the top of a hill, we got our first, startling view of our destination.

Like the distant view of the castle in an old horror movie, the dusty grey town stood high upon a sharp pinnacle. It appeared as if part of the stone of the mountain itself, not built by human hands, but thrust upward from the very bowels of the earth, exposed perhaps to attract its unwary prey, a lure of a city on a mountain.

We approached it slowly on the lonely road, passing not a single car, no sign of a living creature but the starkly-black birds that soared overhead or croaked hoarsely from the dry shrubbery at the roadside.

The road itself changed from smooth and well-marked, and took on a look of neglect, with crumbling and broken concrete guardrails, and patches upon patches. It climbed higher and closer to our destination, the town appearing and disappearing behind the sere ridges.

We stopped twice more to take in the changing views of the city. It was enough to give one pause, and fire the imagination. At each new vantage point the distant, empty windows appeared more and more like the vacant eye-sockets of so many skulls, weathered by time to an ashy grey. A sheer precipice spoke of the extreme position it commanded.

Craco was an ancient city, with documented human habitation dating back at least to the iron age, and in all likelihood, long before. Like many of the old *tufa*-stone cities, it is a place where early man might have been drawn a thousand centuries before, with caves in the soft stone and views over broad plains where wildlife and enemies could be seen from afar. Almost a kilometer above the sea, it is a commanding presence, visible from a great distance.

The town was well known to the ancient Greeks, who were aware of the fertile valley of farms that lay at the foot of the city. The agriculture of Craco's Valagri, irrigated by the appropriately-named Agri river, fed many of the Greek colonies that flourished for 500 years on the southern shores of Italy.

The human population of Craco grew slowly over the millennia, and persisted through a series of ruling regimes. Like much of the region, it had been fought over by invaders many times. Christianity took hold slowly in this land of competing gods and spirits representing both the underworld and the sky. A thousand years ago it was referenced in a Papal bull addressed to the priest and people of Craco. By the 1950's the town boasted thousands of residents, a cinema, several bars, restaurants, and at least two churches. Vibrant agriculture brought steady commerce to the town.

Yet today Craco stands abandoned, an eerie presence that many take pains to avoid. Asked, people will advise you darkly to go someplace more beautiful, leave that old town to fate. Rumors abound that it is haunted, cursed, a doomed place built directly upon the gates of hell itself. It was those mysteries we wished to confront.

We drove on, at length passing a small marker at the edge of the city.

There we saw signs that prohibited stopping or parking, and urging us on to an information center beyond the ghost city. We crept forward until we were passing the very foot of the town. To our right, a huge pile of rubble cascaded from high above, and the broken walls of houses spilled their rocky souls. To our left, a deep valley awaited them like a grave, already partly filled with the stony remains of the earlier landslides. The earth which had thrust this promontory upward now seemed determined to swallow it whole.

The modern promenade which once offered citizens a place to take an evening's stroll and enjoy the striking views now lay twisted and broken, broad slabs of concrete tipped at angles too steep for any but the small grey lizards that basked there. The city walls were also part of the rubble, along with the fragments of a modern concrete and steel wall which had once pretended to have some power to control the forces of the very earth below. A herd of goats wandered over the broken detritus, gnawing at the sparse grasses that survived there.

We paused briefly near a few trees, gazing up through the fence which had been erected by the *commune* to keep the unwary from sudden death in the ruins. The unearthly silence was broken only by the sound of the wind whispering over the broken stones. It was the very essence of desolation.

Although the steep slopes of the mountain had long offered a sense of security from enemies, it turned out that the thing citizens had most to fear was the mountain itself. It had awoken and wreaked a terrible vengeance upon the interloping city on its back.

At first no one noticed that the mountain was moving. After thousands of years of life on the pinnacle, they assumed they were safe. The first few cracks in the walls of houses and public buildings were patched up and forgotten. Then in the early part of the 20th century there were some sudden collapses. They were problematic, but not serious enough to cause panic. Yet the time had finally come for the earth to reclaim its own.

But the earth would not be ignored, and began to make itself heard. No doubt the groaning emitted from below must have alarmed the citizens of Craco, and the sticking doors and windows, the shifting of walls, might have worried some. Yet even in a land not unused to earthquakes, few could have realized the terrible wrath that would soon appear.

In 1963, almost without warning, a massive landslide carried away the western slopes of the town, swallowing the road, the principal piazza with its war monument, the cinema, a bar, and a dozen houses.

The citizens of Craco gathered themselves, and still clinging to superstitious beliefs in the power of the land and the legends, began to repair their damaged houses. New walls with deep pilings were erected to ensure that the slope would be stabilized.

Yet despite their efforts, the land continued to creep, and more houses began to crumble. Large cracks appeared in buildings throughout the city. People began to realize that Craco, for all its history and ancient faith in the earth, was doomed to die. Some fled, claiming that the town was cursed. A few residents, perhaps tied to the mountain by thousands of years of tradition, too stubborn to relinquish their ancient roots and unafraid of the demons of the underworld, held out.

We parked beneath some wizened old olive trees just off the broken pavement of the main road. Fruit hung heavy upon their stout limbs, just as it had done for centuries. Would anyone now return to claim it?

After we had made a light picnic of bread, cheese, and fruit, I decided to hike downhill through the trees to see what could be found there. The path led me to scramble over broken stone walls, scattered red bricks, and fragments of shattered ceramics. A large black bird, perhaps a raven, hovered silently over my head in the still afternoon air, as if watching my progress.

I came to a sharp drop, apparently created by the slowly sliding mass I was walking upon. There, far below, I could make out the thin line of the two-lane highway that split the forests and farms, one from the other, a patchwork of rich green arbors and brown, ripening wheat.

The silence of the still afternoon was broken only by the loud droning of cicadas, emerged from their seventeen years of life underground to enjoy their scant few days in sunshine, to procreate, and then to return to dust. I found it an uncanny parallel, on a far different time-scale, to that of the mountain I stood upon. It too had emerged from darkness after millions of years, had lived its numbered days, and was returning from whence it came.

Today, Craco stands empty, abandoned to the power of the elements. In the late 1960's, the Italian government had allotted money to pay for new housing, and relocated virtually the entire population of the city to the new town of Pesceria di Craco on the river below. Only about twenty-five residents remain in a few modern houses near the edge of the old city.

Still wishing to get closer to the gaping maw that led into the heart of the city, we drove onward and found the site of the info point. There, next to an empty parking lot, was a white-washed building, seemingly as abandoned as the rest of the town. Susan was content to wait in the car while I inquired.

A few steps led to a double door. It seemed locked, but yielded to a firm thrust. I stepped in and found the lobby vacant. A long counter stood unused, and there was no sound from the offices behind. I called out but got no reply, and felt a small doubt creep into my mind. I waited, biding my time by reading the posters and legal notices on the walls.

After a couple of minutes a dull-eyed young man appeared. I asked him if it was possible to enter the city.

"*Si,*" he answered, "we organize tours for groups."

I explained that we were only two, and he replied that, if others appeared, or at 3:00 pm., whichever came first, we could enter the city. But first, we must purchase a pass, which would cost ten euro each. I dutifully paid. We would wait.

We spent the time back at the foot of the collapse, snacking on the remains of our picnic lunch. The ruins seemed eerily quiet. We wondered at the seeming randomness of the sudden eviction citizens had suffered after so many generations, and how they had fared in a forced retreat from the heights that were their birthright.

At the appointed hour, only our quiet young guide appeared, and he led the two of us up to the town. He unlocked a gate in the high chain-link fence, and showed us to a small, cave-like room in the lower city walls, from where he obtained hard-hats for each of us.

Together we set out upon a steep and stony path, climbing over the deep rubble of collapse to reach the lower houses, themselves only half-standing. The other halves had already joined the calcareous remains below. The trail was liberally covered with the droppings of the goats, who retreated down the hill as we approached.

Our guide paused. "*Questa era la piazza grande,*" he told us. "This was the large piazza. There were bars there, and a cinema. There was a fountain here."

"Was there also a monument to the war victims?" I asked.

"*E caduta*," he said. "It's fallen." Like those it was meant to honor, now itself another victim. "It fell in the first great landslide, when all these houses, and the piazza, also collapsed."

"When the earth collapsed, were many people killed?" I asked him,

"Some were hurt. No one died." A small mercy, I thought to myself.

We passed the remains of a house that once offered a spectacular view to the east. It had collapsed three weeks earlier, our guide announced. The broken concrete of the roof lay in large chunks at our feet in the midst of the former living quarters. Huge cracks were evident everywhere, and some of the building appeared to be half buried.

"What is your name?" I asked our guide.

"Vicenzo," he replied.

"Did you go to college to study anthropology or archaeology...?"

"No, I just work here," he replied laconically.

"Where do you live?"

"In Pesceria," he replied, without elaborating. We had passed the new town on the road, offered to them by the government: blocks of sterile two-story apartment buildings, a strip of park, a soul-less alternative to the mountain aerie that had been home to his ancestors.

We climbed up sets of broken steps, past more of the tumble-down houses, and entered the remains of a small *piazzetta* lying before the remains of the town church. Some of the buildings and doorways had been recently reinforced by steel supports and scaffolding, in an attempt to delay their inevitable failure. Above us the campanile still stood tall, but without its bells, or the clock which had once adorned its southwestern face.

"The bells were stolen, all the windows and doors, too," we were told. "Anything of value was carried off or destroyed years ago by 'vandali, ladri...'" Vandals, thieves, he told us. His terms carried impact. The words rang of ancient problems for the people of this region. The very name 'vandal' came from the name of the Germanic tribes that had fled the Huns only to themselves sack Roman Gaul.

69

We peered into the remains of the church, now devoid of its doors and most of the surrounding cement and plaster-work that once covered the surrounding stones. Only the ancient bole of a tree spanned the space above, still partly wearing its original grey bark, providing a rough lintel between the fragile arch of stone walls. It was all that prevented them from collapsing upon each other. High above, the dome still stood. Once beautifully decorated with colored majolica tiles, it had shed most of them over the years, and was the image of decay.

Inside, the altar was also missing, and a heap of rubble and a growth of greenery filled the space between the bare walls. Parts of the roof had fallen upon the floor. Through openings no doubt once filled with stained glass, only the afternoon's now cloudy sky could be seen. The area seemed entirely forlorn, abandoned by both God and man. It was easy to see why superstitious minds might count it as a victory for the forces of darkness.

We climbed higher to enter a large *palazzo*, one of the half-dozen wealthy homes that had stood in the city. Its large common room had gaping windows that once offered spectacular, sweeping views of the valleys to residents and honored guests alike. We gazed out over the vertigo-inducing void into the depths of the valley, and clung to the shattered walls for the little security they offered.

I stood in the vacant opening, framing a photograph of that striking view, and as I touched the shutter, a sudden gust of wind blew in, and carried upon it a leaf, which danced in the center of the window. My photograph clearly shows the broad valley filled with farms, the distant mountains, and the heavy stone frame of the house. But there, in the center, appears the shadowy image of the leaf, floating like a fairy. If one looks closely, it appears almost as if it were a small sailboat, carrying a single lonely traveler. A spirit, a sprite? Or perhaps it was just a random accident of timing and the fickle wind. We will be saving the photo.

When in Rome

There is no place as wholly 'Italian' as the blend of cultures that make up the capital city. Among the most famous cities on earth, *Roma* enjoys enormous tourism, which contributes mightily to its economy. It offers a vast array of subject matter for those wishing to explore historic sites, art, and monuments of every stripe. We wanted to not just see them, but understand them in the context of history and culture. It was apparent it would take time. Repeated return trips to Rome after our brief earlier visit gave us a growing understanding of the complexities of the Italian capital.

Rome is more than the old city on the *sette colli*, or seven hills within the original city walls. It is one of the first true world capitals, as the Roman Empire dwarfed all preceding Western empires in both scale and duration. During those centuries it achieved a population of a million, and began to spread outward, and eventually *"tras Tevere,"* or across the Tevere, as the Romans call the rapidly-flowing river that provides so many scenic views.

The city, its empire, and its mechanisms of law, government, and art left a mark upon much of our 'modern' world. The language spoken by Roman citizens two thousand years ago is today the language of our law, science, and medicine. We use it to organize our genus and species, our stars and planets.

Romans gave us the foot, the yard, and the mile, our calendar, and the names of our days and months.

Before Rome, cities were limited in size by their need for water. Wells could only supply the needs of limited populations. Roman engineers overcame the problem by inventing concrete, and the weight-bearing arch. Those developments enabled them to build graceful aqueducts, some more than ninety kilometers long, to bring flowing rivers from distant mountains to the city by gravity. They added large-scale sewer systems to take away waste. Then they built reservoirs and enormous water tanks to supply those systems.

Roman engineers developed the basic street grid, the first planned cities, and a national highway system that spanned the Roman realm, allowing the rapid movement of not only armies, but goods, turning the Empire into a vast, economically inter-dependent entity. Trade flowed to and fro, from the south of modern Russia to the British Isles to North Africa, from the Middle East to Spain. Products including wheat, wax, honey, wine, livestock, oil, hides, and even stone was transported long distances in a matter of weeks using the Roman network of seaports and roadways. They standardized lane widths to accommodate both chariots and pedestrian crossings, and thereby standardized the chariot itself.

Italy gave us the Renaissance, and produced Michelangelo, Leonardo, and Dante. Italians created some of the world's most-loved concertos and operas, as well as the piano, viol, violin, and cello that made them possible.

The names of Italia's beautiful cities and features are applied to our communities and resorts. The leading edges of global design in fashion, food, and automobiles are filled with Italian names. How is it that one small nation produced so much of what our modern culture relies upon? How does that nation continue to produce such works?

To understand Italy today, you much first appreciate what she offers us. You must learn to ask yourself the right questions, and seek the answers. Then you will return home with a better understanding of what you have seen.

Rome's great advances in architecture and engineering are perhaps best illustrated by the astounding dome of the circular Pantheon.

Based upon Archimedes' mathematical revelations, the Pantheon is a sphere within a cube. The world's largest unsupported concrete dome, it was achieved by gradually tapering the thickness of the dome's shell as it rose, requiring complex mathematical calculations to perfect both the interior and exterior surfaces. The magnificent, unsupported dome is 43.28 meters high, and the width of the base is also 43.28 meters. A sphere of that diameter, if resting on the floor, would therefore touch all the interior surfaces of the dome perfectly. That design has given it the strength to stand in continuous use without significant maintenance since the Emperor Hadrian ordered its construction in 126 CE. It might have been damaged or destroyed during the intervening years, but one of the last emperors, ruling from Constantinople as the Western Empire collapsed, found no use for it, and donated it to the Catholic Church. It thereby escaped the fate of the *Coloseo* and many of the temples of the Forum, which were robbed of marble and stone for private uses.

Pantheon means "all the gods." Today it is a Catholic church. The only light within the building enters through a circular hole at the top of the dome, called an *occulus*. As a result, a single shaft of light enters with the sun, and sweeps across the floor each day, but on an ever-changing path that moves with the seasons, thereby inscribing a horizontal figure-eight on the floor. You may find that same device, known as an analemma, imprinted on your modern globe.

We stood in that single shaft of light, and in an instant, all the rest of the interior disappeared into the shadows. It was like being on a stage, unable to see the audience beyond the footlights. Stepping out of the sun, we watched dust motes drift in its glare, and then the rest of the interior came slowly back into focus.

The Pantheon remains one of the most remarkably simple and beautiful structures in the world. Standing within that space, and listening to the echoing footfalls of visitors, and the muffled voices that reverberate from the perfect symmetry above is nothing less than awe-inspiring.

All the advanced technology the ancient Romans achieved was yet belied by the retained primitive savagery of their culture, which was widely dependent upon slavery, and accepted even ritual murder and gladiatorial combat as public entertainment. This dichotomy seems baffling to the modern mind, which is more inured to brutality confined to warfare and the basest cultures. It was yet another of the dark riddles of history.

The institution of slavery, imposed on hundreds of thousands of enemies spared death at the hands of Rome's Legions, meant an individual was completely objectified, and could be used for any purpose, including sexual, or put to death by their owners. The most fortunate lived well, and some made significant contributions to Roman society. Marcus Tullius Tiro, who was born into slavery and became the personal assistant to the famed lawyer, senator, and consul Cicero, invented a form of shorthand using thousands of symbols, and wrote many books, including the biography of his famous master. Like Tiro, many slaves were ultimately granted their freedom by grateful masters.

Roman society was also very stratified socially, with *i teatri e templi*, the theatres and temples, for example, offering seating in ranks according to status. Marriages were often arranged as much to achieve family political ties or wealth as for romantic reasons. Ostentation and public shows were popular routes to public recognition and acclaim. The world has little changed.

•

On our first return to Roma we found a hotel near the beautiful shopping district of the *Via Veneto*. It was a bright and clean place, and a good compromise between the opulent and primitive. It was also within walking distance of the several attractions in the west-central part of the city. Tourists flock to the city, of course, but because of the vast numbers of scattered attractions it lacks the feeling of crowds of tour groups that we found in other popular destinations. Susan pointed out the fact that Rome is perhaps the only place one can see guided tour groups consisting entirely of nuns.

On one cool, sunny day we started downhill from our hotel toward *la Fontana di Trevi*. Perhaps the world's most famous fountain, the Trevi Fountain was completed in 1762, and its gushing waters still attract throngs of tourists. A smaller original fountain had been placed at that site upon the completion of the *Aqua Virgo*, the aqueduct of the virgin, built by the Romans starting in 19 BCE. The aqueducts brought mountain water for Roman plumbing for over 400 years, until invading Goths smashed all the aqueducts in an attempt to deprive the besieged city of water. In the 1400's Catholic Popes began the work of restoring the aqueducts, which led to the construction of many beautiful fountains throughout the city.

Primarily the work of Nicola Salvi and his successor, Pietro Bracci, the Trevi Fountain was based in part on the design of the famous sculptor Gian Lorenzo Bernini. The fountain features an elaborate frieze of carved human and animal figures, many set in niches in the wall behind, and served as the inspiration for the 1950's film and song, "Three Coins in the Fountain." It was a romantic place, and a bit awe-inspiring.

We mingled with the other visitors, each eager to take the perfect photo, to pose with their friends, to burn the image deep into their own memories. We were no different, and found the fountain just as impressive during repeated visits, especially at night or during rainy weather, when one can find it in virtual solitude.

Our explorations led us gradually around the city, and past many beautiful sights, not least of which was the *Giardini dei Quirinale*, which stand on the *Colle Quirinale*, the highest of Rome's famed seven hills. They are the grounds of the Quirinal Palace, which is today the residence of the president of the Republic of Italy. Various monumental structures and the palace itself mark the grounds.

Among the most prominent landmarks in Rome is the enormous 'wedding-cake' monument dedicated to the memory of Vittorio Emanuele II, the first king of a unified Italy. Completed in 1935, the structure is 81 meters high and 135 wide, almost three times as tall and more than twice as wide as the Lincoln Memorial in Washington, DC. It is styled as the "Altar of the Fatherland" and contains the tomb of unknown soldiers, and museums filled with the memorabilia of the Italian armed forces. The brilliantly-white marble construct is a modern retort to the glories of ancient Rome, built by Mussolini as part of his maniacal efforts to restore them in the 20th century. The king's image is sculpted astride a powerful horse as the focal point of the striking columned structure. He was, no doubt, widely loved. The same could not be said for Mussolini, who preferred to be feared.

We climbed the steps to the top to take in the remarkable views across the city from the front, and those of the famous *Fori Romani*, or original Roman Forums, behind it. That space, with its remaining standing columns and ruins, was once the heart of the Roman Republic, and later the seat of the empire, where senators would gather to debate and vote. Here the lofty and motivating speeches of the lawyer Cicero were sent echoing across the stones, changing the course of history.

Temples to the various and capricious gods honored by the Romans line the stony pathway of the *Via Sacra*. Other temples have been long-since converted to churches. We explored the Temple of the Vestal Virgins, where they once tended the sacred flame of Vesta, representing the hearth-fire of the Empire. A virgin accused of having broken their vow of chastity might be led into a small underground chamber with a small amount of food and water and buried alive.

At the far end of the Forum we passed under the Triumphal Arch of Titus. Still intact after its construction in 82 C.E. by the Emperor Domitian in memory of Titus, his older brother and a winning Roman general. Beyond it rises the familiar curve of *Il Coloseo*, the Colosseum, where elaborate entertainments saw prisoners locked in battles to the death with lions, bears, or each other. The floor of the Colosseum could be flooded, to create space for the re-enactment of desperate naval battles before an audience of 87,000.

During the Dark Ages, the original marble cladding was stripped from the abandoned arena and used to build new housing. Today, even the remaining ruins form an impressive spectacle, and offer tours to the lower levels where gladiators awaited their bloody battles. The peaceful afternoon belied the dark and terrible events that had occurred in that place, but imagination, if left to roam free, might easily conjure up such a past in any locale if left to dwell on the hundreds of thousands of years of human history that have passed over most of the surface of our world. Humans are undoubtedly both the cruelest and most compassionate species that has ever lived, capable of both the most horrific acts, and utter self-sacrifice.

Above the Forums stands the Palatine Hill, where the wealthiest families of Rome once built their private palaces. We roamed through the remaining houses and elaborate gardens with their fountains and broad staircases that had been adapted by those ancient Romans, now converted by modern ones into a public museum. Many were razed by the megalomaniac Emperor Nero to build his "Golden House." Nero considered it an appropriate sort of urban renewal in the wake of the infamous fire that destroyed most of the wooden homes and shops in the poor parts of Rome.

Stretching for great distances across the hills, Nero's envisioned palace was never completed before his death, and his political enemies made sure that it didn't stand as a monument to his insanity. Just across from the Colliseum we gained entry to the dark, underground remains of his mad dreams. Buried by his disgusted successors, they are only now being excavated to reveal the scale of his ambitions and greed.

Just across the street from the Vittorio Emanuele we admired the *Foro Traiano*, or Trajan's Forum. This lesser-known forum was built to relieve the terribly-overcrowded original a short walk away, which had at last run out of space for new monumental buildings and temples. The last of the Imperial *fori* to be built, it features the remarkable column of Trajan, intricately carved in a spiral of scenes that depicted the battles and events of his life, and repeated on each side so that even non-Latin observers could learn just how amazing a ruler he was. Like many powerful rulers of the ancient world, the leading men of Rome encouraged cult followings, and promoted themselves as descendants of the gods, and many were deified by the Senate, some along with their mothers. Their supporters won favors by public displays of sacrifice at shrines erected to them. Emperors were nothing if not focused on their legacies.

The Roman Republic was born of a revolution against a king who was perceived as a tyrant in 509 BCE. From that familiar patriotic story emerged an evolving form of government that survived for almost 500 years. It lacked a constitution, basing legal decisions on a large collection of laws and precedent.

During the centuries of both the Roman Republic, and the subsequent Roman Empire, which began with Julius Caesar's civil war in 49 BCE and persisted until its gradual collapse and splintering four centuries later, there were hundreds of political leaders and generals who did great and terrible things. Magnificent public works and monuments, murder, war, and mayhem fill the sketchy histories of those centuries, much as it does our own. A few of those men stood out, and made dramatic marks upon not only the urban landscapes, but upon the people of Rome, and modern Italy. We thought it would be interesting to seek them out, but their presence was almost inescapable.

Several times we retraced our steps through the dusty Forum

pathways of what had been Rome's political and economic heart, each pleasant walk revealing more about the complexities of the relationship between the ancient city and its sprawling empire. Pigeons strut and coo where legendary figures once strode and debated. There amid the soaring columns of grand temples and high steps of once-magnificent public buildings we found the place still dedicated to the man who was undoubtedly Rome's greatest general. Today only a waist-high mound of crumbling bricks marks the spot where Julius Caesar's savaged remains were cremated on a pyre in 44 BCE. That act, as much as any other ceremony, marked the return to centuries of rule by hereditary royalty.

Caesar's destruction of the Republic for primarily egotistical reasons shouldn't have been a surprise to those ancient Romans. He had spent the majority of his life conducting warfare, and could see no reason he shouldn't run the politics of Rome like he did the army he had raised, first with his own family fortune, and then with the backing of friends in the Senate, which had appropriated funds.

The scourge of the tribal chieftains who had ruled much of the land the Romans called Gaul, Caesar had won the great majority of the hundreds of battles and skirmishes his army had fought. At his command, his engineers built rings of siege towers to surround and surmount several fortified cities, and dealt harshly with those who resisted him. He had overrun all of modern France, much of Spain, twice invaded Britain in fleets built by his own forces, and twice crossed the Rhine to punish hostile Germanic tribes, erecting enormous bridges that were then disassembled behind them.

For a decade he had roamed victorious across most of the known world, as far as modern Egypt, Syria, and Turkey. It was in the latter that he uttered the immortal phrase, *"Veni, vedi, vici"*, while dictating a letter to the Senate. "I came, I saw, I conquered." He wrote an auto-biographical history of his campaigns in Gaul that portrayed himself as wise and successful, and it was widely read. He developed a large fan base through his self-promotion.

Ever insecure without his army, Caesar was faced at age forty-nine with an inevitable return to private life, during which he was certain to be sued by enemies. He chose instead to react to that perceived affront by crossing the Tiber, a small, now forgotten stream at the border of his assigned province, accompanied by a single legion. It was an act of war against Rome. When other Italian cities welcomed him as a conquering hero, powerful political enemies fled Rome with armies of their own, and he pursued them. It was the start of a bloody and senseless civil war. After two years of fighting he emerged victorious, and was installed as what is now recognized as Rome's first emperor. The Republic was all but dead.

He ruled with a sense of superiority and aloofness, and eventually his remaining enemies began to resent him more than ever. That is often cited as the reason that he was murdered soon thereafter by a group of senators, some of whom were former political allies.

In sharp contrast, a pleasant walk upstream along the fast-flowing waters of the Tevere leads one to a far different monument, built to mark his successor, a far different Caesar. The enormous round structure of *Castel Sant'Angelo* was originally conceived as his own mausoleum by Caesar Augustus.

Born Gaius Julius Caesar Octavius, as a young man he became the adopted son of Julius Caesar. Apparently the great general saw something special in his young nephew, and decided to make him his heir.

After his uncle's murder, young Octavius had been forced to fight for his title, repeating Julius Caesar's pursuit of enemies before eventually defeating the forces of Marc Antony and Cleopatra in Egypt. Ruling modestly as Gaius Caesar, the people of Rome themselves bestowed his title of "Augustus" because of his many well-considered acts, which succeeded in stabilizing the empire after the succession of civil wars. Undoubtedly one of Rome's greatest emperors, he reinforced the frontiers, built much-needed public works, enacted laws that benefited the populace, and reigned over more than 40 years of peace. "I found Rome a city of bricks," he was noted for saying, "and I left it a city of marble."

Revered as a god by many Romans of his time, his plans for the magnificent round mausoleum were received with widespread enthusiasm. Built to honor and preserve his memory and great works, it was originally crowned with a forest of trees surrounding a central monument. It was one of Rome's grandest structures, begun during his reign, but further embellished after his death. The interior features a broad sloping processional street which leads downward to his burial chamber.

After the rise of Christianity and the fall of the empire, additional defensive walls were erected to help protect what eventually became a citadel. To that refuge the Popes could flee along an enclosed corridor built above the streets like an aqueduct. We spent many hours exploring the building, grounds, and the fascinating museum within. Relics from the time of Augustus, and many from the intervening centuries, are housed within the colonnaded halls. Fabulously-decorated chambers within feature elaborate ceilings covered with vivid frescoes.

Augustus' temple provides a strange contrast to that of his step-father's memorial. After his assassination Julius was deified by the Senate and a large temple was planned in his honor, but was never built. Today his only monument is the eroded mound of brick, marked only by a few fresh flowers still left by modern admirers. Shakespeare had made him Rome's most famous figure sixteen centuries later.

Today the cool stone of the son's monument provides a shelter from the heat of Roman summers for thousands of visitors. We paused for *panini* and cool drinks on the top terrace level, enjoying the fine views of the city we had come to admire. The gates of the *Castel* face the stone bulk of the *Ponte Sant'Angelo*. Between the two landmarks lies a *piazza* that provides a popular gathering place for entertainers, fakirs, and 'mystics,' including those who perform amazing 'feats of strength,' such as supporting a fellow mystic seated upon an outstretched arm for hours. Tourists stop to take photos and toss coins in their boxes, while others puzzle over the illusion.

After a beautiful sunset, we walked through the long *Via dei Coronari*, or the Way of the Coronations, pausing to gaze into the brightly-lighted and artistically-decorated shop windows. A mark of pride, shop windows throughout Italy often feature beautiful and creative displays to attract shoppers to their merchandise.

We stopped at the window of a *pastificio* to watch a young woman roll and slice broad sheets of pasta dough. Using a small cutter with a lop-sided wheel, she cut ribbons of pasta into zig-zag strips, then cut them laterally before pinching each resulting rectangle into the familiar shape that Americans call "bow-ties" but the Italians refer to as *farfalle*, or butterflies. Tempted by the thought of the freshest-imaginable pasta, we entered to enjoy small servings topped with delicious homemade *sugo di pomodoro*, or sauce of tomato.

We ambled leisurely onward and found ourselves at the end of the bustling Piazza Navona. There we took in the ever-changing human spectacle that swirls each evening around the gigantic fountains designed by the famous artist and architect Gian Lorenzo Bernini. Vendors sold lighted flying toys, and children chased dogs across the broad pedestrian space. Cafes and bars spilled light and life into the cool of the evening, and tented restaurant dining-rooms offered expensive menus. We held hands as we walked, absorbing the sights, sounds and smells. It was modern Rome at its best.

On another day we made our way back to the Trastevere district to view the wonders of the Vatican City, the world's smallest independent nation, and the seat of the Roman Catholic Church. We stood near the river and gazed up the magnificent boulevard of the *Via Conciliazione*, or Way of Conciliation.

After a short walk we crossed the white stripe of border painted on the stone, and stepped into the Vatican City. Once in command of a vast swath of territory known as the Papal States, and the dispenser of legitimacy to kings and emperors alike, the power of the Vatican has shrunk to this postage-stamp of territory, but remains in command of the resources of the Church world-wide. On one visit we passed by the *piazza* only to be surprised by the arrival of the Pope only a few meters away, there to perform the sacrament of the Mass and bless the thousands in attendance.

The tide of life in the Vatican flows to and fro through the enormous space of *La Piazza di San Pietro*. Known in English as Saint Peter's Square, that inappropriate name ignores the fact that the space is circular. Bernini's magnificent colonnades, hundreds of columns set four-deep in a vast arc around the space, are so precisely set in their positions that, when viewed from a particular stone set in the exact center of that arc, morph instantly into a single row of columns. Thousands pass the spot each day, unaware of the phenomenon. We repeatedly tested the view, finding that a movement as small a single step destroyed the effect. It is an allusion, perhaps, to many other secrets of Italy.

The enormity of the Basilica of Saint Peter was designed to impress upon the masses the power and majesty of the church, the gateway to heavenly perpetuity. The exterior walls seem to ripple with vertical columns, devoid of horizontal continuity. Inside, the smoke of incense braziers was illuminated in shafts of colorful light streaming through windows set in the vastness of the dome, more than 130 meters high, making the church a Renaissance skyscraper in all but shape.

The interior spaces were a dazzling display of colorful detail that required binoculars to see clearly. Monumental columns defined and divided the interior, creating spaces within that were still easily large enough to contain most churches.

It is possible to join tour groups for ascents to both the dome above, and the vast catacombs beneath the church which contain the remains of thousands of early Christians, popes and saints. We chose to view the famous Sistine Chapel instead, with the famous masterwork of Michelangelo. While his architectural genius is on display in the design of the Basilica, his skill as a painter touches its highest note in the remarkable ceiling frescoes of the chapel.

The fresco process required the application of paints to wet, freshly-laid plaster, which absorbed the colors, creating a peculiar depth and richness, along with stability of hue. It was a painstaking process that required years of work by teams of artists beginning in 1477. Michelangelo's work was the crowning touch, achieved between 1508 and 1541, covering more than 1,100 square meters of the ceiling.

Although most visitors flock to see such famous attractions as the Vatican and the Colosseum, there are enough other impressive sights and minor monuments to make any other city jealous. It was a challenge to see half of them on our more than twenty visits to Rome.

On one trip we arrived on the direct train after buying 'Roma Passes' at Rome's *Fiumicino* airport. Traveling lightly as usual, we found our hotel only a few blocks' walk from the *Stazione di Roma Termini*.

As we approached our lodgings we passed a venerable round building with an attractive garden tucked behind a high iron fence. Our hotel offered an impressive birds-eye view of the same building. A brief investigation revealed that it was the former *Aquario Romano*, or the Roman Aquarium. Despite the ancient-sounding name, we learned that it had been constructed in the 1880's, and was used only briefly as an aquarium to display sea life. Today it is the home of the *Casa di Architecttura,* or the House of Architecture. Its curved walls are accented by half-exposed colonnades and arches. It's interesting design no doubt inspires many students of that noble art.

We wandered scores of miles on Rome's obscure streets and by-ways, gaining insight into both the brighter and darker sides of the great city. We popped up from the *Metro* at various locations just to explore, finding a wealth of striking churches, piazzas, and parks, as well as segments of the original inner ring of city walls from the 4th Century BCE. Known as the Servian walls, the few remaining segments have often been used to help support adjacent buildings, incorporating them into their structure. An ancient, cracked gate loomed above a busy pedestrian thoroughfare, seemingly awaiting the right moment to fall. Evidence of past repairs showed that the problem wasn't a new one.

We took the Metro to the *Circo Massimo,* or the Circus Maximus, the Roman racetrack built upon the valley of a stream. Engineers had built a culvert of concrete into which the stream was diverted, thereby drying the former wetlands. Once it had been leveled and filled, it became one of Rome's largest public spaces. An elongated oval, it featured both stone and wooden grandstands which, Pliny the Elder credibly insisted, were capable of holding more than 250,000 spectators.

A long central spine divided the track, leaving two sharp 'hairpin' turns to challenge competitors on horseback or in chariots. There Augustus Caesar had placed the first of Rome's several looted Egyptian obelisks after his defeat of Marc Antony and Cleopatra. It wasn't long before that spine was decorated with numerous monuments erected by wealthy Roman families, most of whom constantly held or sought public office. The sloping walls of the arena-like area still feature some of the ancient stones that bore the weight of tens of thousands of spectators. It was at the *Circo,* under the massive wooden grandstands at the curving western end, that fire broke out during Nero's reign, razing much of the city.

After a long tour on a warm Spring day, pizza and cold beer seemed a great diversion, and we found an appropriately-cool and cave-like pizzeria facing the *Circo Massimo,* where we retreated for a leisurely lunch, sharing the view of a television which held the rapt attention of Roman manhood watching the national past-time, a game of *calcio*.

During the slight lull that marked the afternoon nap hours even in the city, we set out to walk the banks of the river again to find the famed *Boca della Verita*, or the Mouth of Truth. Legend told that the mouth would close to bite of the hand of a liar. It was a story tested by Gregory Peck in the film "Roman Holiday." Peck, while showing the fugitive princess, played by Audrey Hepburn, around Rome, famously shoved his hand into the mouth of the ancient fountain. He told her a 'white lie,' yelled and withdrew his truncated arm to the shock of the blanched and screaming princess, before pushing his hand back out of the sleeve, laughing. We and hundreds of others stood in line to re-create the scene for ourselves.

Next to the Boca della Verita stands an ancient Greek Orthodox church that, for a small fee, allows visitors to tour the catacombs below. The bones of early Christians seemed to be the draw for many, but the small church itself is an ornate jewel.

We climbed the knoll of the park across the street to explore the monument known today as the *Arco di Giano*, or the Arch of Janus. He was the two-faced god of time, looking both backward and forward, thus reminding Romans of their fleeting days. He was the subject of other monuments in ancient Rome, but due to twisted history, apparently not this one, even though it bears his name. Built in the 4th century CE, it was probably intended to honor a later emperor. The site provides a beautiful view over the river below.

We rode classic street-cars along broad, divided boulevards. A short walk west of the *Stazione Termini* and beyond the circulation terminal of the city's fleet of buses we found a pleasant park that featured a large bookstore under a tent. Several booksellers shared the cooperative space, and we browsed through stacks of beautiful books in several languages. As I often did, I sought out the *fumetti*, colorful 'comic' books. Among them I was sure to find those called 'Tex,' containing serial stories of a fictional hero of the American West that amount to graphic novels. Printed in Italian, they tell stories such as the battle of the Little Big Horn. I found they made an excellent and enjoyable study tool for my growing knowledge of the vernacular.

Farther along beyond the park at the top of the Viminal Hill lies the expanse of the *Piazza della Republica*, one of the most impressive spaces in modern Rome. Flanking the southern hemisphere of this broad semi-circular space stand a matching pair of buildings whose curved shape echoes that of the piazza. Their elegant lower arches shelter the *sottoportego* sidewalks, and are topped by rows of half-columns. That scene provides an elegant backdrop to the enormous Fountain of the Naiads, whose four lounging female figures are representative of the waters of the lakes, rivers, seas, and the underground. Looking south across the fountain and between the flanking buildings, one can gaze directly down the *Via Nazionale* to the massive monument to Vittorio Emmanuele II.

On the northern side of the piazza, overlooked by most tourists, lies the crumbling remains of the *thermae*, or baths, of the Emperor Diocletian. Covering twelve hectares, or almost thirty acres, but built in only seven years by the labor of thousands of slaves, they were an entertainment palace for the people of Rome. Baths of hot, warm, and cool waters, called the *caldarium*, *tepidarium*, and *frigidarium*, were popular social gathering places for almost five centuries.

A portion of the former baths were converted by Michelangelo during the 1560's into the *Basilica di Santa Maria degli Angeli e dei Martiri*, or Saint Mary of the Angels and Martyrs. It stands facing the *piazza*, but lacks the expected facade of a church, standing almost concealed behind an alcove of the original baths. The interior, however, is an architectural masterpiece. The original columns were foreshortened by the raising of the floor during the conversion in order to fill in the former baths below. Despite that change in the architecture, the ceiling soars high above, speaking of the grandeur of the original Roman construction. Like many of the great cathedrals of Italy, it offers a spectacle for the eye.

One of the most unusual features of the Basilica is a 'Meridian Line' which stretches forty-five meters across the polished marble of the floor following the exact line of 12° 30' E longitude. Created within the church in 1702 by Francesco Bianchini upon the order of Pope Clement XI, it allows sunlight to enter through a tiny hole high in the southern wall, where it casts a beam which describes the figure-eight shape of an analemma upon the stripe of the meridian line. Engraved insets mark the points which the sun will reach at certain dates through the course of the year. It is a combination of calendar and sundial that was used by the church to perfect the Gregorian calendar in use in most of the world today. Other tiny pinholes in the ceiling allow the steady night-time entry of the light of Polaris, and on certain hours that of Arcturus and Sirius, which comprise the two brightest stars in the northern sky. It's effectively both a church and an observatory.

Outside of Rome we took time to visit the city's former port at Ostia Antica. That ancient brick-yard of a settlement near the mouth of the river was once the embarkation point for goods and passengers, and also served to defend against attacking warships that might try to sail upstream to reach the city itself. Once sacked by pirates, the site has many well-preserved buildings featuring beautiful mosaics and frescoes. It provides a wealth of insight into the daily lives of those Roman mariners and traders.

To the east of the city lies the fabled 'water gardens' in the town of Tivoli. Known as the Villa d'Este, the gardens are *giardini delle meraviglie*, or 'gardens of marvels,' recognized as a UNESCO World Heritage site. A gem of Renaissance architecture, the 16th century creation offers an amazing spectacle of water features including sixty-four waterfalls, fifty-one fountains and nymphaea, nearly four hundred spouts, three hundred and sixty-four water jets, and two hundred twenty basins, fed by eight hundred seventy-five meters of canals, channels and cascades. The water flows without benefit of pumps from the Aniene River, and produces a soothing effect on both the eyes and ears. If ducks dreamed of paradise, this is what it would look like.

In Rome, we walked through neighborhoods both wealthy and poor, and followed the shady length of the Via Vittorio Veneto through some of the most expensive real estate in Rome, including the verdant expanse of the Borghese Gardens with their several remarkable villas, including the eponymous Villa Borghese with its striking art galleries. Now a municipal park and the green heart of Rome, the site was for centuries a private vineyard.

We also frequently utilized the convenient *Scale Spagnoli*, or Spanish Steps, stopping to admire the *Trinità dei Monti* church that surmounts them. The small *piazze* at the top and bottom of the steps are popular venues for small street fairs, flower sellers, and artists, and are also used as a backdrop for international fashion shows and films.

The neighborhood has provided the setting for many pleasant walks, but an hour spent hiking the steep streets during a light rainfall one particular evening was enough, so we headed back to the Metro for the trip to our hotel on Rome's Lido at Ostia. Our pleasant hotel on the shore was a trade-off for the distance on the Metro, so we spent the twenty minutes on the train checking news. We were aboard as a cell-phone feed revealed the first puffs of white smoke from a Vatican chimney to let the world know that there was a new Pope to replace the retired Benedict. For the first time, a Latin American was to lead the hierarchy of the Church, and he took the name Francesco, or Francis, after the noble saint of Assisi. It was a memorable moment for Romans, Catholics, and more than 100,000 waiting pilgrims who celebrated in *Piazza San Pietro*.

The Maremma and Argentario

With a pleasant drive on a coastal highway we set out to explore the Maremma, the low-lying coastal plain of Tuscany. Known as a nest of *briganti*, or brigands, Dante Alighieri used it as the setting for many of his dark tales of murder 750 years ago. The area remained sparsely-settled until recent years.

Italians long considered the Maremma unhealthy, plagued with *mal aria*, or bad air. It was only later that the name was applied to the disease carried by the salt-marsh mosquitoes which had flourished there. The large estuary and lagoon that had previously occupied the basin has long-since been diked, drained, and converted to agricultural purposes, virtually eliminating the problem. Today the land is a rich place of irrigated crops and prosperous beach-front resort towns.

We were drawn to explore the fishing towns of the Monte Argentario. The rocky peak rises along a stretch of rather flat coast, seeming out of place among the sandy beaches that surround it. Originally an island, it became attached to the mainland through the accretion of a sandy shelf, called a *tombolo*, through tidal action during recent centuries. Two causeways have since been built, allowing for access by cars arriving from both north and south.

A causeway along the blue of the Mediterranean connects the

mainland with the dark, green shape of the mountain. Ascending the narrow road over rocky spurs hundreds of feet above the water, we wound our way back down to rows of beautiful homes built along the coastal road. Within a few minutes we entered the *commune,* or town, of Porto Santo Stefano, which lay below us like a picturesque postcard. A small fleet of sailboats and fishing vessels filled its tiny harbor. Long wharves and tiers of streets with colorful houses framed the main waterfront boulevard.

Popular with tourists and Italians alike, the town features many small hotels and *pensioni,* but there are plenty of vacation homes for rent. The main street was a mix of typical bars and restaurants, but leavened with a few gift shops offering kitschy souvenirs. The people we met were friendly, and used to hosting visitors. We paused to admire a beautiful mosaic mural that accented the center of town, filling a wall with a colorful outburst that rivaled the banks of flowers emerging from their winter slumbers.

Like many other places we explored, the towns of the Argentario were targeted during the great war. Porto Santo Stefano was almost completely destroyed, and was not reconstructed until about ten years later, when Italy's economy finally began to rebound from the destruction, helped by the United States' Marshall Plan.

The re-birth had been thorough, and included even the *Acquario Mediterraneo dell Argentario,* an aquarium complex which contains realistic exhibits of more than a hundred live marine species present in local waters. It is run by the *Accademia Mare Ambiente,* or Academy of Marine Environment, an educational institute that works with area schools, conducts research, and participates in cetacean work, including rescues of beached whales and dolphins. High-end resort housing clings to the mountainsides above.

When you go, take your time. Hike the steep streets of the town, snack in a pizzeria, explore art galleries, walk the lengths of the wharves admiring the variety of boats, and dine on the freshest seafood imaginable, brought straight from the boat to a waterfront restaurant, made even better with a bottle of local white wine to share. A drive around the circumference of the mountain allows for exploring the smaller town of Porto Ercole, with its own tidy harbor and cafes.

We returned to the coastal highway north of the Argentario, which follows the route of the old Roman road known as the Via Aurelia. Along the seacoast lies the *Parco Naturale di Maremma*, the Nature Park of Maremma, which protects examples of native plant, animal, and bird life. The road passes through miles of pine forest, the distinctive umbrella-shaped *cembro* trees that are the source of the *pignoli*, the pine nuts that flavor the delicious *pesto* sauces that are popular across Italy.

The principal Maremma city of Grossetto, a short distance from the sea, charmed us. Surrounded by Medieval walls and fortifications, the *centro storico* or historic center offers a fine selection of places to shop and dine. It features a large piazza which was a popular spot for window-shopping, especially during the evening *passegiata*, the traditional stroll before dinner. Babies in carriages, flirting teens, and entire families enjoy the rite. Young women and grandmothers walk arm-in arm, and people linger over frozen *gelato*, steaming coffees, or glasses of wine.

The town's central church is beautifully finished with carved stone details and gargoyles, and stands next to the stunning crenelated municipal building. We spent time exploring the creative shops, as well as sampling the delicious *gelato*. We had apparently become addicted, rarely able to pass a shop without sampling the flavors.

An indoor farmers' market offered mounds of the freshest fruits, vegetables, meats, fish and cheeses, and we savored the offerings, bringing some back to cook in the kitchen at another of our new favorites, an *agriturismo*. We also found an interesting museum dedicated to the history of the town, which had changed hands, like most of Italy, a dozen times or more, and suffered under a host of kings, dukes, and emperors.

In Grossetto, as in many cities we wandered, Susan stopped for another attempt to befriend some of the cats she spotted. Whether completely domesticated and perched in doorways or windows, or hungry ferals slinking furtively away to hide in a drain or alleyway, she tried every traditional English method without success.

"Cats here don't know 'kitty-kitty,'" I assured her.

"Well, what do they know?" she asked.

"I can't tell you. Ask an Italian cat-lover."

In her halting Italian she tried, but never seemed to get a clear answer as to how to call a cat. That didn't stop her from attempting to befriend them, though, and she had particular success with kittens, which seemed to please them as much as it did her.

The coastline of Tuscany, like most of the long peninsula, is a series of quaint towns, overviews of rocky coasts, and occasionally attractive sandy beaches. We explored the seaside town of Follonica, and nearby Piombino on its cape overlooking Elba, Napoleon's island of exile. (The delightful English palindrome attributed to him, "Able was I, ere I saw Elba," was unlikely to have ever been uttered by the French general, and naturally doesn't survive a translation into either French or Italian.)

Farther north along the coast, past Livorno and Pisa, lies the town of Carrara, famed for its rare white or blue-grey marble. There, as in many places in Italy, we noted large quarries, some of which have been producing the decorative stone since the days of the Roman Republic.

One of the scenic towns of the area is Castiglione della Pescaia. The view from the namesake large castle perched above the town took in a broad sweep of sea and shore, and the vast basin behind the dunes that was once the lagoon. Now rich farmland crisscrossed by irrigation and flood-control canals, its fields of corn and other grain crops formed a verdant blanket encircled by low mountains, with higher peaks including Monte Amiata looming in the distance. Within the protective walls of the *castiglione* stood a tight cluster of a village with steep streets lined by compact houses, but little commercial activity. Most of the daily bustle and traffic moved through the new part of the town some seventy-five meters below.

Our familiarity with the Maremma was expanded thanks to a chance meeting in Florida, where we had become friends with an Italian couple, Renzo and Rossella. Their adventurous spirits had led them to the habit of coming to the U.S. each summer to ride their heavy Goldwing motorcycles on long tours. I had the good fortune to be invited to join the family at their vacation home in the Maremma, just outside Castiglione.

Situated atop a high, forested ridge a few kilometers outside the town, Renzo and Rossella's property included a large stand of *quercie da sughero*, or cork oaks. They had been recently harvested, a process that involves shaving the soft, sponge-like bark off the tree. Only the small upper branches still sported their spongy coats. The trees would require several years to grow new bark before they could be harvested once again, helping to fill the enormous world-wide demand for wine corks.

In the midst of a record heat-wave, we dipped in their tank pool, and tried to sleep at night in the close, almost airless rooms. In the evenings we watched the setting moon, the slender crescent cradling the darker face, which glowed softly with reflected Earth-shine. By day we picked peaches by the thousands from a friend's orchard, and dropped crates-full at the homes of other friends and neighbors. Bushels of potatoes, greens, wine, and tomatoes were passed our way in return. It was the traditional Italian way of sharing the bounty of the land.

Adventure was never far from Renzo's mind. The town of Castiglione also features a nice beach, and a river which hosts a small-boat harbor. There Renzo kept a six-meter open run-about. On one occasion, he decided that we should take the boat out for a spin. We boarded in the small harbor, and were soon racing several kilometers up the coast toward Punta Ala. Renzo seemed a bit surprised when the *Guardia Costiera*, the Coast Guard, came rushing out to meet us in a cutter. Being a non-citizen and momentarily without my passport, I stayed seated and silent, hoping they wouldn't ask me anything, for fear of being held as an illegal migrant. After Renzo's brief interrogation, we were informed that we had entered a restricted zone. I was afraid that we would end up in some sort of serious trouble, but we were dismissed. He reluctantly turned our bow, and headed back to the south. I breathed a sigh of relief.

On another occasion Renzo decided that we would dine in a favorite restaurant. We crowded family and friends into a large van and set off into the countryside. An hour into the trip we made a stop to visit a friend of Renzo's, a gentleman named Sante Massini. Signor Massini owned large vineyards in the DOC of the *Morellino di Scansano* (one of a number of particularly delicious regional wines virtually unknown in the United States) and was president of the local wine *consorzio*. He and his wife also operated an *agriturismo* called Villa Carletta in a venerable stone building adjacent to their home. It was a fortunate introduction that we would later employ.

After our social visit, we continued our journey toward the promised dinner. Another hour of driving through increasingly-rugged country brought us to the spectacular cliff-town of Pitigliano. There we enjoyed a leisurely two-hour meal before climbing back into our transport for the long drive back home, arriving shortly before midnight. Italians will go to great lengths for good food.

A Tuscan Birthday

After more than a dozen years of frequent trips to Italy, Susan was to pass a 'milestone' birthday. What better way to celebrate it than a party in Italy with a group of good friends? By then we were, although not fluent, able to carry on substantial conversations in Italian, and could offer our friends plenty of help in planning and enjoying what some of them suspected would be a once-in-a-lifetime trip. We put out an invitation to a broad circle of friends, certain that many would find it impossible to join us.

During our search for the perfect venue, we remembered visiting Sante Massini with our friends Renzo and Rossella a few years before. His beautiful *agriturismo* was situated in the coastal Maremma area of Tuscany where commercial tourism is less dominant. Not far from the city of Grossetto, it offered everything we could ask. The entire property was swathed in vineyard-covered, rolling terrain. Beautiful hills and nearby mountains, castles, picturesque fishing villages and sandy beaches lay nearby. The proximity to Etruscan sites and museums, and the cities of Pitigliano, Siena, and Orvieto made it especially attractive.

To the west was the castle-guarded fishing village of Castiglione della

Pescaia overlooking the aquamarine waters of swimming beaches. It would be a perfect playground for our expected group of six or eight friends. A short drive to the east, the first sight of the brooding solemnity of improbable Pitigliano is breath-taking, as it stands perched above a sheer cliff of tufa stone, seemingly grown directly out of the rock. The chasm below, carved by the tumbling river scarcely heard from the town, is perforated with caves dating back millennia.

The surprises came with the responses to our invitation, and our planning numbers began to grow. Soon we were ten, then twelve, then fifteen, and had outgrown the accommodations. Happily, Signor Massini had a sister living a few kilometers away in the next valley who also kept guest rooms, so we began to expand our horizons. By the time our planned October rendezvous arrived, we had filled both places, and eighteen of us gathered to celebrate Italian wines, history, art, landscapes, and of course, Susan's birthday.

Susan had made her preparations while jetting around the world, making multiple trips to a shop in Seoul before she had gotten everyone's names spelled correctly on their luggage tags, and finding eighteen matching shirts in the correct sizes in a Shanghai market to embroider. Unbeknownst to Susan, I had also made some extra arrangements with Signor Massini to make the celebration just a bit more special.

We arrived ahead of our guests and got settled in. The Massini family showed us wonderful hospitality, and we occupied a comfortable room with pleasant views overlooking their large vineyards and olive trees.

Soon the gathering had begun. Some friends flew to Roma, others to Milano, and still others to Firenze or Pisa. One couple drove down from Germany, while Susan's brother George and his wife, also named Susan, arrived by train in Grosseto, where we met them at the station. We shepherded the group to our remote country destination, and within hours they had scattered to take advantage of the area's beauty.

We hadn't fully considered the wide range of events and experiences that would occur among such a diverse and ambitious group of fellow travelers. The results were nothing if not entertaining.

Among our friends in attendance were a special couple from Florida, Paul and Sharon, who were traveling with Sharon's sister, Maryellen, a single, career-oriented New York executive also on her first European trip. They approached Italy as they approached everything in life: with a real sense of gusto, or what the French might call *joie de vivre*. They had rented what must have been the most expensive car in the rental agency when they arrived, perhaps because they had read of the Italian focus on maintaining *una bella figura*, or, as we might say in English, cutting a good figure. There is something in the Italian psyche that demands that you appear at your best whenever possible. They did. They drove their sporty four-seat Alfa Romeo on twisting mountain roads looking like they owned them. They laughed their way through each adventure with aplomb such that everyone else in our party could only envy.

Returning one night from dinner to their room at the *agriturismo*, they spotted a *cinghiale*, a large boar, rooting among the olive trees. That, Paul thought immediately, would make a great photograph! He instinctively leapt from the car, and Mary Ellen fearlessly joined him. Sharon turned the wheel and drove the car out of the parking area to attempt to herd the massive beast back toward them. The Alfa, not designed for off-road driving, nevertheless spooked the boar, which began to try to escape. Around and around they went, the boar dodging and weaving, Paul and Mary Ellen, fortified by a bit of Italy's best wine, shrieking as they maintained the chase. Eventually the boar made his escape, and it was then that they realized that no one had used a camera. Sharon resigned the car to its proper location, still in good condition.

The story entertained the rest of the guests the following day over breakfast as we organized an expedition. Familiar with the route, we planned to lead our group to Volterra and Siena in a short caravan of vehicles. Our friends Paul, Sharon, and Maryellen, decided to leave ahead of us.

A little more than twenty kilometers from our *agriturismo* they suddenly encountered a muffler on the highway. Apparently dropped in the road by some other unlucky motorist, traffic prevented them from swerving around it, and there was no time to stop. The compromise was to straddle it, and hope for the best. The best wasn't in the cards. The low clearance of their sports car sent the muffler crashing into the radiator, which burst, spewing a slick mix of water and antifreeze over the windshield and roof. The car quickly began to overheat, and Sharon coasted the car onto a handy exit ramp and happily found *una benzinaia*, a gas station, at the foot of the hill.

The rest of our party, perhaps fifteen minutes behind, were unaware of what had occurred, and passed by, leaving our friends stranded.

Our trio of friends had no knowledge of Italian, but tried, without much success, to explain to the staff that they had hit a muffler in the road. No amount of gesticulation seemed to translate the facts of the event, but they were at last put in touch with the rental car company, which eventually dispatched a tow-truck to the rescue. Their day was quickly going south, as they say.

With Sharon and Maryellen riding in the cab with the driver, Paul had no option but to ride in the Alfa, which was secured onto the bed of the truck. He got some great views of the Tuscan countryside from his elevated post, but when they arrived at their destination and the truck drove straight into the garage, he was faced with yet another challenge. The tight space didn't allow for easy access from the car, and he was eight feet off the ground. He squeezed himself through the window, and sidled along the narrow metal flange of the truck, clinging to the car still slippery with antifreeze. It was almost death-defying, but Paul had a solution: he used the rear-view mirror as a hand-hold. Unfortunately, when he found himself safely on the ground at last, the mirror was still in his hand. The mechanics took a look, rolled their eyes, and waved him out of the garage. Our three friends would have to wait until a replacement car could be found. They doubted it would be another sports car.

Still unaware of their predicament, we continued on to dark and brooding Volterra, where we walked through the ancient arched gate of the three faces, had *panini* from a sidewalk cafe, and enjoyed the beautiful views overlooking a thousand square miles of Tuscany. We visited the wonderful Etruscan museum, time-traveling back to the days before the rise of Rome through the extensive artifacts and dioramas that brought them to life, before returning to sample *gelato* on the streets. We were having a great time, but couldn't imagine what had happened to our friends.

Paul, Sharon, and Maryellen finally managed to catch up to us in Siena at dusk, where we wandered through winding streets to gape at the amazing layer-cake *duomo* before sharing dinner on the lovely locale of the broad piazza. There, where only a few weeks earlier horses had raced on cobblestones for the honor of their *contrade*, more than a dozen Americans in animated discussion was not an unusual sight.

After dinner we headed back to our car, parked in one of the parking lots which surround the *centro*. Our trio of friends followed us, despite the fact that they had parked their replacement car in another lot... someplace? Italian hill-towns are well known for their confusing arrays of car parks, and they can present an intimidating maze for a disoriented traveler.

We squeezed seven of us into our own car, and together we drove around the city, searching in the night for their mysterious dark car of forgotten make. For several minutes it seemed a futile mission. We were unable to identify even the lot, let alone which car might be theirs. Sharon eventually remembered her key fob, and began pushing buttons, hoping for a response from the gloom. At last it came, a faint flash on a hill that repeated on demand.

•

When the big day arrived, we enacted plans for our celebratory banquet. With Susan's brother George and his wife Susan we drove down the coast to the promontory of *Monte Argentario*, and the scenic village of Porto Santo Stefano. There a small fleet of fishing boats heads out each morning to cast their nets into the blue waters of the *Mare Tyrrhenia*. Our plan was to explore the town, and then meet a boat captained by a friend of Signor Massini, who would be providing the freshest seafood imaginable to accompany a full menu of delicious Italian cooking.

The day was fresh and bright, and we rendezvoused at mid-day with others from our party before we walked the waterfront exploring the small shops, eating *panini* for lunch, and then stopping for dessert in a *gelateria*. There, to our amazement, we noticed that a 30-foot length of wall was covered with a photo-mural of a famous garden we knew very well.

"Wow, look at that!" we exclaimed.

"It's in California," the owners told us.

"No, it's in Florida!" we replied, to their surprise. "That's Cypress Gardens!" Several of our party lived near the famous gardens, some within only a few blocks. It was a reminder of just how small the world seemed to be growing.

Back outside, we were surprised again to see that the clear skies of the early afternoon had been replaced by gathering clouds. As we watched a dramatic storm began to take shape. A vast, dramatically-threatening whirl of dark cumulonimbus formed over the sea, and seemed to drive the fishing fleet before it as they hurried back to port. Towering walls of ominous purple-grey ended in an impressive spiral of out-flowing cirrus still lit by the sun high above.

By the time our boat docked, a steady rain had begun to fall, but the heart of the storm was not yet upon us. We gaped from under umbrellas at the still-wriggling catch as the crew loaded boxes, some of which would be heading to Massini's. To our surprise, the captain told us that we needn't have bothered meeting the boat to choose the fish for the dinner, as he would be delivering the catch directly to Massini's himself.

Hoping to beat the storm, we scrambled, dripping, back into our car, and headed north up the coast highway as the storm broke in its full fury. Slashing rain quickly flooded the roadway, reducing our safe speed to little more than a crawl. The rain seemed to come harder with each passing minute. It was almost impossible to see either the road, or a place to leave it.

The sudden darkness brought on by both storm and nightfall was punctuated by blinding flashes of lightning which seemed to strike all around us as we crept across narrow bridges casting up huge sheets of spray. It was more like piloting a boat than steering a car. Memories of Susan almost missing the wedding dinner had me imagining my guilt if she were to miss her own birthday celebration.

We arrived late and dripping, and made our way to the large dining room where tables had been set for our party of eighteen. While we had played, our loyal friends Jean and Heidi had decorated and taken over the kitchen, where they were busily preparing many of the dishes that would feed our gathering.

La Signora Massini had also been busy in her own kitchen, cooking traditional Italian specialties and an amazing *torta cioccolata*, or chocolate cake. Fresh seafood arrived with the captain of the boat, and he quickly retreated to yet another kitchen where he and Sante began to conjure up their own sort of magic. Italy's culinary repertoire is full of surprises. Like American men and their barbecue grills, they seemed to know seafood like it was second nature, and took real pride in what they sent forth. We enjoyed fried calamari, baked sea bass and trout, and the surprise hit of the night, *pesce crudo*, or small pieces of raw fish which had been sautéed in vinegar.

Toasts with *Prosecco*, the light bubbly Italian answer to France's Champagne, were followed with still white and red wines, and the celebration rolled in earnest. An impromptu roast developed. Susan's brother George brought it to an uproarious crescendo when asked to tell stories of her childhood by responding that "I don't remember much about her...in fact, I don't think she lived with us."

By the time our banquet had ended, the rain had done the same, and I invited everyone outside for Susan's last surprise of the night, the one that I had arranged well in advance during surreptitious phone calls from Florida: a display of fireworks fired high into the Tuscan night. We oohed and aahed as traffic stopped on the road to take in the sight. Stars peeked through the clouds as we said our good-nights and thanks to friends old and new, all dearly treasured. The memories will remain with each of us for all our years.

A Tight Squeeze in Orvieto

During our stay we did our grocery shopping in the familiar city of Grosseto, a *commune* of over 80,000, where we found most of our immediate needs. It gave us opportunity to introduce our friends to the beautiful *centro storico* surrounded by Medieval walls defending its beautiful Romanesque church, and the municipal building with its crenelated walls.

There were more than enough attractions at our disposal to keep everyone fascinated, and eager for the next day to begin. We drove the few kilometers to Marina di Grosseto and its beach with Susan's childhood friend Linda, her husband Boyd, and son, Burke. The trip to Italy was a fulfillment of Boyd's lifelong dream to return to his ancestral land.

Maryellen was fearless, and waded in the chilly sea. Sharon, venturing too close while trying to capture the perfect photo of the moment, was caught by a wave. It was all part of the adventure.

Some of our group climbed with us up steep paths to the ancient fortress that overlooks the seaside village of Talamone. Maryellen again showed her boldness, walking along the top of the battlement walls above a twenty-meter drop. She seemed somehow transformed from the person we knew only a few days earlier.

We drove along the scenic shore of the Maremma, a line of coastal dunes covered with a forest of the graceful *cembro* trees, also call umbrella or parasol pines. The entire area is protected as a bird and wildlife refuge.

On one memorable day we filled our rental car with friends and followed a beautiful drive away from the *Maremma* coast of Tuscany, eastward through the mountain towns of Scansano, Manciano, Pitigliano, and then along the stunning northern shore of the Lago di Bolsena. This route threads through some of the most appealing countryside in southern Tuscany. On the right side of the road was a stunning view of the deep volcanic lake, while on our left, steep, forested mountainsides loomed.

The view across the lake of shimmering silver toward a dark distant ring of mountain that formed the south rim of the crater was a postcard-perfect image of Italy. A few fishing boats glided upon the surface of the crystal-clear waters.

We encountered a typically-vibrant street fair in the town of Bolsena. Traffic was diverted around several lake-front blocks filled with colorful tents offering a wide array of foods, plus clothing, hardware, and a thousand other useful offerings. Crowds of people moved among the booths, and small sailboats flitted along the shoreline.

We climbed again to cross the mountains toward Umbria to arrive high above the evocative city of Orvieto, standing atop its rocky mesa tucked into a hidden valley almost upon the Tuscan border. Lacking the fog that had filled the valley years before, the scene was never-the-less dramatic.

We followed the switch-backed drive down the mountain to the base of the city's mesa and began ascending from the suburbs up to the old city above, passing through the ancient city walls and entering a large, church-fronted *piazza* already filled with cars. Looking for a place to park, we wandered down a side street, which led to another, then still another, but no space to park.

We threaded through the increasingly-narrow passages, hoping to find another piazza or parking area. It was a forlorn hope. In the tightly-constricted Medieval city, every available space had been used for buildings. Rough-hewn stone walls seemed to constrict us.

The narrow street turned, became a tight passage that followed a long wall, turned a final corner and then... ended abruptly in a space not much wider than a sidewalk, already occupied by three parked motorbikes. Behind us, a low stone wall separated us from a fifty-meter drop into the abyss. There was no room to turn around. Our car had barely made the last two tight corners going forward. How would we manage to back up two hundred meters on those tight alleyways?

Our situation called to my mind an old episode of the TV show Candid Camera, wherein a car was placed sideways in an impossibly-tight garage, and various tow-truck drivers called to rescue the helpless woman who claimed to have gotten it stuck. Their reactions had been very funny, I had thought at the time. I wasn't laughing now. We were in need of a helicopter extraction.

Unable to open the car doors, I left the vehicle through a window to examine our situation. We were wedged rather tightly between unforgiving stone walls, the wheels turned halfway through a corner. The driver's door had two inches of clearance, the front and rear bumpers not much more. Curious residents peeked out from windows above to see how we would escape, but no one was bold enough to offer any suggestions, for there appeared no simple solution.

Pushing a rolling refuse bin tight against a wall gained us a few inches, and our passengers escaped to coach our movements, but we had only a hands-breadth of room forward or backward. I climbed back in, and with the lightest touches on the clutch, began to crank hard on the steering wheel while Susan nervously indicated the amount of space remaining with her hands. Three inches forward, turn the wheel, three inches backwards, reverse the wheel, repeat step one.

After ten minutes of effort we extracted our ride from the first corner, and began backing slowly up the long alley to the prior corner. This one, approached carefully and slowly, was made with only a half-dozen course reversals, and allowed us to continue to back carefully along the next, longer straightaway, where we finally encountered a tiny intersection with an alley. With Susan watching carefully for approaching motorbikes, we managed to get the car turned around and our passengers aboard, and we headed back toward the piazza. Thankful to escape with all four fenders intact, we fled with the remaining shreds of our dignity. Our walking tour of Orvieto would await another day.

Retreating to Pitigliano to meet the rest of our group for dinner, we dined in a *trattoria* at the edge of the precipice, feeling as though we might tumble at any moment. There we related the story of our misadventure. We laughed most of the way back 'home,' and treasure one of our most vivid memories.

Each of our friends was changed in some subtle way, no doubt, by the adventures they encountered in Italy, and those changes manifested themselves in their lives. Perhaps the most remarkable result of Susan's birthday expedition was Maryellen's decision to ask for a year's leave of absence from her high-powered executive position in New York. Denied, she simply resigned, and spent the next year traveling around the world in pursuit of her dreams. Travel can change our perceptions of what is most important in our lives.

Matera's Troglodytes

In the United States a building might be considered 'old' at 300 or 400 years. The oldest housing in the United States is that left behind by Hopi and Anasazi cultures more than a thousand years ago. Scattered across Italy and much of Europe are Roman structures that exceed two thousand years. Yet none of them can compare to the dwellings of Matera.

Humans moved from forests to caves more than 100,000 years ago. Their first uses may have been temporary shelters, but in those places where groups of caves could house communities, it is apparent that they have been occupied almost continuously. Tucked among the worn-down mountains of eastern Basilicata, Matera's tufa stone, or *sassi*, and steep, narrow canyons made it a natural town, defensible against attack.

The soft stone is readily cut, even with primitive tools. Inhabitants learned to reshape their caves to suit their needs. Just start with a shallow cave, cut away everything that doesn't look like a house, and, *eccola!* As stone was excavated from inside, it was often used to construct walls at the entrance.

Over the ages, as the original caves were expanded, a city began to emerge as if grown from the earth itself. Wooden doors were added to enclose the primitive dwellings. In some places houses rise directly upon the roofs of their neighbors much like modern apartment blocks.

The area was still occupied through the Second World War, but the need for modern sanitation for the growing population had created unhealthy conditions. In the 1930's Italian author Carlo Levi was exiled to the remote region by the Fascists because of his left-wing leanings. When the war ended in 1945 he published a book, <u>Christ Stopped at Eboli,</u> about the conditions at Matera. It motivated the government to help, people were relocated, and the caves preserved.

Matera is today a UNESCO World Heritage site, and has been designated as the Cultural Capital of Europe for the year 2019. Guided tours offer a chance to visit some of the caves, now filled with props to show how people lived in such rough conditions.

A more-modern Matera now perches above the deep canyons that helped protect its people from enemies. There we explored the Tramontana castle, climbing up steep stone staircases to the high tower under an overarching blue sky. We peered down at the deep dry moat, the city, and out at the surrounding rugged hills. The name *tra montana* means 'among the mountains,' which was apt but accidental. Begun by the Count Gian Carlo Tramontana more than 500 years ago, it was left unfinished when he was killed during an insurrection in 1514. It was long occupied by his successors. The musty scent of past lives, of the archers and knights, the servants and barons who once walked these halls, still lingers to fire one's imagination.

We wandered through the narrow streets of Matera before climbing down steep staircases to find a delightful restaurant clinging to the sheer cliff. Glasses of dry local white wine slaked our thirst as we took in the view along with our lunch. From our scenic terrace we gazed down into the chasm at the dusty stone walls below, and at now-vacant houses that seemed half-buried in the earth, still more cave than structure. A black cat crept through dark openings far beneath us, where weeds grew among the stones, and cascades of yellow flowers clung to the precipices. Above us flocks of the emblematic small falcons called *falco grillaio* soared gracefully, hovered motionlessly, and then swooped into the canyon below.

The Majestic Mountains of the Pollino

Susan is fond of mountains, and often when asked where she wants to go next, replies simply, "up." In the southern *regione* of Basilicata, that was an easy order to fulfill. Heading south and west along the *Strada Littorale* of the Basilicata coast, it is easy to access the *Parco Nazionale di Pollino*, which includes most of the highest peaks that straddle the border between Basilicata and Calabria.

We turned up the SS653, the label indicating that it is a *Strada Statale*, a national route, as opposed to a *Strada Provinciale*, or SP. Roads marked SS tend to be a bit wider, straighter, or better maintained than the provincial roads. The highway follows the valley of the *Fiume Sinni*, the Sinni River which drains the eastern side of the park, and directional signs referred mostly to the towns perched high above it.

As we steadily ascended, the broad, stony bed of the river made it apparent that it is prone to dramatic surges of spring melt-water. The river, then almost dry in summer, becomes a torrent fed by melting snow that flows into a series of reservoirs, which in turn supply water to the coastal towns. Many of the streams in the area are in fact named not *fiume*, or river, but *torrente*.

On our left we passed the hill town of Rotondella, the appropriately named community set upon a mountain dome that seemed as rotund as a basketball. The town appeared as perfectly positioned as the Pope's *zucchetto*, the small skullcap he is rarely seen without. There, as in many towns of the Pollino, ancient pagan rituals are blended into the religious *sagre*, or festivals honoring the patron saint of the village. Colobraro, another mountain town, perched high above us on our right. We found that it offered scenic views both to and from the top.

We drove partway around and crossed over the large, aqua-green reservoir lying at the foot of the mountainsides, moving into a narrow valley. The road climbed along the river past Francavilla to the village of Episcopia. There, men sat in the shade playing cards in the afternoon's cool breeze. Above them, in a bold, Old-West font, the name of the adjacent bar was spelled out: "Wanted," as if copied directly from Wyatt Earp's handbills. In the tiny *piazzetta*, children kicked a soccer ball between a few parked cars.

As the hour struck eleven, the *campanile* of the village church began to sound its bells, and to our surprise, they then played a tune, softly charming us with their melodious effect. It was reminiscent of the carillons of the Low Countries, and that of our own home in Florida, Dutch immigrant Edward Bok's Singing Tower.

Off the main highway now, we turned across the narrow stream and began to climb into the *Pollino*, and onto the flanks of the mountain range to the south. Signs warned that tire-chains were required in winter, but snow was not a threat on a June afternoon.

The road narrowed and began a series of hair-pin switch-backs that frequently required shifting to first gear. We were soon rewarded with views that rivaled those of North Carolina's famed Blue Ridge Parkway, but were accented with steeply-sloping vineyards, and occasionally the *campanile* of a village church silhouetted against the sky.

As we climbed, the temperature dropped and the breeze freshened. We wandered through or past tiny mountain villages with entertaining names. Manca di Basso translates appropriately as "without bottom." The towns of Pietrapica, and Cropani clung to the rugged slopes nearby like wood-ears growing on fallen forest logs.

We followed the narrow road as it wound beneath the village of San Severino Lucano, the views over gaping gorges causing us to pause when we could, leaving us wondering why people chose to live in such difficult locations.

The five-speed gear-box of our aging Fiat got a true test of endurance as we shifted repeatedly into first gear to edge around the sharp curves at barely more than walking speed. Eventually the car overheated, and we stopped on the roadside to let it cool. A small stream of rusty water dribbled from the radiator. At the shoulder of the road, a mature forest left enough sun to support scattered wildflowers, and allow a view from the heights. Mountain jays watched us curiously, and pursued each other through the trees. Not a car passed as we enjoyed a light snack and took photos of the deep valley below, embroidered by the thin line of the highway we had driven earlier. A few scattered clouds sent dappled shadows sliding over the landscape.

We continued on, still climbing, then passing along the flank of the peaks with sheer drops to our right. Shortly after mid-day we followed signs that directed us into a steep and narrow drive through a dense *bosco*, or forest, where we found an appropriately-named restaurant. There we ordered a proper Italian *pranzo*, or lunch. As we dined, brisk winds arose, sweeping over and through the building, blowing untended objects around the room. The stout trees outside the windows swayed and tossed their branches, but clung stubbornly to their rocky footholds. Inside the almost vacant restaurant, doors slammed as the wind had its way. We dined alone in a hall large enough to seat a hundred, even though it seemed that there weren't that many people within twenty kilometers.

As we paused at the front desk to pay our check, another sort of drama played out. From a closed door across the hall came the sound of voices, and a repeated twisting of the door handle. The door was either stuck, or locked. We could hear a man and a woman discussing their predicament from inside the closed room, but apparently there was no key to be found. Their voices and efforts at the door grew gradually louder.

Eventually two smiling employees were also drawn to the scene as the shaking of the door turned to futile banging, but the door remained stuck fast. We realized that eventually the amusement of those on the outside would alert the victims, no doubt trapped by the wind-slammed door. Were they managers, or guests? We had no way of knowing. It was yet another of those mysterious moments that seem to come with travel, especially in Italy. Not wishing to be found standing there laughing when they finally emerged, we decided to be on our way.

We returned to our climb, and soon found ourselves emerging from the forests into broad meadows above the tree-line, where the views went from merely grand, to stupendous. Titanic rock cliffs soared above steep valleys, and broad meadows filled with masses of dazzling yellow wildflowers accented the brightness of the sun. The few passing clouds left the shadows of their racing tatters streaking rapidly down the forested valleys and back up the stony expanses of the far mountainsides.

Our road, now reduced to just a single-lane track, leaned first left, then right as we navigated along ridge-lines, around rocky outcroppings, and past grassy meadows and patches of forest. Split-rail sheep fences, some replaced by modern wire, lined pastures. Rickety-looking fence ladder-crossings led to paths used by shepherds, and a flock of sheep grazed along the shoulders of our course. At one curve we found our way blocked by a solid-looking dog, one of a trio that escorted a flock of sheep on their way to a higher pasture. We waited patiently under the watchful eyes of the hound until the sheep had cleared, and we were allowed to proceed.

We came upon a *baita*, a shelter high in the mountains that may have saved the lives of travelers in snowy winters past. A row of tiny, one-room cabins offered only the barest shelter from a blizzard, but would likely make the difference between life and death if caught in one.

The road dipped and climbed before entering a darkly-shaded *bosco*. There it clung once again to the side of a steep slope, the sheer downhill view through the thick forest sending butterflies fluttering through Susan's stomach. "Don't look down, just drive carefully, and hope no one is coming the other way," she told me.

We snaked along slowly, the narrow strip of cracked asphalt

providing our only guide, as no available map, paper or electronic, showed the road we traversed. It was follow-your-nose navigating. After twenty minutes of peak-a-boo views into deep green chasms, we rounded a corner to find a marker and a picnic table.

"Time for a break, and a snack," we agreed, and scrambled from the car, up a slope, and around a low wall to a picnic table. There we found ourselves facing a stunning view. The mountainside fell away in an almost vertical fashion, dropping a kilometer or more. Rocky outcroppings provided tempting but precarious balconies overlooking the forested mountainside below.

Across the rugged valley fifteen kilometers away we could see a matching range of high peaks, deep shadows gathering on their eastern faces. Far below us the tiny line of the *Autostrada A3* could barely be seen, as it passed over a bridge before disappearing into a tunnel. Microscopic trucks passed in columns like foraging ants. Waves of sunlight and shadow crept over the scene as clouds scudded past. Looking to our left, we could see the valley sloped toward the watery line of the *Mare Ionio* forty kilometers away, visible as a small dark crescent through the haze.

Overwhelmed by the beauty of the setting, we made our picnic surrounded by wild roses, munching on watermelon, cheese, and almond *biscotti*, toasting the beautiful view with rich local wine, and watching as large raptors soared overhead. Although the wind blew with a vengeance, even threatening to blow our meal away, we clung stubbornly to our mountain aerie. It almost seemed that if we were to fling ourselves from the cliff, the winds would bear us safely down. It was as close to heaven as we expected to come.

•

We returned to the Pollino several times, each time seeking deeper perspective into the people who inhabit these isolated mountains. On our map we noticed two towns, San Paolo Albanese, and San Costantino Albanese, and remarked on their unusual names. *Albanese* were people from Albania, which was on the opposite side of Italy, and across the Adriatic Sea. Why was that appendage attached to these places? We headed off to explore.

A long, climbing drive brought us at last to the very isolated community of San Paolo Albanese. It was a fifteen-kilometer journey from a place with no name, just a village lost amid the forests. On the steep slopes above and below the settlement were vineyards and a few fields hosting food crops, but the rocky ground didn't seem like an ideal locale for farming endeavors. Beautiful flowering vines hung along the streets, and twined themselves along the walls of buildings. Singing birds gave the scenery a lively soundtrack.

Entering the town we saw no other traffic at first, but took advantage of a generous row of parking spaces facing a scenic strip of park along the edge of a precipice. Beautiful views through the trees were certainly attractive, but there had to be more than vistas to lure people to live there.

We walked uphill into the tiny, sloping piazza, where we found the village church surrounded by a tight cluster of two-story houses. There was not so much as a bar in sight, and no one to ask about the origins of the name. We wandered with our cameras through tight passageways, and found several rough stone buildings whose leaning walls were braced by stout logs. Some leaned upon each other, with only thick timbers holding the opposing walls apart. Many of the homes featured wrought-iron railings around tiny stone stoops. The only sign of habitation during the afternoon was a faint voice from a radio or television somewhere above us.

After twenty minutes spent exploring the narrow by-ways of the village without encountering a soul, we headed back toward the piazza and the park. To our surprise a large motor-coach had arrived, and was maneuvering in the narrow street, backing into the piazza. In moments it disgorged a gaggle of German tourists, who invaded the church with their cameras, and spilled off into the side streets like a tide. Without restaurants or hotels, there would be no economic benefit to the residents from this northern invasion, nor from our own explorations. It was apparently an inconvenience they endured because of their extraordinary location and unusual history.

In the park all remained quiet, but there, seated on a bench, was a wizened old man, who appeared to have been around for perhaps a century, and was staring out toward the valley below. We said hello, and he chatted happily in a thick dialect. We began to ask him about the village, and its unusual name. He explained to us that some of his ancestors, many years before, had come to those mountains as refugees from oppression in Albania.

They had settled there in San Paolo Albanese, and for many generations kept to themselves, holding to their own language.

Listening carefully, we learned that he had lived there all his life, and had outlived three wives. We told him that he was fortunate to live in such a beautiful place with its stunning views. He knew we were visitors, and asked where we were from. He had never heard of Florida, though, so I pulled out my cellphone to show him a digital map of North America and our peninsular home. It was then that he told us he was blind.

Legendary Destinations

Across the sea not so far from Napoli beckoned a famous island that, in my childhood, had seemed the epitome of fantasy destinations, the 'Isle of Capri.' We were determined to see it.

We purchased our *biglietti* near the docks, and realized we had almost an hour before the next boat. Not wanting to waste a minute of our time, we wandered into the adjacent waterfront park. There we watched elderly men deftly hefting their *bocce* balls in heated but smiling competition. The newly-leafed trees provided a wonderful canopy for the peek-a-boo sun, and we quietly observed the competitors' inscrutable expressions as they concentrated upon the next critical toss, rounds of shouts accenting well-placed shots.

When we noticed our *traghetto* approaching, we walked back to meet her. Not a sleek yacht, this was a working boat, wide in the beam, that swiftly disgorged a fleet of vehicles and long columns of passengers. Among the first to board, we watched as a similar cargo was loaded in an efficient manner. We hurried to the upper deck to find comfortable window seats while the cars and trucks rolled into the lower decks.

At last we were off, cruising into the *Golfo di Napoli*, an arm of the Tyrrhenian Sea. Although we had boarded our *traghetto* for Capri with all the anticipation of children on a field trip, we were barely underway before the rain began, pelting in a wind-driven spray. Soon we were swaying as the small ship plowed through the roiled waves. The city of Napoli had swiftly disappeared behind, along with the high, brooding bulk of steaming *Vesuvio*, patiently pondering the fate of all around. After most of an hour Capri began to emerge from the wind-whipped spray and clouds.

Capri was the refuge of Tiberius Caesar, the chosen heir to the Emperor Claudius, whom the grateful people of Rome had dubbed "Augustus." Arguably Rome's greatest emperor, Augustus had finally stabilized the Roman world after a long series of civil wars, establishing peace that was to last for almost 60 years. Tiberius didn't measure up to his predecessor, however. Reserved and distrustful, he made a poor leader, and soon retired from public contact to this rocky island refuge. He left his marks upon the island, however, which we were bound to find.

Capri was reached *in orario*, on schedule, despite the weather. Our sixty-meter-long *traghetto* locked onto a steel ramp at the Marina Grande where the cars would be off-loaded. We walked with our bags and glanced upward at the imposingly-steep face of the island that hemmed in the narrow strip of the *piazza* that made up the waterfront. We would not be walking all that way, we agreed!

I inquired about a bus, but was quickly directed to a *biglietteria*, or ticket office, for the *funicular*, a sort of cog train. The curious cars of this train were built in tiers, each car featuring several levels of a few seats each, so that one end of the car was far above the other. It matched the track it sat upon, which seemed to point at an almost forty-five degree angle up the mountain. We clambered aboard, and in three breath-taking minutes had ascended one hundred and fifty meters above the diminishing port, past rustic stone houses surrounded by fragrant groves of blooming lemon trees.

We disembarked in the bustling center of Capri, the larger of the two places that might claim the title of town on the island. George had made the arrangements for us to spend our few nights in Anacapri at the Bianca Maria, so we wandered through busy streets in search of the island bus stop. The fashionable but tiny *piazza* that is widely known as the *Piazzetta* but the local dialect calls a *chiazz*, is filled with expensive shopping and dining options.

There we quickly found the bus lines that provide the primary means of transportation around the island for visitors and residents alike, and boarded the correct bus to the upper town of Anacapri. It was reached by following a narrow, switch-backed road to the 300-meter-high, bowl-shaped plateau which makes up the broader western end of the island.

Anacapri we found to be a quieter, almost dream-like series of small patio-sized places threaded bead-like along the narrow streets. Space is at premium on the small island, so room for cars is almost non-existent. Most of the alley-wide streets are also closed to any traffic but that of the immediate residents, so the village lacked the background sounds of cars. Only the ever-present buzz of 'motorini, or motor scooters, primarily Vespas, disturbed the peace. Most carried women with groceries, or school-bound teens.

A ten-minute walk with our luggage brought us to the door of the Bianca Maria, or 'White Mary,' a nondescript, block-shaped, but appropriately white, pensione. The clerk showed us to a clean but simple room. One of its two windows offered delightful views toward Napoli and the heights of Vesuvio, sighting cleanly along the mountainous north coast of the Sorrentino Peninsula.

The weather had improved temporarily, so we took the opportunity and walked back to the modest piazzetta that made up the heart of Anacapri. Over dinner on an outdoor terrace in the cool breeze of the late afternoon, we noticed a cable bearing tiny metal seats, occasionally occupied by passengers or bags of groceries, that passed over the nearby houses. Asking the waiter, he explained in passable English that we were seeing the segiovia, or cable-way, that made it possible to visit the Roman ruins at the top of Monte Solaro, still another 250 meters higher than the high town. That, we resolved, would be our Saturday excursion.

We whiled away a few evening hours sipping wine in our room, watching the sun set the clouds ablaze, and then gazing down at the twinkling lights that marked the edges of the vast liquid expanse of the Golfo di Napoli, occasionally picking out the lights of the traghetti loaded with cars and passengers bound for the several islands and ports of the area, as well as the small fishing and pleasure boats that plied those waters.

Saturday morning was breezy, and lingering clouds spit occasional bursts of light rain. The citizenry moved busily, making last-minute purchases at the local markets laden with vegetables, cheeses, breads, and fresh fruits, all in preparation for the traditional Easter feasts which would no doubt draw crowds to family tables the following afternoon. For us, far from family and completely carefree, it was the perfect setting for adventure despite the dampness of the day.

A traditional light breakfast of *cappuccini* and pastries left us ready for a bigger lunch, but we satisfied ourselves with purchases of fresh *mozzarella, panini,* tomatoes and *basilico,* and made up traditional *Panini Caprese* in honor of the island. The crusty bread, split and covered with the cheese, tomatoes and fresh green basil, makes an aromatic sandwich. Sprinkle on Italy's famous dense green olive oil and a dash of vinegar *balsalmico* to complete the dish. Wash it down with glasses of white wine or sparkling *prosecco. Delizioso!*

Lunch complete, it was time to gather our courage for the ride to the top of the mountain. Susan, ironically afraid of heights, hesitated in the *piazzetta,* watching other passengers take their place in line for the utilitarian thrill-ride of a trip on the *seggiovia.* For those with homes near the top of the island, this was virtually the only way to travel, and certainly the most efficient.

As a flight attendant, Susan's fear of heights had often caused laughter while safely on the ground. Only a year earlier we'd had an opportunity to fly aboard the U.S. Navy's hot air balloon during a charity event. We sailed for an hour at an altitude of less than a hundred meters, moving at the less-than-blistering pace of six kilometers an hour, Susan was petrified. Every movement of those aboard caused a gentle swaying that led her to exclaim loudly to us that "it's tipping! Stop moving!"

"But, Susan, your job involves flying at 800 kilometers an hour at 15,000 meters," I replied. "Surely this can't be any scarier than that?"

"That's different," was her only response.

Now she anxiously eyed the small, swaying seats of the *seggiovia* and watched the commuters hop aboard with their purses and children. After two or three minutes of hesitation, Susan mustered her courage, and stepped up to the elevated platform, ticket in hand. "You go first," she said, and watched me as I stood in the indicated spot, waited as the empty basket seat swung around the huge pulley, and sat quickly when it bumped my knees from behind, lowering the seat bar and grasping the single rod which connected it to the overhead cable. I watched as Susan bravely hopped onto the next seat some twenty meters behind, and we were on our way.

The cable threaded its way above backyards and rooftops, sometimes almost close enough to touch them, then followed the flank of the mountain, riding from stanchion to stanchion at a steady, swaying pace, occasionally buffeted by a gust of wind. "It's tipping!" Susan shouted from behind in mock terror. She laughed, but both hands were tightly gripped on the bar. The view, however, was distracting, and soon all fear was forgotten.

The town dropped away, and we found ourselves zipping past tightly terraced vineyards with their budding vines, and compact gardens and woodpiles behind neat stone houses with *terracotta* roofs. The view of the sea became expansive and the mountain rose sheer above us as we angled toward the distant peak.

At times the ground dropped away, and we found ourselves fifteen or twenty meters above the surface. At other points it rose to meet us, and it seemed we could almost drag our feet before the quick rise and drop as we passed each supporting tower.

The views grew ever more breath-taking as we traveled, but all too soon we arrived at our destination, and an attendant efficiently assisted our departures from the post. We walked up a short, steep flight of steps and a sloped path to emerge at the peak of the island, spectacular views in every direction.

Many Romans of the time thought the Augustus was 'pazzo,' crazy, to trade the verdant and secure pastures of his beautiful and fertile island of Ischia, a refuge only a few dozen kilometers away, for this almost-perpendicular and rocky outcrop good for little more than goats. *Capri*, in fact, means 'goats,' and it was easy to see why the name had adhered to this place.

Augustus had been in the thrall of a demanding lover. He paid her tribute by building a crowning villa atop her highest peak. Now we stood in that legendary aerie, commanding the same breath-taking views, and letting our imaginations carry us beyond old limits. The scattered ruins were the remains of the summer home of the Roman emperors so many centuries before. The inlaid floors spoke of the wealth expended upon such a palace as this had been.

Looking down from the breathtaking height, the sheer cliff face brought one's eyes to the *Faraglioni*, three monumental rocks that stood like lighthouses along the south-eastern end of the island. Their name translates as 'great lighthouses,' and that is what they might have been for sailors: enormous landmarks unlike any other along the coast. Massive waves crashed against them, casting spray high into the air, making the cold wind seemed to sharpen, cutting through our light jackets and sweaters.

In the eastern distance lay the Sorrentino Peninsula and its mountain range, rising even higher than our position. It was clear that 'our' island was nothing more than the broken tip of the spear, the last big peak in that mountain range protruding far out to sea. To the west, nothing but the wind broke the surface of the blue Mediterranean. That way, we knew, out of sight, lay Sardinia, and to the south, *Sicilia*, or Sicily, the two largest islands in the Italian archipelago.

We explored the town, and visited the former home of the famed German writer Axel Munthe, a local hero due to the fame he had brought the island. We wandered through the local streets, imagining how George and Emily had navigated the same by-ways, and communed with the same people we were passing.

We quickly discovered that the community life of Capri, like other Italian cities, towns, and villages, is driven in part by their compactness. Unlike their American counterparts, they were designed before the advent of the automobile, when proximity was most important. Town centers arose for the convenience of people who traveled most often afoot, and who moved goods by mule or ox-cart. Streets were narrow, to maximize space for living and trade. In Italian cities today cars are a handicap, with severe shortages of parking, as many streets are reserved for pedestrians and bicycles. Walking is popular, and an important part of the success of what has come to be known as 'the Mediterranean Diet.' Each evening people leave their homes to stroll about, window-shopping and socializing in a daily event known as *la passegiata*. We learned to participate in this popular Italian tradition, and have since enjoyed the custom in large cities and small towns alike.

In Italy people walk to visit friends, to shop, to dine, and just for the sheer pleasure of walking. Public transportation is favored for longer distances, along with the common motorcycle and motor-scooter, known as *il moto* and *il motorino* respectively.

Easter Sunday dawned cold and windy, and gave us another memorable experience. The clouds had departed to leave a breathtaking arc of blue dome over the world. Details of the distant towns along the Bay of Napoli stood out in relief, and the top of *Monte Vesuvio* surprisingly sported a fresh coat of snow.

We made our way the few blocks to the *Chiesa di Santa Sofia*, the principal Catholic church in the town. Built in 1510, the facade glowed a warm yellow-gold in the morning light, and seemed to welcome us from the icy cold. Bells rang brightly from two tall *campanili*. Offering a cheery *"Buona Pascua!"* the traditional Easter greeting, we received a response of *"No, invece Buon Natale! Fa gelido!"* "Good Christmas instead! It's freezing!"

Exchanging smiles, we climbed the short flight of steps and were greeted by the warm glow of a thousand candles. They might have been the only heat available in the church, for, despite the fact that it was packed full of people, it remained very chilly. Devout nine-year-olds and fervently-pagan two-year-olds, dressed far better than they wished, squirmed between parental pillars. We managed to squeeze into a pew as another hundred lined the walls and filled folding chairs set up in the aisles for the traditional service, a practiced choir in full throat elevating the experience to just short of heavenly.

Could We Ever Return to Sorrento?

We first came to visit the celebrated town of Sorrento aboard a *traghetto*, a ferry boat, one of the dozens which operate around the Gulf of Napoli and the adjacent waters, serving the islands and the towns of the Amalfi Coast. Our trip followed upon the heels of a storm, and our very bouncy ride to Sorrento ended at the long wharf of the harbor. A narrow strip of waterfront lay below a sheer bluff. Perhaps fifty meters above lies the line of venerable but elegant hotels which made up most of the seaward side of the city, offering their views of the bay and the smoldering volcano.

As we took in the view, other passengers, no doubt more experienced with the ways of Sorrento, mobbed the eight or ten taxis that met our boat. Left with no obvious way to get from the waterfront up to the town, we eyed the snaking, switch-backed road the led there. Others were walking it, so we dragged our luggage up the steep half mile, pausing to rest and take in the stunning view of the harbor and the bay.

Reaching the promenade that marked the edge of the town proper, we quickly realized that our climb was not over. The town continued to ascend

121

a rather steep hillside. Our hotel, we knew, was somewhere up there, hidden among the stone and stucco of the *centro storico*.

We paused for *cappuccini*, breaking the Italian's cardinal rule of reserving milky coffees for the morning hours, then resumed our walk. At least we were getting plenty of exercise. Italy's mountainous landscape guarantees that much.

After locating our hotel, we wandered through the *centro storico* admiring store-fronts filled with art, and the beautiful furniture made with Sorrento's traditional hardwood inlay process. Tables, chairs, tea carts, platters, and dozens of other creative pieces showed off the extremely detailed decorative techniques of master woodworkers. Renaissance architecture flattered the shaded streets, and cafes and restaurants beckoned.

We decided to take advantage of the afternoon to catch up on traveler's essential needs, which led to another memorable and instructive adventure. We gathered our laundry into a suitcase and asked where we could find *una lavanderia automatico,* or typical self-serve laundry.

Following directions scratched on a map by the hotel clerk, we wandered down a main thoroughfare abuzz with traffic, and found ourselves at a dry cleaners, or *lavanderia secco*. "Si, si," they assured us, they could launder our small bundle of clothes, and would have them ready by the following evening. The price would be 45,000 Lire, about $29. We groaned to ourselves at both the steep price and the idea of being forced to spend another night in the hotel room we already didn't like. We thanked them graciously before heading out to seek another option.

Asking, it seemed, at every shop we passed, we sometimes bought a piece of fruit, bread, or cheese to snack upon as a way of pardoning our intrusions. At last we were told that, yes, there is a *lavanderia automatico* only a short distance away, underneath a corner store.

Following what we understood of the instructions, we managed to locate the tiny space, and entered from a side door on one of the sharply-descending side streets. It smelled antiseptically of bleach and detergents, and offered three or four washers and a similar number of dryers.

While our laundry turned, we took turns escaping to return with treats, including creamy, frozen *gelato*, and later a bottle of wine, which we sipped discreetly from a paper cup as I tried not to ogle the stunningly-gorgeous Italian goddess who arrived to refresh her own dainties. We were feeling increasingly Italian ourselves, as though we were settling into the background, eager to no longer appear as tourists, at least until we opened our mouths to speak.

It was only that evening when we sneaked along the bluff through private hotel gardens to watch the sun set beyond the vivid reflected colors of the bay that we truly began to sense the real draw of this famed tourist destination. Despite the winter chill, the luxurious semi-tropical gardens and blooming lemon trees lent a fragrant accent to the gleaming lights that lined the far shore of the bay like a twisted necklace of triple-strand pearls.

The Magic of the Amalfi Coast

Driven by the desire to see the famous *Costiera Amalfitana*, the 'Amalfi Coast' on the other side of the Sorrentino Peninsula, we bought tickets on the intercity bus for the short jaunt to Positano over the mountains. The route climbed and presented a spectacular view of the Mediterranean Sea thousands of feet below before we were confronted by the challenge of the round tunnel and the square bus.

After overcoming that brief delay, we slowly descended in a series of sharp curves, gradually growing closer to the sea, until we were no more than fifty meters above the water. We both marveled at restaurants and cafes cut into the rock face of the mountain, or sometimes built on spires of stone that seemed to lean out over the sea. Hotels somehow found perches, too, iron feet driven into solid rock, their rooms stacked one above the other in a vertical echo of the mountain itself, each narrow balcony an engineering marvel.

Narrow strips of stone steps led directly over the cliff face, to what would seem to be certain doom, but were no doubt comfortable passageways for mountain goats and local residents accustomed to such terrors.

Without firm plans or reservations, we planned to escape the bus at the first likely-looking opportunity. Asking the driver, and with the added comments of other passengers who joined in a brief, incomprehensible debate, we were advised to descend at the first of two stops in Positano.

Within minutes we found ourselves looking over a low metal railing at a cliff-hugging, colorful postcard image of a fantasy vacation spot. Rooftop parking spaces held automobiles above pastel houses, and the entire unlikely scene descended in terraces toward the sea below. At the busy crossroads behind us were a bar, a series of small shops, and roads that threaded the face of the looming Latteri Mountains above.

Here, in the southern-facing sunshine, protected from the north winds by the heights, we found ourselves shedding layers of jackets and sweaters as we stopped to ask directions to *un buon albergo* in our practiced phrasing. We were directed to follow a downhill side street which comprised part of a long, one-way loop through the town below.

We walked down the sloping street, entranced by the views. Gulls circled overhead, and songbirds serenaded from the trees that leaned over the street from above a high wall that held back yet more brightly-colored stucco houses. On the seaward side, due to the steepness of the mountainside, the houses were built well below the road, so our view of the sea was largely unobstructed.

The original fishing village below had grown up into a valley so narrow that the two walls of what might be called a canyon face each other across a gulf of only a few hundred meters. At a casual glance the opposite side resembles a layer cake with colorful icing, or perhaps a town created of toy models for a holiday display. Its reality was confirmed primarily by the traffic ascending on a steep, snaking road, built partly on pilings dangling over space. The familiar two-note horn of a bus warned other drivers of the approach of its road-hogging bulk.

Positano proved to be an enchantress. It was during our first visit in 1995 a relaxed, homey sort of town, with a natural and unaffected ease about it. Our room was wider than it was deep, and equipped with a balcony offering breath-taking views over the steep terraces of the town, and a small slice of the seafront below.

We stood on our balcony in the evening and watched the lights come on, like strands on a Christmas tree decorating the facing cliff faces. A dozen bats emerged from a gap-walled house down the hill and put on a show, deftly darting in pursuit of insects both above and far below us, the very image of aerial agility. A bright moon crept over the mountain, pouring a soft, pancake-batter-yellow light upon the entire visual feast laid out before us. From our perfect private perch on the mountain, the world seemed a soft and wonderful place indeed, and sharing made it even better.

Following the locals down the steep steps that pass for pedestrian streets, we emerged into the *centro storico* with its maze of curving streets. There we discovered the *maiolica*-domed church of Santa Maria Assunta, with gold-gilt interior trim and a legendary icon that gave the town its name.

According to the ancient legend, Saracen pirates had raided the village, and stolen the sacred icon of the Virgin Mary and Child attributed to a Byzantine artist. When the Saracens prepared to leave with their booty, a terrible storm arose, and they fled back to the shore, only to hear a voice from the heavens calling *"Posa, posa!"* In Latin, that translates as 'place it' or 'set it,' and the Saracens interpreted it as referring to the icon. They placed it on the beach, the storm swiftly abated, and they fled, no doubt dissuaded of future attempts at icon-thievery.

Both above and below the church stand clusters of delightful shops filled with ceramics and inlaid wood. Below, a paved waterfront promenade offers several open-air restaurants. Although there is no swimming beach at that location, waves crashing into the end of the seawall leap in the air sending spray ten meters high in a showering arc, to the delight of small children and, at the time of our visit, one very excited dog.

People posed for photos as the huge splashes formed dramatic backdrops. We watched them as we dined on dishes of traditional *cioppino*, a fish-and-shellfish dish that mingles several different types and flavors into a very tasty seafood stew, at a popular local restaurant. Washed down with glasses of crisp white *Pinot Grigio* wine, they were followed with tiny glasses filled to the rim with the sweet-tart local specialty of *lemoncello*, the tart yellow liqueur made with the zest of the enormous local lemons. Our dinner was memorable.

So enchanted were we with Positano that we returned several times, and one memorable trip with friends for Susan's birthday we planned dinner at a popular water-front place known as 'Chez Black.' I had called ahead to order a cake and flowers to surprise her, and that effect was topped when the owner of the restaurant, dubbed "Black" by his wife, came to our table to visit at the end of our dinner. There he used his artistic talents to decorate his menu, front and back, for Susan, signing it *"Buon Compleanno, con simpatia."* "Happy Birthday, with sympathy." It hangs framed upon our wall.

We watched artists as they painted evocative scenes of the town while sitting in the sunlight, offering their works to the admiring public. We bought a beautiful canvas and secured it in a tube, knowing exactly where it would hang. Positano was proving to be our kind of town.

Each day in Positano was filled with new discoveries, and new surprises. We dined in a restaurant that was a conventional structure at the entrance, but led directly into a cave cut deep into the limestone of the mountain, where we enjoyed southern-style pastas and aged cheeses with rich wine from the cellar.

We posed for photographs in front of Communist Party posters on the front of their tiny party office (one local joking that they hold a meeting every time both of them are in town on the same day) and bought colorfully-detailed tiles with Positano sea-side themes, most handcrafted in small shops or created in large *fabriccche,* or factories, in the nearby city of Salerno, a center of beautiful ceramic work. We watched fishermen unload their still-flopping catches at the waterfront, and followed their carts directly into restaurants to partake of the bounty. Positano was our perfect image of Italy.

Friends for a Lifetime

Exploring the length and breadth of Italy, and giving each region enough time to leave a serious impression on a traveler, is not something that can be done in a few weeks, or even a few months. It is a land of a thousand different cultures, each a variation of its immediate neighbors. Traveling from the icy mountains of the *Alpi* to the sunny coast of Calabria, one may visit famous large cities, and minute villages unheard of a few score kilometers from their *terracotta* roofs.

We returned frequently, delving ever-more-deeply into her mysteries, allowing our experiences to seep into our own sense of romance. We explored the time-washed villages and ancient hill-towns, basked in the warm sun, and cuddled before chill breezes.

We met people everywhere we traveled, and kept in touch with an increasing list. Our travels became a sort of quest, to coax from these ancient places the real secrets, rather than simply enjoy the obvious scenery. From

Venice, Padua, and Monghidoro, to Capo Rizzuto, Rome and Lake Como, we made new acquaintances, and friendships grew. It became a matter of slowly absorbing the essence of the land and her people. All our friends were invited to allow us to return their hospitality in Florida, but few were able to accept.

After repeated invitations, Pina and Gino finally agreed to bring their growing children and come visit us in the United States. Young Jonny, all boy, exclaimed delightedly over the relative enormity of American cars and trucks when we arrived in New York City. We will be forever grateful that we took the opportunity to visit the World Trade Center, taking in stunning views of the city.

Hosting them in Florida, they made the most of their days, choosing to visit the Kennedy Space Center and exploring favorite beaches. They marveled at the warm waters of the Atlantic, heated by the July sun, and the sight of the four of them lolling in a tidal pool as warm as bathwater was gratifying. They delighted in the profusion of friendly squirrels they encountered at Bok Tower Gardens, and were wowed by wild alligators.

For our part, we paid frequent return visits to their home in Lierna, where their hospitality was without equal. Numerous family dinners, outings along the lake shore, or rides on the *traghetti* to other points of interest across the lake were the norm. Together we explored Varenna, just to the north, and southern neighbor Mandello del Lario, where the famous *Mottoguzzi* motorcycles are made. (Each summer the town attracts tens of thousands of bike enthusiasts for their traditional reunion.) We drove deep into the Alps to visit Livigno, and visited their family church, where Pina sang in the choir. We were accepted into their family, and they into ours.

We watched their children grow to adulthood, each visit providing us a sort of freeze-frame snapshot of their growth. We followed Rosalba's progress through school to become a dental technician, celebrating her successes. Her spectacular wedding, during which guests were shuttled from the church to the reception across Lake Como on boats, was a highlight, as were the two beautiful daughters that she 'brought to the light' during the following years.

On one visit, we called upon their friend Paolo in neighboring Lecco, who prepared a fabulous dinner, and together we strolled along the broad promenade that fronts *Lago di Como*, which offered spectacular views of the city, dominated by the tall, pointed *campanile* that the locals refer to as *la matitone*, 'the big pencil.' In the late afternoon the sun's rays illuminating the eastern mountains as it descended behind those to the west made it perhaps the most beautiful city I had ever seen.

During one visit Susan suddenly began developing stomach pains, and by Sunday morning was in distress. We called Pina, who dashed over to transport us to neighboring Mandello di Lario and a clinic run by the *Alpini* that offered *pronto soccorso*, or first aid. We walked in and found an on-duty doctor and her staff, who immediately focused on her problem. An examination diagnosed a first-ever gall-bladder attack, and she was given an injection and a prescription. When the treatment was complete, I asked about the bill. The staff seemed surprised.

"There is no charge! It is free," they told us.

Italy seemed to have the right attitude about medical care. At home Susan's ailment would have meant a visit to a hospital emergency room that would have cost at least several hundred dollars. We insisted on donating to support their efforts, which was graciously welcomed. It was just another memorable weekend in Italy.

The War at Anzio

Our growing knowledge of Italian was no doubt pleasing to our old friend George in his role as a retired teacher of Italian, but it saddened us that his health would not allow him to return with us. During our first decade of travel, the passage of time had taken its toll on him and those of his heroic generation. As his health and strength gradually ebbed, he and his sister Emily had sold their home near us and retreated to an assisted-living center, two hundred kilometers away.

Our contacts inevitably reduced, we didn't see them during the following months, and were shocked to learn of George's unexpected passing from a mutual friend who had heard only the sketchiest details. There was no obituary in the local newspaper, but we mourned his passing.

We resolved to keep up our efforts to discover more about his Italy, and the battlegrounds that were the scene of so much turmoil for him, and hundreds of thousands of other veterans. It would be a fitting tribute.

The war had long been a costly affair for Italians, who were caught in the middle in a war between a Fascist ruler and the Allies. It is hard to overlook the effect it had in shaping the modern Italian psyche. Each region had stories to be uncovered.

Beneath Napoli, more than 140 kilometers of Roman aqueducts, the Aqua Augusta, remain unused. An entertaining novel, Pompeii, by Robert Harris, focuses partly on those marvels, as well as the intrigue and politics, of Roman engineering. Built by Augustus, the adopted son of Julius Caesar and first ruler of Imperial Rome, they once carried water from the mountains to the city and the neighboring towns. In WWII, the waterworks became bomb shelters for tens of thousands as Allied bombs rained down upon the important harbor and factories above. Errant bombs caused much destruction and death in the city, the inevitable cost of war.

In Lazio, a different sort of war unfolded. The town of Anzio is a pleasant resort that boasts an attractive sandy beach within a short distance south of Rome. It is a popular place to bathe in the warm waters during the hot Roman summers. It seems as remote from the horrors of war as it could be, but there we learned more of its connection to George and his companions in the 88th. They had, through their victories against the Gustav line to the south, helped to relieve one of the greatest American Army disasters of the war which had taken place on those beaches and surrounding plains.

The Allied landings at Anzio by the U.S. Army's 6th Corps in January of 1944 were a master-stroke in conception. Placing a large army behind the German defenses to the south, where George and his compatriots were fighting a grueling battle, would cut the Germans' main supply line, forcing the surrender of a vast German army and the loss of enormous weaponry, effectively halving the armed strength of the Nazis in Italy.

The 6th Corps found the beach only thinly defended. A quick stroke inland would cut Route 6, shatter the Nazi's Gustav Winter Line, and block their route of escape from Cassino. Men and equipment poured ashore, but overly-cautious commanders failed to take advantage of the surprise. While they dithered getting organized, the Germans raced troops to encircle the beachhead, placing artillery on the hills that dominate the landing zone. The narrow coast became a death-trap. There was no ground within the landing zone safe from German cannons, and repeated attacks failed to dislodge the enemy from their heights.

Instead of being the beneficiaries of the surprise landings, by May, George and his Blue Devils were fighting their way northward to try to relieve the trapped 6th Corps. At last, after they had lost a series of coastal towns, the Germans began a general retreat from their Gustav Line, and the Americans escaped their trap. Then, in one of the most discouraging turns of fortune, yet another blunder was committed by an American commander.

As the German line to the south was broken, the 6th Corps was ordered by Allied Command to advance from the collapsing Anzio encirclement and cut off Route 6, and thereby the Germans' retreat. It was a chance to speed the liberation of Italy by almost a year. Perhaps a hundred thousand German soldiers would have been captured, comprising a disaster of the first magnitude for the Nazi occupiers.

Commanding General Mark Clark, an aspiring politician, realized that the British Eighth Army was also advancing toward Rome, which had been declared an open city and was already vacated by the Germans. He ordered his forces to race there instead, in order to beat the British. The glory of victory was all-important. The Blue Devils arrived in Anzio just after the breakout, and were ordered to head north to Rome. After a sharp fire-fight just to the south, they were credited with being the first Allied unit to enter the open city.

Because of Clark's decision the Germans inflicted heavy casualties in a rear-guard action, while pulling their forces back in an orderly retreat to reinforce their defenses farther north. During the breakout on May 23rd, the 1st Armored Division took 955 casualties and lost 100 tanks. The Germans' 362nd Infantry lost about half its strength the same day. It was some of the bloodiest fighting of the war.

The events delayed Allied progress for many more months. George and his compatriots would be forced to repeat their fight against soldiers who would have already been prisoners.

Shortly after the battle the U.S. War Department published General Clark's book. Entitled "Road to Rome," it featured an image of the insignia of the Fifth Army on its cover. His pursuit of glory for the liberation of Rome had come at a cost of many lives. I mentioned the story to a friend, a lieutenant. colonel in the modern U.S. Army. He was well-aware of the blunders of Clark and other generals. He remarked that when he was studying military tactics, and he or his friends were forced to mention the name of General Clark, they would invariably spit afterwards.

Understanding a 'Civil' War

Before the first World War, Italy, like much of Europe, had fallen victim to the rise of populism and militant nationalism. Hungered by the Great Depression and the damages of the war, people were easily stirred to emotional responses. Ultra-conservative movements, wrapped in church and flag, attracted many. Spain's violent civil war between dictatorship and liberal republicanism was raging. The Fascists came to power in Italy even as Hitler's brown-shirted thugs seized control of Germany. In America as well, far-right movements had millions of believers, and German-American 'Bunds' celebrated the rise of Hitler, and his ways of 'Re-vitalizing' the German economy.

Many people remained opposed to the groundswell of the far-right. Their voices were overwhelmed by the drumbeat of propaganda, and they were marginalized, labeled as socialists, or communists, or anti-patriots. Not prone to being swept away by emotional appeals to nationalism, these were the people who ultimately became the heart of the resistance, the 'partisans.'

In Italy, the war was a time of hardship for the farmers and peasant people. The government demanded their sons as soldiers, and their cattle to feed the armies. Goods were rationed, from food and fuel to clothing. Eventually the government demanded their bronze, their brass, their iron. They took the bells from the campanile of the churches to make weapons.

The war in Italy devolved into a sort of civil war after moderate leaders overthrew the Fascists and signed an armistice with Allied forces in 1943. When the Armistice was declared, most of the people of Italy celebrated, even as many elements of the Italian Army and Navy fled to the protection of the Allies. They believed the war was over, and that soon their sons would be returned to them. They were wrong. Nazi Germany was not ready to give in so easily. The Germans, anticipating the events, moved strong forces into the peninsula, in effect becoming an occupying army. They disarmed and imprisoned Italian soldiers unwilling to fight for their cause.

Liberated Italian forces joined the Allied war effort, while the Fascists continued to rule with an iron fist over the territories north of the battle lines, where German armies slowed the Allied advance. Fascist sympathizers could earn favors from their Nazi masters by pointing out those suspected of disloyalty. Arrests, beatings, or execution often followed.

The Liberation of Italy was more than just the end of Nazi

occupation, it was a moment of revenge, when the oppressed suddenly rose to throw down their oppressors. The collaborators often became the victims of reprisals. Few guilty in the deaths of Partisans escaped, except in the company of the German forces. Italy was at last free.

Those Sexy Etruscans!

We returned again and again to Italy, each time focusing on particular parts of a surprisingly large and varied country. Tuscany, the largest and undoubtedly the best-known region of Italy, never fails to live up to its reputation as a source of beauty. Here the emblematic cypress trees line narrow roads that were merely improvements upon ancient wagon trails. Old stone walls line vineyards, and quiet farms press their home-grown grapes to be vinified in their own barrels and offered to visitors.

Tuscany and the northern part of Roma's Lazio region had played an important part in civilizations long before the rise of the Roman Empire, and along with southern portions of La Toscana it formed the heart of the Etruscan federation. Being curious, we wanted to know more about its history. We learned that Tuscany draws its name from the old name of Etruria, land of the Etruscans, although the Italians call it *'La Toscana.'*

The Etruscan culture had predated the Romans, and had been absorbed into that of ancient Rome, thereby helping to define and establish many of the Roman traditions. A powerful league of cities, they shared their culture, trade, and mutual defense.

Etrurian civilization first appeared in Italy about 3,000 years ago, and by 650 BCE, they were dominant, a loose federation of cities that traded directly with Greece, and probably even Egypt, as Egyptian products have been discovered among the grave goods. Once they were 'rediscovered' in the last two centuries, the Etruscans have been elevated to an important role in the history of human civilization, and the richness of their culture and art still shines through in their work today.

Discovering a bit of the remaining evidence of Etruscan romantic exploits would take some detective work, so we headed towards Vulci, where Etruscan tombs dot the countryside. The tombs, of which more than 5,000 have been discovered, are reminiscent of underground houses, carved directly into earth and stone. Walls decorated with vibrantly-colored murals feature scenes from the life of the deceased, which give us moderns some insight into the modes of living in those ancient days.

The next morning dawned clear and cool, and we rose with the sun, eager to renew our search. We knew the Etruscans were rumored to have been perhaps the greatest lovers in the history of Europe. Their, 'ahem,' reputations were the result of a sexually-permissive culture, which they had managed to pass down to the Romans who mingled with and ultimately absorbed them. Evidence had been recovered that pointed to a pattern of open partnerships in a society in which women were influential equals. While we couldn't prove or disprove the theory, we decided that it would be interesting to become acquainted with the ancient neighbors.

Near Vulci we found the *Castel Vulci* and a beautiful and delicate Medieval bridge built of stone. It traced a graceful arch like a rainbow, or *arcobaleno*, that almost seemed to defy gravity, rising above a small river. No doubt it provided a popular way of crossing the stream, and brought substantial revenue to the noble who had financed the construction. Most such bridges had their own customs houses, collecting a toll on the value of the trade goods brought across. It was beautiful, but it wasn't Etruscan. We kept looking.

Following signs on lonely country roads, we finally found a typical Etruscan tomb, which we entered through a rickety set of wooden steps. We sat in silence under a single bare light bulb for a few minutes, absorbing the other-worldly feel. It was interesting, yet here was where they had laid their celebrated dead, and we were in search of evidence of the living Etruscans. We resolved to continue our pursuit of the ancients from cheerier locations.

Contemporaries of the Greek city-states, the Etruscans may have espoused making love, not war, but they prepared for either, and built their settlements on the highest and steepest hills, then enhanced those natural defenses with high walls. Most of their chosen city sites remain occupied today. The Italian towns of Orvieto and Volterra are excellent examples, and in addition to offering romantic views, contain significant relics of those founders.

We finally found our Etruscan muse atop the heights at the darkly-brooding town of Volterra. We had driven across thirty kilometers of rolling green pastures filled with wildflowers and flocks of sheep before approaching the town on a steeply-climbing road. It sat like a brooding king on its lofty throne, higher than any of the surrounding hills.

Volterra today remains a point of high interest, positioned as it is between Pisa and Firenza, and no doubt it will eventually be submersed in a sea of tourism as nearby San Gemigniano has been. That has not yet happened. Volterra possesses a certain quality of remoteness that we had not found in other towns in the area.

We parked at a municipal lot below the wall, and hiked up a steep slope to an ancient arch of stone: the city gates. Three faces, their features almost erased by the passage of time, stared down at us from atop and each side of the arch. It was an oft-repeated theme of Etruscan art, a sort of pre-Christian trinity, but its significance remains unknown.

The gate, we learned, was known as the *Porta all'Arco*, or door of the arch, and has stood in this place for nearly 2,500 years. Here Etruscan guards had watched for enemies, and tended the heavy wooden doors that protected the city. The gate was a center of activity in September of 1944 when the approach of the Blue Devils caused near-panic among the Nazi occupiers. George DeLuca and his fellows had established a reputation for toughness.

Frightened of the impending attack, the German commander proposed to implode the gate to block the street. The townspeople recoiled at the idea and almost revolted against the occupiers, but hundreds gathered instead to tear the cobblestones from the street before it and block the arch with the rubble, effectively concealing the opening. The Germans accepted this solution, but then fled in the face of the approaching Americans, who pursued the Nazis to battle in the valleys below. The arch survived the war intact.

The city walls, though reinforced during later years, were those built by the ancient people of Etruria. They offered an excellent defensive position, and clear lines of sight to distant hills. As we walked atop their battlements the intervening years seemed to drop away, and we stood as the Etruscans must have often done, pondering the dominating view of the broad sweep of valleys stretching in every direction. No doubt they also pondered the wonders and dangers of the wide world beyond their safe defenses.

The top of the Etruscan walls offer a striking view into a well-preserved Roman theatre lying just below, a gift from the rising power of Rome to the people of this far older city. Once the voices of actors portraying kings and despots, plotters and princes, echoed across its bowl-like shape. It offered an ideal place to share the culture of the Roman world, and today still performs the same function as visitors walk among the remaining tiers of stone benches, and gaze upon the colonnaded stage.

With rich farmlands and a command of commerce through their Tyrrhenian seaports, the Etruscans lived well, and were inclined to take their pleasures where they found them. Much of their culture and origin remains a mystery, however, including the source of their language, which does not fit into the the surrounding framework of Indo-European tongues.

At the height of their influence they governed an area stretching from the Po River valley in the northeast of Italy to the region of Calabria far to the south, and extending even to the entire island of Corsica. Their dominance was lost in waves, first to northern Celts, and eventually all to the rising Roman Empire, with which they had had shared their art, culture, and agriculture, including their skills at growing grapes and olives, and their architecture, mostly adapted from the Greeks.

The thick walls of the *Museo del Arte degli Etruschi*, filled with Etruscan art and artifacts, were also typical of the massive stone construction that seemed far older than any we had seen before. The *museo* displays an amazing array of the artworks of those people that history had long forgotten.

Our explorations of the Etruscan culture have led us to many more marvelous discoveries, and several other amazing museums full of recovered art, jewelry, pottery, and thousands of every-day tools and objects that help bring these people to light. Among them is the *Museo Nazionale Etrusco*, located in the Via Giulia in Rome. Smaller but also impressive are those in a dozen towns scattered across Tuscany and northern Lazio, including the ancient Etruscan capitol of Vetulonia, near the tiny village of Tirli, overlooking the seaside *Maremma* of Tuscany. There excavation is only beginning to unearth the full scope of their constructions and culture.

Today the remaining Etruscan towns are being excavated and documented, and several fascinating museums display the evidence of the beautiful art they produced. Colorfully-painted tombs filled with relics lie scattered around the remains of the Etruscan towns. The *necropolis*, or 'city of the dead,' near Tarquinia contains more than 6,000 graves cut into the stone, including some two hundred painted tombs that date back to the Seventh Century BCE. The area is now a UNESCO World Heritage site, protected for future generations of researchers and visitors.

Tuscany: Grace and 'Grappinos'

Siena is as challenging for a motorist as most Italian hill towns. Built for pedestrians, they don't have space enough even for the cars of residents. We finally found a space in a line of cars parked on a leafy street at the edge of the walled city.

With its great *Cattedrale Metropolitana di Santa Maria Assunta*, or the Metropolitan Cathedral of the Ascended Mary, it's one of the most impressive sights in the region. Pilgrims and tourists stream through the doors in good weather.

One of the largest churches in Christendom, the *Cattedrale* is a Renaissance layer-cake of black and white stone both inside and out. In a land rife with symbolism, it came as little surprise that even the colors of the *Cattedrale* have their own, representing the black and white horses the legend ascribes to the city's legendary founders, Senius and Aschius. A new wing, planned but never finished, can be seen laid out in the stones. Had it been completed, this modest town in Tuscany would have boasted a church larger than St. Peter's Basilica in Rome.

Nearby is the famous *Piazza del Campo* that hosts, twice each summer,

141

the frenetic and dangerous horse race known as the *Palio*. The piazza is a large, steeply sloping, brick-paved space, lined along the upper side with shops and restaurants. It is flanked on the lower end with a magnificent Medieval town hall featuring a tower that reaches a hundred meters into the sky, beckoning tourists to climb its 503 to steps to catch a spectacular view of the town and countryside from near the top.

From that vantage point, even the brick pavement of the Piazza reveals its symbolism in the form of alternating patterns, nine in all, corresponding to the nine families which had shared in the governance of the city at the time of its construction in 1349.

We returned to our car to find that not only ours, but every car bore a parking violation notice. So much for trusting the judgment of others! Later visits found us parking outside the city to walk in.

Heading further south, the hills of *La Toscana* flatten out into a broad plain, the *Val di Chiana*. We drove through a variety of farms toward a high hill that stood in a dominant position. Here we would find Montalcino, home of the ascendant, deep red *Brunello di Montalcino* wine.

We climbed the road toward Montalcino, enjoying the views that encompassed hundreds of square kilometers of fertile farms watered by canals flush with the winter rains and snows from the surrounding heights. We found the charming town a *terracotta*-toned princess of a village, with steeply-sloping streets surrounding pleasant small *piazze*.

We checked into our small *albergo,* and went out to stroll through the streets, exploring the many interesting shops that fronted the quiet *strade.* We had no intention of causing any disturbance...

On the principal *corso* we discovered a large *enoteca,* or wine shop, which featured dozens of well-known local Brunellos, along with other labels from across Italy. It was also well stocked with small ornamental bottles of *lemoncello,* and *grappa,* a liqueur made from the 'must' remaining after the juice has been pressed from the grapes.

I amused myself reading creative descriptions on wine labels, while Susan browsed through a long, rough-hewn table filled with the miniatures. Suddenly I heard the tinkle of glass, which swiftly grew to a roar, the sound of many dozens of bottles engaged in a cascade. I ran toward the sound, only to find Susan presiding over the orchestral cacophony.

"Oh no! Stop!" she shrieked, waving her arms helplessly as if to halt the chain-reaction of a hundred toppling *grappa* bottles rushing the length of the long bank of tables like so many dominoes, each bottle upsetting its neighbors in a swelling wave. I had a momentary vision of our entire vacation fund evaporating in one final 'poof.' Then, as the cascade reached the end of the tables, two small bottles toppled over and shattered in an anti-climactic crash.

Susan turned to me, wide-eyed and chagrined. "All I did was set down one bottle!" she said. Examination determined that she had placed that bottle in a knothole, which had caused it to tip.

The clerk, hurrying to the scene, quickly put our fears of crisis to rest. *"Niente, niente,"* she repeated graciously. "It's nothing, nothing." She swiftly began to sweep the broken glass and reset the tipped disaster area, while we stood back at a respectful distance, afraid to touch anything. She refused our repeated offer to pay for the minor damages, so we felt obligated to purchase a couple of the more expensive wines to make amends.

This singular event was the origin of the term "playing grappinos," which has followed Susan, and delighted our friends, ever since.

•

We visited Pisa on several occasions, we almost invariably found it raining, both summer and winter. Despite that, the accompanying hush that settled over the *Piazza dei Miracoli*, or 'place of miracles,' was welcomed and appropriate, and gave us a good opportunity to explore without fighting crowds. Originally a seaport, Pisa now stands several kilometers from the Tyrrhenian sea, its wharves and docks long removed. Silt washing down from the mountains over the centuries continued to accumulate and gradually filled in the long estuary of the Arno River, which flows through Firenze long before reaching Pisa and the sea.

The entrance to the piazza is through the walls that encircle it. On the vulnerable western end, which once faced the sea, a massive gate stands at the ready to defend the site from pirates or attackers. Just inside the now-unguarded walls stands a cluster of vendor's shops, ready to offer souvenir tee-shirts, statuettes, warm coats, or in our case, umbrellas. As elsewhere in Italy, the moment the sun emerges, the umbrellas disappear in favor of sunglasses.

Most of the vendors selling to tourists at street-side stalls throughout Italy are not Italians, but foreigners from Asia or Africa. Haggling with them will typically result in a significant reduction in price, especially if you show interest in an item, but put it down when the price is mentioned. Walking away often results in a slow-motion pursuit during which the price may be cut again. They hate to lose a potential sale, but the unwary will often just pay the first ask. Do beware, however, of vendors spreading 'knock-off' handbags and similar goods on blankets along the street. They are often only a step ahead of the *Guardia di Finanza*, and will quickly wrap their goods in their blankets and vanish into the crowd at a signal from their lookouts.

Pisa's religious complex comprises the famous leaning *campanile*, the *battistero*, or baptistry, and the *duomo*, or cathedral. The 'Leaning Tower,' known to the Italians as *le Torre Pendante,* serves as the bell-tower for the church. They were built upon the same unconsolidated silt that holds the rest of the city.

Because of the silty, unstable ground, the famous tower began to lean shortly after construction started in 1173. The builders compensated by adjusting their aim, making the next tiers slightly taller on one side. An astute observer can quickly discern the clever changes in the construction.

Fortunately for the future tourism industry, the tower, more than fifty-five meters high, continued to lean even after its completion. Its tilt drew the attention of visitors, and its fame spread. By the 1990's, however, the tilt grew so alarmingly that it seemed its collapse was imminent.

At the time of our first visit, the 'uphill' side of the tower had been fitted with enormous lead counter-weights, blocks of metal that surely took a large crane to lower into place. Subsequent efforts over more than a decade decreased the tilt slightly, and stabilized the structure. It has since been reopened for visitation, but only for a restricted number of people.

Legend says that here Galileo Galilei demonstrated his theory, to the surprise of skeptics, that objects of different weight would fall at the same speed by dropping two differing cannonballs from the top. Galileo was a supporter of the sun-centered theory of celestial motion, an idea that put him in direct conflict with the position of the Church. He was forced to renounce his position upon threat of prison, only re-stating his true beliefs when he was on his death-bed, and beyond the reach of any punishment.

The interiors of the beautiful *duomo* and the *battistero* are excellent examples of Renaissance architecture, and delight the thousands who visit daily. Like them, we walked around the *Piazza dei Miracoli* to make photographs of the three monumental structures from different angles. It was then that I realized that, like the tower, the duomo itself leans in some peculiar ways. Walls intended to be vertical now tilt outward as if threatening to rain their bricks upon the unsuspecting pilgrims below. We gave the space a wide berth.

The Heroes of Giglio

We returned to the beautiful Monte Argentario and the scenic fishing town of Porto Santo Stefano several times. Only once did we take the *traghetto*, or ferry, to visit the nearby island of Giglio (pronounced GEE-lio), boarding the regular boat that runs to the islands of Giglio and beyond, Elba.

Porto Giglio is a mere speck in the broad sea, just another tiny fishing hamlet clinging to the steep eastern shore, with a single road that snakes over the ridge to a scattering of homes on the western side of the island. It has been a sea-faring town for generations uncounted. Only a handful of commercial enterprises call the island home, and it is normally the most peaceful of locales. Although in summer the tiny island population swells to some 1,500 people, only 800 residents remain to work the boats through the winter months.

Our vessel crept into the tiny harbor as our cameras worked overtime. A nearly full moon shone upon the waters of the *Mare Tyrrhenia*, the sea that sent its undulating waves lapping at the breakwater that enclosed the island's small harbor. A pair of lighthouses, one painted bright red and the other a vivid green, marked the small jetties, and a score of small boats lay tied to the wharves and docks. Despite the peaceful setting, we had come with the purpose of seeing for ourselves the circumstances of a tragedy that had occurred a few months earlier.

It had been a cold evening in January in the quiet village, a winter night like many others. The evening's chill had sent the citizenry home to hot dinners and warm beds. Few of those hardy citizens would bother to peek from behind their shuttered windows to see the familiar lights twinkling across the water on distant Monte Argentario, the promontory from which we had arrived. Tomorrow, they expected, would be another day of fishing, repairing boats, or tending to the small enterprises that made up the island economy. Yet this particular January night would be one that they would never forget.

Shortly before 9:00 on that consequential evening, a glowing array of lights was approaching from the direction of Civitavecchia, the bustling port of Rome, a few score kilometers to the south. The lights belonged to a cruise ship of Italy's Costa line.

Only six years old, gleaming white, and filled with dining passengers, she was heading north to Savona in Liguria, the first leg of a week's cruise around the central Mediterranean. The ship's course would take it between Giglio's rocky shores and the mainland's mountains, a familiar passage it made some twenty-five times a year. This time, however, the captain planned a closer approach, a 'salute' the tiny islet, home to one of the ship's officers. That seemingly-harmless maneuver would change the people of the island forever.

At 9:45, as most of the island's residents were heading off to bed, the Costa Concordia made its closest approach. Passing within a mile of the harbor mouth, the ship was a moving mountain.

More than 950 feet long, and bearing more than 4,200 passengers and crew, it dwarfed the tiny village. Anyone watching from shore would no doubt note its passage. Would they have also noticed the sudden shudder of the vessel as it encountered the rocks of the well-known reef of Le Scole? It seems unlikely. Many of those aboard heard the impact, but failed to recognize that the ship had struck ground, and many were assured that the temporary power loss was due to an electrical problem. Yet the ship began to list to port. As it continued northward, it bore a truck-sized boulder ripped from the sea-bed, wedged into the end of a long gash sliced deeply into the steel of the hull.

As water began pouring into the lower levels of the ship, Captain Francesco Schettino seemed in denial about what had happened, as were some

147

of the other officers. The engine room was soon flooding, shutting down power generation. When electrical power began to fail on the ship, passengers were re-assured that the situation was under control, and told to return to their cabins. Some, unfortunately, did.

As the situation became clear, the captain turned the ship toward the tiny port town, perhaps thinking of running it aground to prevent its sinking.

More than thirty minutes after the impact a general alarm had still not been raised, no assistance had been requested, and the captain was assuring the authorities that the ship had only had an electrical blackout. Yet as the engine room filled with water, the mighty engines died one by one, and the vessel gradually slowed to a crawl.

Only at 10:26 p.m., as the people of Giglio slept, came the admission that the ship was in trouble. The radio call was relayed to the local men of the *Guardia di Finanza*, the island's only official Italian authorities.

At 10:44 their small coast guard boat was launched from the harbor They found the ship listing hard to starboard and settling on the rocky bottom only a few hundred yards from the town. They immediately radioed a general alarm for all assistance, alerting the military. Hearing the word, the staff of the tiny Giglio newspaper rushed to the scene, and soon a photograph of the darkened ship was being flashed to news outlets around the world.

Aboard the huge vessel, conditions were confused, and the slanting decks made walking ever more difficult. Some of the officers and crew were already preparing to evacuate passengers, even as the captain was ordering dinner on the bridge. Many were climbing into the lifeboats, even as the listing of the ship made half of them useless as they tipped against the hull. The rest dangled out toward thin air, making boarding them precarious. Finally, at 10:48 came the signal from the captain – seven short blasts from the ships horn, followed by one long one – the order to abandon ship.

Some in the nautical town heard the ship's signal, and knew immediately that major trouble was afoot. Others, awakened by the commotion in the harbor, peered out windows at the dim apparition of the massive ship, and dashed to their boats.

Aboard the ship, William Arlotti grabbed his five-year old daughter Dyana, and hurried to a lifeboat station on the port side. The boat was almost ready to launch, and no seats remained, so a crewman advised him to try the boat on the opposite side. Carrying his daughter, Arlotti dashed back into the ship. Giuseppe Girolamo, a 30-year-old drummer working on his first cruise, gave up his seat on a starboard lifeboat to a child, and took the opposite course, racing toward the port side. Even as they did so, the ship began to list sharply to the starboard side in a slow roll. The corridors were too steep for walking, and water was flooding into the mid-decks of the starboard side. One slip was enough. All three were plunged into the chilly water. All died.

As the ship continued to list farther to starboard, passengers, without clear instructions, were beginning to panic. Some leaped into the chilly waters, attempting to swim to the shore. There they would encounter a sheer rock face. At least six drowned.

Within minutes, every able person in the village had rushed to help. Some of the ship's lifeboats were lowered and cast off virtually empty in the darkness and confusion. Others, overloaded, careened hard into the water. More than 90 people were tossed into the inky sea. Those aboard the boats worked to rescue them from the cold waters.

In the town, blankets were hurriedly gathered and the church was opened as a shelter while a flotilla of lifeboats and small fishing vessels began carrying the thousands from the ship to the tiny breakwater jetty. By midnight boats were racing to the island from Argentario and other ports. Helicopters hovered overhead as spotlights played upon the waters, searching for survivors. Dozens were winched from the ship, where they had clung to railings as the ship settled on its side.

Outnumbered five-to-one by the victims of the disaster, the villagers worked through the night to pluck people from the rocks and pull them from the waters. Ashore, others prepared food and hot beverages to try to warm the chilled survivors.

It was after 4:00 a.m. before the last known passengers were removed from the vessel by the equally-exhausted rescuers. Two dozen bodies lay in a temporary morgue, and other missing passengers and crew were still being sought. In all, 32 died, and scores were critically injured. All were emotionally injured.

The night created many heroes, and there were few among the

population of that village who failed to earn that commendation. Giglio that night became the model for human compassion, for action beyond capacity.

The people of Giglio are friendly and open, and the town itself charming. Yet there was a certain reserve about the traumatic events which had changed it forever. At the time of our visit the doomed Costa Concordia lay sadly on its side, a massive hunk of rusting steel, still the tomb of at least two victims. A gigantic platform had been erected next to the ship, part of it a hotel-sized dormitory for workers. Teams of men were unloading welding equipment and supplies from work boats in the tiny harbor. A barge was piled three stories deep with more equipment.

In the town itself, everyone was impatient for the cursed ship to be removed from their shores. They had had enough of the trauma, the drama, and the noise. Yet they remembered in vivid detail the events of the night in January. Some were hesitant to speak about it, yet they banded together to share their memories in a book. Entitled "*Quella notte un anno dopo,* or "That night one year later," the book is a collection of intimate memories, as personal as a diary. It speaks to the strength of these modest seafarers that they have shared it with the world.

The Road to the Top of the World

Our exploration of the rest of northern Italy began with a drive across the wine country of Piemonte, a name which comes from *piedi di monti*, the "feet of the mountains." Here the rolling country is sheltered from wintry blasts by the wall of the Alps just to the north. We admired the steeply-sloping vineyards, some still laden with dark fruit of the Nebbiolo grape. It sets the area apart from virtually every other wine-making region in the world. Basking in sunshine, the vineyards offer perfect growing conditions that produce the legendary red wines known as Barolo and Barbaresco. These intense, long-lived wines offer one of the consummate experiences available to wine aficionados.

As we drove along we gazed longingly at the lush grapes that clung in their ripening clusters on the rows of terraced vines. Carefully tended, they stood upon south-facing slopes to wrest every moment of sunshine and summer warmth from the cool climate, the better to bring forth the sugars that fill the ripening globes. Once crushed, it would be those sugars that would fuel the fermentation process. Then the wine would lie in oak barrels for two or three years, mellowing the resulting wine into its lush, final form. Rows of gold medals would mark the success of years of fine vintages, but a single untimely rain could ruin the crop for the entire year.

We passed several large estate homes before stopping at a rustic *vendemmia* sign on the shoulder of the road. The surrounding vines seemed particularly attractive, even though the small *cantina* itself featured rough-cut timbers.

Hoping to sample and purchase some of the local production, we walked in and began to peruse the laden shelves. An elderly woman emerged with a polite smile from a back room that seemed to burrow into the hillside behind. Without hesitation, she quickly and professionally began to show us the variety of wines and vintages produced in the house.

We tasted lush wines with intense, ruby-red colors, breaking the flavors of each with crusty bread before moving to the next. Rich Barolo vintages were sipped, followed by wonderfully-complex Barbaresco. No wimpy wines there, only lush fruit flavors with faint notes of chocolate, licorice, leather, and tobacco. It was a wine-aficionado's dream.

A year later we happened to browse through a 'Wine Spectator' magazine, and were surprised to find an article about Barolo wines from that very vineyard. Gracing the opening page was a large photograph of our smiling hostess, standing before the many prizes her wines had won. We were pleased to discover that she was the matriarch of a noted family that had been producing those same excellent wines for more than 200 years.

•

Pressing westward across Piemonte the rolling, rugged country became decidedly more mountainous. Distant peaks loomed higher, and the road became a winding course between high ridges. We entered the mouth of the narrow valley of the Fiume Aosta following the course of the fast-flowing stream toward its source in the high Alps above.

Our route was several times marked by ancient castles looming upon high hills. Brown stone and towers looked down from the heights, giving their occupants a clear view of the valley below. Once offering succor to friends and danger to enemies, the several fortifications also served to collect tolls from those stout traders who traveled afoot or on horseback. Today they offer romantic views to travelers passing on the modern, high-speed *autostrada*.

The valley was for thousands of years one of the primary routes for travelers attempting to traverse Europe's highest mountains, and helped to link northern Europe with the Italian peninsula as it penetrates deeply between the flanking ridges to the north and south. Ironically, at the head of the valley the road encounters not an easy mountain pass, but Europe's tallest mountain, *Monte Bianco*, or the White Mountain. It straddles the border with France beyond, where it is known as *Mont Blanc*. At 4,810 meters, or 15,782 feet, it is crowned by vast glaciers that keep it shrouded in white throughout the year. It stands a thousand feet higher than the highest of the Rocky Mountains, but like the rest of the Alps rises from a much lower surrounding plain, making it even more dramatic.

Along the south side of the valley stands the mountain fastness that the Italians call *Gran Paradiso*, the Great Paradise. Now a national park, the mountains are home to several species of increasingly-rare animals, including ibex, Alpine chamois, Eurasian badgers, and ermine. The park was once the private hunting preserve of King Vittorio Emanuele II, but in 1922, perhaps inspired by the founding of America's national park system by President Theodore Roosevelt, he donated the vast holding to the Italian state and people. Today it draws thousands of summer visitors to its cold fastness, along with researchers who study the changing climate and disappearing wildlife.

After hours of scenic driving we arrived in the beautiful alpine town of Aosta, the principal city and capital of Italy's smallest *regione*. Aosta lies in a deep valley, where cool breezes play even in the summer. Masses of geraniums cascaded from window-boxes in the autumn's modest warmth, and we found our hotel within the walls of the old city. We had barely arrived in our rooms when the city seemed to burst forth in song. An amazing cacophony of perhaps a hundred bells rang from churches across the city to mark the evening vespers. I flung open the windows and held out a voice recorder, determined to capture this most musical moment.

We strolled slowly through the heart of town in search of an attractive restaurant, passing through the town gate known as the *Porta Praetoria*. A pair of matching walls featured rows of arches enclosing a small square. They were, we learned, part of the Roman defenses built for their colony of retired soldiers about 20 BCE. At that time the town was known as

Augusta Praetoria Salassorum, and was a frontier of the growing Republic. Colorful lichen decorated the ancient walls, now stripped of their original marble cladding. The town has since been an important stronghold for a series of rulers, including Ostrogoths, Byzantines, Lombards, and Charlemagne's Frankish realm.

The next morning, we set out to drive the few remaining kilometers on the modern highway. The river and parallel railway often crossed our path. Both roadways eventually plunge beneath the mountains through tunnels, but our goal was different: we would stand atop the mountain. We pressed on toward our destination, the high village of Courmayeur. We found the quaint alpine town of half-timbered houses bursting with an abundance of brilliant flowers sprouting from hundreds of window boxes.

There we found our first goal: the base station of the lift that would carry us to the top of the mountain. We craned our necks to see where we would be going, but only the lower reaches were visible, fading into the sky above. Beyond lay a broken deck of clouds. Somewhere above them, reaching high into the atmosphere, was the top of the mountain itself.

Here in the sunshine, under a building festooned with flowers, we layered on extra clothing for warmth. Coats and tickets in hand, we walked onto the landing, and watched as the enormous gondola descended on its cables, and swept into the station. It paused as we boarded, and with little hesitation, began its pendulous sweep from the station-house up the flank of the mountain.

Within a minute our starting point was out of sight, and the steep mountainside swept below us unrelentingly. Tall evergreens emerged from the clouds above, and in moments were left far below. The nearly-empty gondola, capable of containing thirty or more, swayed slightly as it passed each gigantic stanchion that bore the cables, but otherwise seemed steadier than a ride in a car or bus.

After a couple of minutes of climbing, the gondola arrived at a station. The doors opened, and we exited, not knowing just what to expect. There was a small bar serving hot coffee, and a few people dressed in warm clothes gathered in groups talking. Only a minute later, a second gondola appeared, and an attendant pointed us toward the open door. We boarded, and were almost immediately swept upward, the bar, its customers, and the station itself rapidly disappearing behind.

The path of the cables flattened and steepened in turn, and the car, slightly smaller than the previous, followed obediently on its journey. Now the scene changed dramatically as we passed the snow line, and dense clouds engulfed us. The pines we had seen before now stood among deep drifts of snow, and the air seemed pregnant with more. The gloom deepened, then parted dramatically as sunshine burst forth, and the dazzling snow seemed blinding.

The swaying of the car increased just as we pulled into another station, and we were soon disembarked and boarding yet another, even smaller glass-enclosed gondola. This too sped upward, above the tree-line, where only snow, ice, and rocks provided the scenery. The clouds formed a seemingly-solid floor of white below us, masking the true distance we had traveled up the mountainside.

For several more minutes we climbed, and looking ahead up the black lines of the cables we could make out a small station, nothing above it but deep blue sky. We stepped into a small *refugio*, where one could be protected from the cold outside, and gazed out upon the icy summit. Still a couple of hundred feet higher than us, bare rock jutted skyward above the glacier that surrounded us. We stepped through the door and were met by temperatures far below zero.

We followed a simple walkway of icy stone, and then followed a track worn into the snow toward the peak, a thousand feet beyond. As we walked, a car passed on the cable, continuing over the mountain frontier to descend into the French village of St. Moritz. Riding atop the car were a pair of repairmen, hard at work in the cold, even as their patient zipped along on its unhesitating chore.

One visitor began to hike out across the snowy field in search of a better view down into the valleys below. Happily, he was interrupted by an alpine hiker coming the other way, who called him back to the well-worn trail. "There are crevices in the ice here that are more than a thousand feet deep," he said. "If you find one, we will never be able to recover your body."

Following that warning we stuck to the small viewing area, and took in the thin air in great lungs-full. We stopped to talk to a couple that were sharing a bottle of red wine while huddled against the low stone wall. Visitors from Austria, they too were there for the adventure.

The Watery Heart of Umbria

Usually promoted as "the green heart of Italy," Umbria. is one of only three *regioni* that do not touch the sea, yet we found that water forms a major part of its past and present. The broad *Lago di Trasimeno* fills the crater of yet another ancient volcano even larger than Bolsena's, also now long dead. We arrived at the shore of the lake, then wound into the high ground to the north seeking the *agriturismo* that we had reserved for the night.

Hoping for peace and quiet, we had apparently out-performed our ambition, as our inn was far more isolated than we had imagined. We climbed high over the rim of the crater-lake, and descended into the valleys beyond, following a narrow thread of road. Long minutes passed by without a sign of our destination.

At last, after almost half-an-hour of travel, we found a gravel drive leading to the complex of buildings. We stopped our car near the main house, and looked around. A beautiful pool lay just below the buildings, but there was not another car in sight. We approached the house and knocked on the door. No answer. I shouted. No response. We walked around the back, and repeated our efforts without success. There were sheep wandering the property, but no sign of residents. I tested the main door. Finding it unlocked, I cracked it open and shouted into the interior. No reply came.

We called the number we had saved in our phones, but got no response. We waited, hoping someone would appear. We even tried to call the booking agency, but had no phone service, and resorted to sending them an email explaining our predicament. An hour passed. We walked around the grounds, enjoying the views. It was set in a beautiful mountain valley, with a ring of hills a hundred meters or more higher surrounding. The slope featured an open pasture filled with curious sheep, with native forest and a pale blue sky overhead. There was the expanse of house and inn, but not so much as a dog. It seemed a bit peculiar, but then, it was Italy, where things are often done differently.

After an hour waiting, I looked around at the silent, surrounding hills, and decided that reservations or not, we were leaving. We drove back into Passignano sul Trasimeno, a pretty town perched on the shore of the lake. A few modern hotels lined the waterfront, and a venerable *fortezza* and the *campanile* of the principal church dominate the skyline, silhouetted behind the ring of green hills that encircle the crater lake. There, on a boulevard lined with fragrantly-flowering *tigli* trees, we found a room for the next few nights.

Lago di Trasimeno is large enough to boast three significant islands, and a ferry service connecting them to the towns along the shore. The often-limpid waters reflect the sky from their jewel-like setting. The lights of the encircling towns at night are like shinning beads on an enormous necklace. Forested mountains enfold it all.

Very near our hotel, and visible from the side window of our room, stood the Medieval fortress called the *Rocca di Passignano*. *Rocca* can refer to either a ruin or a fortress. Some are partly both. Built in the fifth and sixth centuries by Norman rulers, this solid stone structure with its tall tower was heavily damaged by Allied bombing during WWII. It has since been thoroughly restored, and was finally reopened in 2008. We spent a few hours exploring it, and learning about the past of the area, where prehistoric man had once fished from reed boats along the shoreline. Susan watched I climbed to the top of the tower and enjoyed an impressive 360-degree view over the waters and the mountains to our north.

We also joined the locals who strolled along the lake shore promenade, watching the ferry boat making its regular crossings to the island as the waves lapped against the seawall. We joined small crowds gathered in the park on a summer evening to watch *calcio*, soccer, on a large screen television while sipping local wine and interesting beers from the temporary bar, or enjoying creamy, refreshingly-cool *gelato* from one of several stands. We were content to explore the rest of the area from this comfortable base.

The region of Umbria is known for many things, but perhaps its most famous feature is due to one man. On a hill-top a short drive east of the lake stands the city of Assisi, home of Saint Francis, a Christian ascetic who forswore earthly comforts and pleasures in favor of those of the afterlife. Renowned as a gentle and spiritual person, he is often represented with a bird or two perched upon his fingers, or surrounded by animals.

His followers are legion, and he founded several religious orders for both men and women. The Franciscan order of the priesthood has been among the most visible in the centuries since his death in 1226. He is designated as a Patron saint of Italy. In the city of his birth stand several religious institutions, include a striking basilica, that were built in homage to his life. The site draws hundreds of thousands of pilgrims from around the world each year.

Lake Trasimeno has also attracted visitors for thousands of years, but none were deadlier than Hannibal, who crossed the Pyrenees and the Alps with his armies and elephants more than 2,200 years ago, intent on sacking the wealth of the growing rival city-state of republican Rome.

Hannibal had mustered an army of 30,000 men from a wide variety of nations and tribes. Having brought his army from Carthage in modern-day Libya through Morocco, he invaded Spain to begin the Second Punic War. Along the way he recruited allies and mercenaries intent on mayhem and pillaging, and made his famous crossing of both the Pyrenees and the Alps with a dozen elephants. He then moved south down the peninsula, determined to defeat his rivals in a climactic battle.

The Roman armies were commanded by consuls who were aristocrats, and had typically little or no military experience. Military service was limited to free land-owners, each of whom were required to pay for their own swords and shields. Officers and cavalry were drawn from the wealthier classes capable of providing the horses and equipment necessary for their rank. They marched north from Rome 45,000 strong to meet the threat.

It was at Lake Trasimeno that Hannibal laid his trap for the Legions. Knowing that the Roman army was approaching from Tuscany to the west, Hannibal hid his infantry and cavalry in the forests above the lake's north shore. He sent a group ahead to light fires in the distance, convincing the advancing Romans that the body of his troops was camped to the east of the lake. As the Romans advanced in a column around the lake, Hannibal sprung his trap, an assault into the flank of the extended files of troops.

We drove through the area of battle, and it was easy to imagine the reaction of the Romans, their backs to the lake as their enemies suddenly appeared on the high ground. Led by inexperienced officers and taken completely by surprise, the Romans had no opportunity to form into their formidable battle groups. Hannibals' charging men, although outnumbered, decimated the Romans, and drove the fugitives into the lake, killing them almost at leisure. Others were captured and sold into slavery. Only a quarter of the Roman force escaped to return to Rome.

Today one can find a few historic markers, and gaze upon the scene of the disaster. Several of the towns and geographic points around the battlefield bear testimony to the horror of the slaughter that day. Pian di Marte translates as the Plain of Mars, who, as god of war, was expected to protect the Romans. The village of Pugnano translates as the "the place of fighting." Sanguineto, or "the river of blood," was said to have flowed red for days after the battle, staining the lake crimson. Nearby lies Caporosso, the Red Cape, and the villages of Sepoltaglia, the charnel house, and Ossaia, referencing the fields full of bones that lay exposed to the sun.

Today, events of more than 2,200 years ago don't affect the charm of the area. Broad landscapes featuring rows of vineyards and sheep grazing in flowery pastures contribute to the appeal. The people of the region are warm and welcoming, and live life in a generally relaxed manner. Their towns and farms are generally tidy affairs. The centerpiece of the region, however, is the broad expanse of the lake itself.

On the southwest side of the lake lies the town of Castiglione del Lago, marked by its namesake great castle. We explored the *corso*, defended in typical Italian fashion by its wall and gate. We climbed to the end of the street to enjoy the view. The sunshine sparkled on the inviting waters as small boats plied the surface, and spring flowers grew wild on the steep slopes below. Overhead, tiny *rondini* chattered as they flew.

We reversed our course, seeking in vain for a *ristorante* that might offer a terrace taking advantage of the delightful view. The locals, no doubt inured to a view they saw dozens of times a day, apparently saw no value in such niceties. We satisfied ourselves with lunch in a solidly-built stone *trattoria* that seemed as old as the battlement walls themselves.

On return trips with friends we visited the town of Torricella, and the tiny hamlet of Monte del Lago, each offering pleasant views over the broad waters from their heights. In nearby Magione we also found that most useful of resources, supermarkets.

We watched the rhythmic passage of the boats from our fourth-floor balcony in the evenings, while thunderstorms moved like grey walls across the lake. The distant cone of Monte Amiata, far to the south in Tuscany, marked the horizon. Martins dipped and dove through the air in pursuit of invisible bugs. Sunset tinged the clouds into swirls of violet, rose, and fuchsia, slowly fading as the first stars appeared.

Parma's Patrimony

In 2015, we had the good fortune to meet an Italian musician at a stop in New York's Kennedy Airport, an event which led to adventure and new friendships. Awaiting our flight, my curiosity led me to strike up a conversation with a young man who was traveling to Milano with an instrument case so large he had purchased a ticket for it. He introduced himself as Paolo Schianchi, and opened his box to display what he called his "49-string guitar." It was a boggling sight, incorporating five different sets of strings.

Obviously born to teach, the aptly-named man (he was quick to point out that his surname is similar to *chiacchierone*, the Italian equivalent of 'chatterbox') was happy telling the story of his beautiful instrument. He designed this incredible construction himself, and when he plays he employs the entire range of five different sets of strings. He spoke animatedly in excellent English of his passion for his music, and was full of praise for the Argentine luthier who had built it to his specifications.

On his way back to his home in Parma at the end of a month-long tour performing and teaching at American universities, Paolo insisted that we visit him there. When we arrived, he met us at our hotel and took us on a drive to his home in the rural outskirts of the town.

Emilia Romagna lies in the heart of music, a crossroads where innovations in both instrumentation and style were cross-pollinated. The Byzantine lyre had been introduced during the days of the Empire, but during the early Italian Renaissance it inspired a variety of instruments, including the lute and the viola. Credit for violins goes to neighboring Cremona. The harpsichord was invented in nearby Padova, as was its offspring, the piano. In Italy guitars, too, began to evolve into new styles. The result was an outpouring of musical creativity that became the toast of Europe and the world.

We took a long evening walk amid wildflowers and olive trees while Paolo explained his music. A university-trained Master classical guitarist, he had completed ten years of supervised study and training on the instrument under the tutelage of famed classical guitarist Matteo Mela. His studies also yielded Masters' degrees in Music Discipline, Music Didactics, and a Bachelor's degree in Acoustic Science.

As a proud citizen of Parma, he had read much about the famous musicians of the city's past, including one noted lutenist, Santino Garsi da Parma, who lived between 1542 and 1604, and was a favorite at the court of the Farnese ruler of Parma. Garsi's late-Renaissance creativity had provided one of the sparks that led to the development of the classical orchestra which is still enjoyed today.

Despite Garsi's storied past, Paolo was distressed to find that there were no known musical scores of his work. His inquiries at the marvelous library of Parma resulted in his being shown into a room full of scorched books, the remnants of a large collection destroyed by Allied bombing during the war. A volume of hand-written scores, burned around the edges, was only partially readable. It was the beginning of a quest. His feet were set on an 'Indiana Jones' adventure.

Paolo eventually learned that many of the master's notebooks had been housed in Berlin, and were evacuated during the war to various safer places. With the help of libraries in Belgium, Germany, and Poland, he tracked them down and eventually had enough to begin translating them from the original hand-written notation into modern sheet music. For the first time in five hundred years, the sounds of Garci's compositions were heard by human ears. It was an effort born of the pure love of music.

We returned to his beautiful home, and in his temporary third-floor recording studio he presented a private concert. Incorporating a form of classical guitar, a five-string bass, two harps, and a fourteen-string guitar, his instrument makes sounds that resonate over multiple octaves in mysterious ways. He is pushing the frontiers of music into new territory by incorporating the elements of musical history. To call his music impressive would be an understatement. It was easy to see why he was in demand for his teaching skills.

Afterwards Paolo drove us to a favorite restaurant where we met his wife and three-year-old son. We spoke at length about his love of Parma, his music, his creative ideas, and of course, his family, over a range of traditional and delicious Emiliana dishes.

He topped the evening's entertainments by driving us to the flood-lit *Castello di Torrechiara*, which sits on a hill south of the city. It could be seen from afar, and made a dramatic impression overlooking the surrounding farming lands. Fearless, Paolo drove his large equipment truck up the narrow street to the gate of the castle. He carefully edged forward, folded rear-view mirrors almost scraping the ancient walls. Once inside he continued to drive deeper along the darkened streets, where we found a small restaurant serving a few patrons of the village.

When it came time to leave, the size of the vehicle became a serious impediment. For a moment I was worried that we would repeat our misadventure in Orvieto. Only after several failed attempts was he able to get the truck turned around. Back in Parma, he narrated a night-time tour.

Paolo and his music are a gift from Italy to the world. His stunning public performances display his command of music from classical to New Age as he explores the full potential of the guitar. We were later able to help arrange his performance at the Polk State College Lake Wales Arts Center, a historic building saved for the arts in part through the efforts of the Updike sisters and George DeLuca. It was a fitting tribute.

Parma was a delight, from the Medieval architecture to the lively night-life and restaurant scene. We walked along the beautiful *Torrente Parma*, crossing the stream on the venerable Pons Lapidus, a stone bridge dating to the reign of the Emperor Augustus. Once an important center of trade for the

Roman Empire, Parma had also been a department capital under the reign of Napoleon. The river itself, even in April, carried only a small volume of water, in keeping with a well-known quote from the poet Attilio Bertolucci, who observed that "As a capital city it had to have a river. As a little capital, it received a little stream, which is often dry."

Across the bridge we found the broad expanse of the *Parco Ducale*. The Duke was long gone, but the popular park he left behind was a mosaic of broad lawns, mature trees, and pleasant walks. Vendors offered snacks and *gelato* from small stands, and children fed birds and squirrels, or chased their ubiquitous *palloni da calcio*, soccer balls. Bicycles were a popular mode of transportation throughout the city, which had many broad sidewalks painted with double bicycle lanes in addition to the pedestrian paths.

Tall residential houses line the sheer, walled bank of the river, interspersed with rows of office and commercial institutions. We crossed back to the city center, wandering the often-narrow streets to gaze at bronze statues, Gothic churches, and broad stone-paved piazzas. Street-cars shuttled their passengers along the busy boulevards lined with shops and restaurants.

As a major rail hub, the city was devastated by Allied bombing of the supply lines beginning in 1944. When the men of the 88th Infantry had finally pushed the Germans out of their mountain strongholds of the Gothic Line, they swept like wildfire across the plains of the Po, covering more ground in an hour than they had in months of fighting in the mountains. A center of the resistance, Parma was only one of the cities that fell to the Allies as the Nazis were finally routed on those fateful days in April, 1945.

Built as a citadel starting in 1583, the *Palazzo della Pilotta* is a massive structure which had required extensive reconstruction after the war. The original armory within the palace had been converted only a few years later into the amazing *Teatro Farnese* by Alexander Farnese, a scion of the famous and wealthy sometime-ruling family. Wooden columns and tiers of seats rise in a truncated oval facing an enormous stage that would contain a marching band with room to spare. The floor of the theatre was designed to be flooded, in order to recreate naval battles for the entertainment of the public. Thousands of spectators would have bird's-eye views from the upper tiers. An arching ceiling with rows of windows allows butter-soft light to pour in to coat the gleaming wooden structure.

The Pilotta also contains a history museum where Paleolithic history is beautifully displayed. A small town has been recreated. Graves, tools, and pottery once buried by floods serve to illustrate their lifestyles. The sprawling complex also contains the *Galleria Nazionale*, one of Italy's national art galleries. Sculptures, alabaster urns, large oil paintings, and a wealth of fascinating historical reference fill the museum's halls. Wall-sized paintings and hundreds of portraits allowed us to see the family resemblances of historical figures. Susan was more impressed by the large collection of gilded furniture, lamps, statues, and vases, which were enough to make her frustrated interior-decorator heart go pitter-patter.

Bella Bologna

The Roman Empire became a powerful state partly through the enduring system of roads created by their engineers. Many in the English-speaking world are familiar with at least the name 'Appian Way,' which the Italians refer to as the *Via Appia*. It ran south from Rome, linking it with Napoli and the southern provinces. Less known, perhaps, but at least as important was the *Via Aemilia*, which ran through the level ground of the Po Valley between modern Rimini and Piacenza. Typically straight and broad, they comprised the world's first system of 'defense highways,' and allowed Roman generals to move troops rapidly anywhere the need arose. They were the inspiration in part for America's "Interstate and Defense Highway System" as originally approved by President (and retired general) Dwight Eisenhower.

The 'Aemilian Way' was well known long after the fall of the empire, and gives its name to *Emilia Romagna*. Along this busy corridor lie the cities of Modena, Parma, Bologna, and Forli. During the Renaissance, the advantage of quick transportation gave these towns an inside track as ideas and commerce spread and grew. As a result, some of the most beautiful art and architecture of that era can be found in the region.

The short hop along that route brought us from Parma to Bologna, long the principal city of the area, where we were met by our good friends Silvana and Claudio. They had driven from Monghidoro in the mountains to the south, and were eager to show us the city that had been their home for many years.

Bologna is a wonder of Medieval architecture and art, and a bustling industrial hub to boot. With easy access to public transportation, the city is home to numerous manufacturing and distribution facilities. Understandably proud, our friends led us to the *Università di Bologna*, Europe's oldest. It houses the world's first operating theatre, where doctors learned anatomy the old-fashioned way. The accompanying library houses a stunning collection of the compiled scientific knowledge of the Renaissance, and the heraldry of the families who helped compile it as students and teachers. Both the theatre and library were heavily damaged during WWII, and have been meticulously restored.

The *centro storico* stands in the shadows of several Medieval-age towers. Built by competing familial interests, the towers were symbols of the power and wealth. More than one hundred of the towers, like those of San Gimignano, once stood within the city's walls. Today, only a handful remain, one leaning at an angle as striking than that of Pisa's famed *campanile*. The tallest of these, the *Torre Asinelli*, is open to the public. For a fee of only four Euro, one can climb the four hundred and ninety-eight steep and worn wooden steps that ascend to the top, as I did on a warm April morning. Below the tower, the bustle of a major city is augmented by plenty of small, personal shops offering clothing, food, and of course, creamy *gelato*. From there, it is easy to see why the striking views of the terracotta rooftops gave Bologna the nickname *La Citta Rossa,* the red city. The northern foothills of the Appenini mountains, themselves decorated with castles and fortresses, dominate the southern view. To the north beyond the city walls, a clear day reveals the snow-clad Alps.

Roman roads were built to last, upon a deep base of crushed stone, with layers of sand and gravel topped with flat pavement stones. Roadside drainage carried away flood waters and helped to protect the structures. Stretches of Roman road may still be found throughout the former empire, even in England, which they ruled for a couple of hundred years. Today, the arrow-straight course of the *Via Aemilia* is mimicked by that of the *Autostrada A1* and the busiest rail lines in Italy, which pass through fields of yellow rape-seed flowers, vineyards flush with spring growth, and broad pastures with sheep, goats, cattle and horses. In summer, fields of golden wheat and hay, and lush green corn and sugar beets mark the broad, flat plains of the Po, Italy's largest river. Such is the landscape of Emilia-Romagna, Italy's 'bread-basket.' The generous flow of water from the Alps supports the production of many types of rice. The region is the source of some of Italy's most famous products, including Parma ham and their famous Parmigiano cheese.

As industrial agriculture has absorbed the traditional family farms, the area has been left laced with hundreds of abandoned farmhouses, their forlorn and crumbling structures left begging for inhabitants in the midst of the farms. Modern apartment blocks cluster close to the train stations in towns and villages.

With easy access to the markets of central and northern Europe, and a skilled workforce, Emilia Romagna is home to many high-tech industries. In the international airport of Bologna, a display of a bright yellow Lamborghini, hand-tooled and looking as much like an aircraft as a car, causes travelers to stop in their tracks. It is built in Sant'Agata Bolognese, just north of Modena. The rival Ferrari is built in the town of Maranello, just south of Modena. It is such a source of pride to Italians that old men in country villages are reported to rise and applaud its passage.

The venerable *Palazzo della Mercanzia di Bologna* was begun in the late 1300's, and still serves the city's business interests. An ornate *congresso*, or meeting hall, is replete with painted walls and ceilings and elaborate plaster decoration.

The building also features the *Scala di Onore*, or staircase of honor. Seventy-five steps in five sculpted flights allow access to the upper floors. The ceilings above are decorated with the carefully-painted poly-chrome heraldry of the families of the judges that have served the city over the centuries.

Nearby stands the enormous and unusual Basilica di San Petronio. Begun in 1390, the facade of the church was never finished. A succession of architects proposed designs over the centuries, but no plan has ever been accepted. The upper half of the front remains unfinished, raw brick looming over the beautifully ornate marble of the lower half.

In the *Piazza Maggiore* before the church we enjoyed the elaborate *Fontana di Nettuno*. Neptune stands atop a pediment, his trident raised and arm outstretched as if to still the waters. Designed by Giambologna in the Mannerist style, it features, true to form, four mermaids who recline around the base of the pediment and hold their out-thrust breasts, from which emerge the nurturing waters. Completed in 1565, the fountain is a symbol of the city. Neptune's trident was further adapted as the symbol of the Maserati car company, which was also founded in Bologna.

The facing wall of a building is covered with memorial photographs of many hundreds of victims of the Second World War. As we browsed the faces and names, a man standing nearby surprised us by pointing out his great-uncle. "He was a partisan," he told us in English. We gazed at the sober-faced man in the photo and thought again of the terrible cost of war.

A Hidden Paradise

We arrived in the tiny mountain community of Musellaro with few expectations. Surrounded by the mountains known as the *Majella*, and set among rolling alpine pastures and sheer cliffs, the village seemed a step back into time. Hidden amidst Abruzzo's natural reserves, it is a hamlet of less than two hundred persons, and the streets were quiet after our fifteen-minute climb up steep and narrow roads from the *autostrada*. The roar of the *Fiume Orta* rises from the depths of the river's canyon as it cuts through the mountains which enfold it. Above and to the east loom the heights of Monte Pescefalcone.

The village seemed timeless, unchanged since the Medieval period. Only a single business, a bar offering fresh coffees and a very limited choice of pastries, gave any sign of commercial activity in the tiny hamlet. The people who lingered in doorways and balconies fit into the setting seamlessly.

We had reserved a small apartment, which we discovered occupied one side of the 'Piazza di S.S. Crocifisso,' or the Piazza of the Most Holy Crucifix, behind the village's small hotel. The narrow street led directly into a drive and space sufficient to park three cars, with a steep ramp and steps ascending to the pedestrian piazza. That space was filled with pots full of flowering plants, and a lush vine climbed the walls, from where it bestowed a wealth of white jasmine flowers and a seductive aroma upon the scene. The cool air of the afternoon was sweetened by the perfume of the *tiglio* trees, abuzz with honey bees, bumble bees, and all manner of tiny, sweet-seeking insects. The air around us was constantly aflutter with the passing of the hundreds of *rondini*, small swifts that made their homes in abandoned buildings, and flew through a broken window to nest inside an unused portion of the old castle.

Only a couple of curious cats watched as the manager unlocked our venerable apartment. Light poured into the space through small skylights in the open-beamed ceiling above. We opened the shutters to gaze into the deep canyon behind, and alpine peaks beyond. The apartment, we were told, had once been the guardhouse, from which the watchmen could observe both gates through the encircling castle walls. Inside we found that it had been updated to include an array of modern plumbing and a nicely-equipped kitchen, but still retained the ancient flavor of its former use.

We felt that we had been granted a window from which to gaze into the heart of the village. In the piazza only steps from our door we found the tiny church, and below it an elaborate chapel that housed the legendary crucifix. It had been created from a wing of the original castle, donated by the count.

According to legend, the crucifix was found in a ditch during the Crusades, following the destruction of Jerusalem by Saladin. Returned to Italy, it was preserved in the tiny chapel beneath the village church. The story tells us that when a wicked count demanded unpaid taxes from the village and sent soldiers to extract their penalties in blood, it was the crucifix that bled to warn the villagers. The soldiers were confronted by a dense fog, and a voice that commanded them to turn back, as the taxes had been paid by a mysterious stranger.

For hundreds of years the chapel was the destination for *i pelligrini*, the pilgrims from throughout the region. Today only a handful of visitors seek out the site, but the locals continue to revere their treasure.

That night the valley rumbled with the sound of thunder as rain fell, and we slept like babies, snug in our comfortable bed with a down comforter. We arose the next morning to sunshine filtering through broken clouds that danced about the mountaintops. When they parted, they revealed a broad band of fresh snow that had settled upon the heights of *Monte Pescefalcone* just to our east. It served as a dramatic background for the meadows filled with summer wildflowers.

We savored the alpine isolation and the cool, fresh air of June, walking along the main street to the sole bar to order coffees. The locals were no doubt curious about just who these strangers were, but remained respectful. We initiated a few conversations, and they seemed surprised that people from Florida would want to come to their isolated village in the mountains.

Walking to the end of the street to the traffic roundabout to see if we could capture the splendid scene of alpine mountains with a fresh dusting of summer snow surrounding the venerable stone houses, we found a surprise. There in the field just next to the road, an elderly woman was herding a flock of goats as they grazed on the lush grass. Barely five feet tall, she was wearing a traditional long-sleeved peasant dress over which was layered a long smock in a print of the same scarlet hue. She had covered her hair with a scarf of similar color. Her weathered face with its deep creases smiled readily, and her sun-browned hand gripped a solid staff of dark wood as tall as herself. She made a dramatic appearance against the vivid green of the meadow.

Susan, excited by the scene, approached the woman to see if she would allow herself to be photographed. She smiled but indicated that, no, she wouldn't like to be the subject. Susan instead focused on the goats, their extended udders proving their value as the source of the milk used to make the local goat cheese.

I came closer and addressed the goat-herd, explaining in Italian that we had come from Florida, and were impressed by her goats.

"You don't have goats in Florida? she asked incredulously.

"No, not really. Very, very few," I told her.

She smiled, softening to our request and presence, and allowed us to snap a few photos as she coaxed a lone goat to rejoin the rest a short distance away. Suddenly we heard the shout of a man, and realized that her husband was across the meadow, demanding to know why she was lingering so close to these strangers. She called back, smiled at us, and began a leisurely movement back in his direction, obviously flattered at the attention she had attracted, and his jealousy.

We took advantage of warm afternoon weather to drive along the uneven and narrow mountain tracks to the neighboring village of Salle and beyond to the castle perched on the hill above. Although we found it locked at a time posted for opening, we walked through the grounds to admire the ancient stone walls, and gaze down into the chasm of the river far below. The roar of rapids rose clearly, indicating the power that had cut its way through the mountain for millennia.

We made the hamlet of Musellaro our home for a few days, soaking in the restful atmosphere, far from the bustle of life beyond. We watched the antics of the darting *rondini* that frequently skimmed within inches of the lazy cats lounging in the piazza. It was a tiny slice of heaven.

In a Park of Monsters

The mention in the dog-eared old travel book was brief, but once my eyes fell upon it, I couldn't forget it: a "park of monsters." It had been hiding in the woods of central Italy since 1552, just sixty years after Columbus sailed to the New World. We just had to see it. Four of us climbed into the car for the trip to northern Lazio.

The *Parco dei Mostri* is located just outside the town of Bomarzo, in a deep valley below the walls of its massive castle. The entire setting imposes a somber mood over the area, a feeling of stepping back in time. Seen from below on the narrow country road that approaches the town from the north, it seems to slumber in a sort of Medieval dream. The sheer stone walls of the town seem forbidding, as if it were a cloister.

We followed small signs along a rough, snaking lane, and entered a substantial parking lot that contained only three cars. Entering a large building, we found a sort of dining hall with rows of picnic tables. All were empty. It seemed that we were the only visitors that day.

At the counter was a woman who sold us tickets to enter the park. We were handed the tickets, and told to go ahead to the "labyrinth." I knew enough of mythology to remember what that meant. The slightly off-kilter feeling was delicious, just a bit of a spine-tingle to prepare us for what was ahead.

We walked a short distance along a wooded trail, passed through a large stone gate, and encountered the first of the monsters. The giant sculpture was known as *l'orco*, the orc. It brought me to a brief halt, and then I quickly moved to get a clearer view.

Chiseled from stone, a grotesque expression stared back at me through hollow eyes. We climbed a flight of steps to approach the gaping round mouth of the beast, and stood in its frozen jaws, struggling to understand the significance of the work. Who, or what, did it represent?

We ducked inside its mouth, and found a small space that received faint light from the two empty eye sockets above. No, it wasn't designed as a pleasant sitting room, despite the small table perched upon its tongue.

Nearby, we found a dragon battling lions, and one of Hannibal's famed elephants bearing a rider and a stone castle on its back, engaged in crushing a Roman Centurion. It seemed a grotesque reminder of the terrible defeats they had suffered at his hands.

In all we explored more than twenty massive pieces of sculpture, ranging from a leaning house to human figures in 'compromising' positions. Dragons, trolls, each work seemed to reflect some aspect of the darker side of life or mythology. Two giants fought a battle to the death as one dismembered the other. A house was so bizarrely canted that one is immediately disoriented upon entering, perhaps to augment to effect of the surroundings.

Too large to be moved, all these gigantic forms were created *in situ* by the artists. Creatures real and imagined had been brought to light, for reasons difficult to fathom. The park represented an early form of 'science-fiction' in an era when such things were largely unknown.

Medieval sensibilities were undoubtedly less jaded than our own society's, awash as it is in bloody video games, films, and television. Although these creations were in a park, it was clear that they were not intended to be beautiful, or even necessarily pleasing to the eye. This was a park designed to disturb you, to challenge you, perhaps to warn you of the presence of unknown things. Given the superstitions embraced by so many people then and now, it has surely achieved its goal.

We learned that the park was commissioned by Prince Pier Francesco

Orsini, known locally as Vicino, which means neighbor. The prince had been held captive for years following a war that took the life of his best friend. After no doubt years of longing for his wife, he returned home, only to have her die.

In what was apparently an early form of post-traumatic stress, the prince seems to have beecome a bit unhinged. He hired a famous architect, Pirro Ligorio, who had designed the incredible water gardens at *Villa d'Este*. Ligorio had been fired by Pope Paul V for having criticized Michelangelo's work in St. Peter's Basilica. He also had a reputation as part of the Mannerism movement, a style of surrealism, and did not fail to achieve that strange expression in the amazing *Parco dei Mostri*.

Even the uniqueness of the site could not protect it from time. The monuments were eventually neglected by the prince's descendants, and swallowed by the forests. Only in 1970 did new owners begin the job of uncovering the strange behemoths and show them, once more, to a wondering world.

The Venice of Dreams

Our first encounter with Venice had been put off as long as possible. Fear of disappointment, perhaps, fear that the stories might be accurate, made us hesitate. Was there any truth to the rumor that it was a dirty, smelly relic, jammed with tourists and kitsch? We were afraid that our dreams of a lovely city afloat in the blue waters of the lagoon would be rudely and permanently extinguished like so many tooth fairies.

We had well-established mental images of the famous arch of the Rialto Bridge, and the expanse of the Piazza San Marco, featured in so many television commercials hawking credit cards and diamonds. We thought we knew what we might find, and the time had come to introduce ourselves, to strike up a conversation, and see if we might come to be friends, or at least admirers, of this elderly *Grande Signora* of the Adriatic.

Instead, our fantasy was suddenly replaced by the tangible reality. Venezia exploded to life as a multi-color, living creature, one that breathed in clouds of pigeons, exhaled legions of boats, and, like a queen, bathed in Adriatic tides four times a day. We were charmed, entranced, almost overwhelmed by the city we have since come to know almost as well as our home towns.

Known for centuries as the "*Serenissima*," the Most Serene Republic, Venezia is a world unto itself, the antithesis of a modern freeway with its speeding traffic or interminable stoppages. Cars are things of the mainland: foreign, useless, and filtered from circulation at the Piazzale Roma, the end of the causeway.

Venice is the world by boat. In Venice, vessels are the natural adjunct of life, the thing upon which everything else depends. We were soon completely reliant upon them, and quick to learn that one *gondola*, with the accent on the first syllable, became two *gondole*. In a boat one travels, shops, and receives goods. The morning fruit and vegetable boat is the source of evening's dinner.

Not even a dire emergency would permit a car to enter the city proper, for there are no facilities but pedestrian bridges to bear one across the waters. The ebb and flow of the tide makes an effective roadblock, protecting a city without a whit of care for such affectations.

Most visitors arrive either by train, over the long railroad bridge which had first linked the city to the mainland in 1846, or more often by bus or automobile over a parallel causeway called the *Ponte della Liberta*, or "Bridge of the Liberty," built out from the mainland in 1933.

Arriving at Venezia, after weaving through the traffic on a high-speed *autostrada* drive across the plains of the Veneto, is a bit like reaching an oasis after a trek across a desert. The shock of contrast leaves you a bit breathless. The effect is only slightly lessened arriving by train. Whether parking your car in one of the multi-story garages or simply descending from your chauffeured chariot, you are at the threshold of a world at once foreign and fantastic.

For many visitors, their first unfortunate experience is the diesel-choked vortex of the *Piazzale Roma*, where buses and taxicabs circle like so many metal vultures, swooping in to gobble meals of exhausted visitors before dashing away to their refuges on the mainland. This expanse of asphalt, lined with hotels, parking garages, cafes, and the transportation ticket office, is a potent reminder of the world outside, a world soon to be left behind. Once across the first bridge, one steps into a different realm.

In Venezia, it is not only that there are no cars, buses, trucks, or motorbikes. There are virtually no wheels. It may take a first-time visitor a few days to notice the complete absence of even bicycles, skateboards, or scooters. One wonders if Venetian children have ever played with toy firetrucks or race cars. In this watery domain of *gondole* and *motoscafi*, the watercraft of Venice, youthful fantasies run more to sleek wooden speedboats. Their imaginations are fired by the looming cruise ships, white as soap against the moody blue of the lagoon, that seem to arrive twice daily in the warmer months.

If one discounts the tiny rollers on the suitcases led by invading tourists, only the occasional delivery carts make use of one of humanities' most basic inventions. The carts themselves are as unique as everything else in Venice, featuring long handles, and an extra set of small extended wheels, so they can be levered up the steps of countless bridges.

Some first-time visitors arrive from long international flights and find themselves two hours later completely lost. Confounded by scribbled directions that point them toward reservations and much-needed sleep, they stumble along the *fondamente,* the water-front walkways, and through the twisting *vicoli,* or narrow alleyways, stumbling on their jet-lagged feet as if paying the required penance for the sin of arriving in the midst of such beauty.

"It's got to be around here somewhere!" they mutter, barely glancing at their surroundings. They eventually locate their lodgings, and awaken from their naps to find themselves still immersed in a dream.

We arrived like most, but with a determination not to fall into the predictable patterns. Ignoring the large public-transport boats, we walked with our luggage, threading our way across the *sestieri* of Santa Croce and San Polo. We paused for heaping cookie-cones filled with creamy *gelato,* Susan's choice still the chocolate-streaked vanilla *straciatella,* and mine the darkest *cioccolato* available.

We strolled with a confident air, certain that our infallible map, concealed in a handy pocket with landmarks circled, would guide us straight to our hotel. Yet Venice is never short of tricks. The random web of canals that slice the city into scores of islands make for interesting navigation.

We stopped to laugh and photograph, as thousands have before, the multiple arrows pointing toward Rialto or San Marco, or sometimes both, often facing in opposite directions stacked one above the other. There are many ways, it seems, to arrive at one's destination, and we sometimes choose the road less traveled by. We found our hotel after only a couple of turns around a wrong block, having crossed a different bridge than intended.

Tourists can be easily forgiven for succumbing to the mysteries of Venezia's twisting rabbit-warren maze of streets, which might have been planned equally well by following the drunken stumblings of Medieval sailors on leave. They narrow to choking straits that require passers-by to angle their shoulders to pass each other between rough stone buildings, then twist and turn, widening into broad places called *campi*, before suddenly ending blankly against walls. They jog suddenly around corners, cross bridges, and then turn back the way they came as if designed for the purpose, not of connecting places, but of dividing them.

In truth, each of the islands that make up the city had its own pattern of paths and buildings before the bridges began to link them. Bridges are twisted and angled to make the connections between unrelated passages. One, in fact, is known as the *Ponte Storto*, or distorted bridge, and resembles the form of a broken-backed dragon in its angular course. Today more than one hundred and eighty stand patiently bearing their human traffic over the liquid barriers.

The waterways, and especially the *Canale Grande*, or Grand Channel, are filled with boats of every size and description, including plastic kayaks, sleek private launches, and slogging Fed-Ex barges piled high with cardboard boxes. Police and firefighters, postmen and sanitation workers, each had their own fleets of boats to serve the population of the city.

Dominating the watery traffic lanes are the *vaporetti*, the Venetian equivalent of the city bus. Much longer and wider than those land-bound vehicles, a *vaporetto* might easily carry well over a hundred passengers, packed, at peak hours, like so many tinned fish. These curious transports earned their names because they were originally steam powered, their progress marked by plumes of vapor. Today they are driven by powerful diesel engines, and the sound of their propellers reversing is a familiar back-ground bass to the symphony created by wind, water, and 100,000 people passing by.

Vaporetto pilots guide their vessels around both the inhabited and desert islands of the *laguna* and through the Grand Canal, deftly threading the bewildering maze of nautical traffic. Avoiding each other and the thick flow of commerce, they dock briefly at floating piers on alternating sides of the *Canale Grande* to disgorge passengers. During the peak summer months, piles of luggage heap the center deck, while their owners jostle for space along the rails.

Visitors stand on *vaporetto* decks to gawk and photograph the boldly-colored *palazzi*, homes built centuries ago by wealthy merchant-traders, which line the waterway. Locals wedge into seats in the lower decks fore and aft to chat on their cell phones or concentrate on their newspapers.

Immediately succumbing to the magnetic draw of Rialto after our arrival, we headed through the backstreets of the San Polo district. Venezia is divided by custom not into 'quarters,' as in many places, but rather sixths, or *sestieri*, created as administrative divisions in 1170. Each has its own address numbering system that follows the twisting streets and open *campi*, contributing to the added confusion of generations of tourists. The city is further divided into thirty-eight parishes, a reduction from the original seventy. If it seemed we passed a church every second block, it was probably not our imaginations.

We threaded our way through shady *portegi*, or porticoes, and along out-of-the-way passages before finding ourselves at the side of the *Canale Grande*. Our path led us into the heart of a busy street market, a fixture on the San Polo side of the bridge. Here one could buy virtually any sort of snack, or *spuntino*, as well as toys, t-shirts, neckties, glass trinkets, or a thousand other sorts of distractions or souvenirs. Stalls and carts and tall racks of clothing made a colorful and entertaining maze, perpetually crowded with shoppers from the far corners of the world.

A cacophony of voices in a dozen languages mixed with the squawk of music, the shouts of children, and the cries of the vendors hawking their wares, but failed to disturb the ubiquitous pigeons that swept low over our heads or scrambled fearlessly underfoot in competition for crumbs and scraps. We pushed through the maze toward our destination.

Suddenly there before us was the familiar, yet never-before-seen shape of the *Ponte Rialto*, looking from our perspective more like a low hill. What photographs fail to capture is the marvelous 25-meter width of the arch. It is almost a piazza itself. Almost 30 meters long, the magnificent landmark was designed by the native architect known as Antonio da Ponte. Ponte means 'bridge' in Italian, and was a name no doubt earned by his construction.

Rising twenty-four feet above the Grand Canal to accommodate boat traffic, it was completed in 1591 to replace a wooden bridge which had been once been burned in a revolt, and twice collapsed. At last Venezia had a reliable stone portal across the big waterway, which slips like cupid's arrow through the heart of the city. The people of the city naturally fell deeply in love with it.

The boisterous street fair we had already encountered seemed to continue right up the broad Rialto. It filled every available space on the three walkways which threaded between rows of shops designed and built permanently into the bridge in this space-conscious city. Temporary vendors with rolling racks and kiosks filled other available spaces.

We mounted the worn stone steps, marveling at the capacity of the structure. Passing through the crowds of tourists posing for photos, we found a spot at the top, leaned upon the balustrade worn to a soft patina, and gazed at the famous view down the center of the canal.

In sharp contrast to the scene at our backs, we gazed out at the heart of the city. Elegant *palazzi* lined the canal, and *gondole* slipped silently below. The water reflected the warm colors of the buildings, and the blue sky above.

(Unlike most cities, Venice isn't divided into quarters, but sixths, called *sestieri*. Our stroll continued across the Rialto bridge, passing from San Polo to San Marco in the process, and led us into a small *campo* surrounded by shops and restaurants. We explored the area, discovering the city's main post office, and a COIN department store, one of few larger chain stores in the city. Eventually we wandered, with no particular destination in mind, through a series of narrow, pedestrian-clogged streets that squeeze between buildings before bursting forth into the vastness of Piazza San Marco.

Clouds of pigeons announced our arrival as they swirled en masse toward a group of tourists spreading bird food purchased from the vendors. A young girl, half terrified and half delighted, was virtually covered with flapping, feathered, bird upholstery, her voice almost drowned out by the sound of wings in motion. The birds, of course, pose a constant threat of sudden droppings, but in Italy to be so anointed is considered a sign of future good fortune. The scene is rarely repeated today, as the sale of bird food has been prohibited.

Tearing our eyes from the pandemonium before us, we scanned the expanse of the *Piazza*. Unlike most Italian cities, in *Venezia* there is only one *'piazza.'* Other open spaces are restricted to the title of *campo*. Large enough to encompass at least three football pitches, the size alone is remarkable, especially when compared to the crowded warrens of narrow streets that dominate the city.

To our left rose the five enormous silver domes that mark the *Basilica di San Marco*, each with its Greek onion-style shape, crowned by a smaller secondary bulge. The five domes reflect the typical cruciform shape of the cavernous space below. In keeping with the Italian love for Byzantine symmetry, five enormous arches across the front of the church shelter five huge entry doors. Those gigantic arches are themselves sheltered under a massive stone portico borne by dozens of finely-chiseled and polished marble columns. Inside the central arch stands a colorful mosaic with a gold-tiled sky, portraying Christ with a cross surrounded by kneeling saints. Atop the balustrade of the portico, crowded with visitors, stand four monumental horses cast in bronze. It is, without a doubt, a breath-taking sight.

To the right of the Basilica stands the graceful Palace of the Doges, Rows of columns support large Gothic arches, which in turn support a graceful row of more than one hundred smaller Gothic arches which continue along the side of the building. Above these sits the solid bulk of the palace, as tall again as the graceful double tiers of arches, and pierced only by a row of seven enormous arched windows, scaled to match the large arches on the lower level. The effect creates the illusion that the building is floating above a forest of columns and arches, as if being borne to the sky.

Beyond the Palace, the broad blue expanse of the lagoon, filled with gondole and other boats, forms an evocative backdrop.

Immediately before us, and separated from the palace by an open arm of the main piazza called the *piazzetta*, rises the soaring *Campanile di San Marco*. A zig-zagged line of tourists waited to file in for the elevator ride to the top and a view over the city. The tower has collapsed twice, most recently in 1902, and each time been rebuilt to the same specifications. Nearby, a group of street musicians plied their trade, tunefully recreating another familiar ode to love, or love lost. It was quite a charming scene.

Having wisely made reservations, we joined the line at the entrance to the Basilica, which moves with a merciful speed. Stepping through into the cavernous interior, we were once again overwhelmed with the incredible evidence of the love of detail applied to this magnificent space.

Rows of windows lining the base of each dome illuminate the fabulous gold-gilt interiors, lined with sky-blue portrayals of saints and angels. Much of the upper walls are adorned with colorful paintings of religious figures, some on horseback, some arranged in tableaux. Otherwise, every square inch of the upper reaches is covered with gold-covered ceramic tiles, creating a golden glow over the interior.

The Byzantine love of mosaic is reflected in the incredibly complex patterns that ornament the floors, their colorful ceramic chips well-worn by the passages of countless millions of feet.

Mounting the broad stone steps to the chancel, we came upon the four massive bronze horses. These are the originals, protected from the weather, unlike the replicas which have replaced them in their duties outdoors. Cast of nearly-pure copper, their finely-detailed features glow with a warm patina. It is easy to see how their striking beauty led to them being coveted prizes.

Although their exact origins are unconfirmed, they are perhaps 2,000 years old, and have a history of being stolen. Legend suggests that they were made for Alexander the Great, and conflicting written history from the 9th century described them as having come from the island of Chios. The Roman Emperor Constantine had them looted from Egypt's Alexandria for his new eastern capitol in Constantinople. There they had been displayed with a chariot.

They fell to the Venetians when they became prizes of the sacking of the then rival Byzantine Empire capital of Constantinople by the Venetians in 1204. They were installed on the Basilica in 1254 at the command of the Doge Enrico Dandolo. There they remained for 543 years, until Napoleon looted them in 1797 after his capture of Venezia. Napoleon had them installed in his Arc de Triumph in Paris. In 1815, after the Battle of Waterloo ended Napoleon's reign, the horses were returned to the Basilica.

In the corner of the Basilica stands another unique bit of art with a history. Known as the Tetrarchs, it is a statue made of a beautiful reddish-brown stone. Consisting of four anonymous men with impassive expressions, they are said to represent the four rulers of the Roman Empire after the decree of the Emperor Diocletian, who in 293 attempted to end another series of civil wars through a clever division of power, shared among four men.

Although the system existed for only twenty years, the statue remained in Constantinople until the city was sacked by Venice. Somehow in that event the statue was broken, and one corner, including a foot, was left behind, only to be rediscovered in Constantinople, now known as Istanbul, in the 1960's. Of course, Venice asked nicely for the missing piece, and the Turks just as politely refused to hand it over.

To spend time in Venice is to immerse oneself in a spectacular array of sensory stimulation. The eyes seem to be constantly teased by the graceful shapes, reflections, lights and colors of a city of resplendent fantasy. Rows of small, pointed Gothic windows marked by miniature columns combine to form larger arches. Wrought-iron accents dangle over-sized lanterns above doorways and corners. Distinctively-flared chimneys stand in rows above roof-tops. Sunlight reflects from walls the colors of roses and marmalade, only to bounce off the rippling waters to toss dapples of contrasting light and colors across neighboring walls of yellow or cocoa-brown.

For the nose, aromas of fresh-baked breads and cups of steaming espresso mingle with the wilder smell of seaweed and saltwater. Flower markets send tendrils of scented air wafting down neighboring streets and canals.

The ears may delight in the dominant sounds of the bells which explode from the *campanili* with synchronized regularity, or the subtle cooing of the rock doves nesting on ledges. The melodic songs of the *gondolieri* serenading those willing to pay for the extra ambiance drift up from canals, often rewarded by the applause of tourists lining the bridges to soak up the spectacle.

Fingers will find their entertainments, too, in the soft fabrics and rich brocades offered in shops and market stalls, or the rough textures of the stones that form the enclosing walls of the narrow *viali*. Whether wooden knobs on ancient doors or the smooth glass of modern ones, each new touch contributes to a waterfall of sensations that overwhelm.

It is also a place that evokes many different emotions. Rusting wrought-iron gates enclose private gardens full of arboretum-quality trees. Modest neighborhood churches built of brick, or finished in painted stucco, always feature their towering campanile ready to sound the hours. We returned time and again to the *Piazza San Marco*, exploring the interior of the Doge's Palace, with its incredible architecture, great halls, painted ceilings, and marble and mosaic floors. We crossed the *Ponte di Sospiri*, or 'Bridge of Sighs,' from which condemned prisoners may have caught a final glimpse of family and friends as they were led to the tiny dungeons across the narrow canal. Those iron bars seemed less threatening to us than they must been to those hapless offenders hundreds of years ago.

Venetians were mostly reserved, used to the masses of tourists chatting in foreign languages. We broke the ice with our growing vocabularies of Italian, and found them ready to respond, and quick to make friends. The *barista* at the cafe, the hotel doorman, the vendor at the vegetable stand, each was ready to suggest a favorite restaurant, or a special place to take a photo.

Dining in *Venezia*, as in most tourist destinations, is a challenging affair. Venice has long been the target of some who complain of bad food and bad service, but we found much to counter that reputation. Tourists pack into places offering beautiful views of the characteristic canals and bridges, paying exorbitant prices for the privilege. The San Polo side provided the candle-lit tables of *ristoranti* directly at the water, while the San Marco side with its broad *fondamenta* opposite featured a larger selection of bars, *pizzerie, trattorie,* and *gelaterie,* some offering the food wrapped to eat at walking speed, while locals often head for quiet, out-of-the-way places they know offer the freshest fish or best wines.

As we became familiar with the city, we learned to dine in out-of-the-way places, always watching for those that drew the local crowds. We preferred fine yet affordable feasts in the basement level of a converted sacristy in the *San Marco* district, and became enamored of the *ala carte* platters of *calamari*, buttered spinach, and crispy fried artichoke hearts, or *carciofi,* served in a quiet courtyard across the *Ponte Accademia* in the *Dorsoduro*.

At the northern tip of the *Dorsoduro*, within view of the Doge's palace across the water, stands the elegant church of *Santa Maria della Salute*, one of the most familiar landmarks in the city. Viewed from inside the high dome of the church makes it appear even larger. Built by the people of Venice in gratitude for the end of the plague in 1576, it stands as a reminder of that event, which took a third of the population of the city.

We returned to Venice on a warm summer night to participate in the annual event that celebrates that deliverance, the feast of the *Redentore*. The eponymous Redeemer church stands on the shore of the Giudecca island, and becomes the focal point of one of the world's most remarkable celebrations. For this one day a year, the broad expanse of the Giudecca ship channel is spanned by a long bridge, built upon an inflatable foundation that is anchored into place. Streams of pilgrims make the crossing to pay homage to the Virgin who is credited with answering the prayers of the city and ending the terrible plague. The day is also marked by a colorful regatta, which fills the channel with thousands of boats. Late that night the observance comes to a climax with an incredible display of fireworks, said to be the best in the world. It was a sight we were determined to witness.

Weeks prior to the event, our friend Ari arranged to reserve a gondola large enough to accommodate us and three of Susan's airline co-workers. Boarding in a quiet canal, we were rowed into the *Canale Grande* and then out into the basin of San Marco. We drifted upon the crowded waters as the dazzling display overwhelmed the senses for close to a hour. Synchronized pillars of flame swept like metronomes, arched over the waters, sparkled in beautiful colors, and boomed in thundering ovations. It is the July climax of the summer tourist season, but a sight that makes coping with the crowds worthwhile.

On other visits to the *Dorsoduro* we frequented the parish of *San Trovaso*, host to an excellent *taverna* featuring delicious local dishes, and a popular local wine bar. There we also enjoyed the steady night-life generated by hundreds of locals. Nearby, in the *Sestieri di Santa Croce* and close to the *Piazzale Roma*, we also enjoyed the university district, where a broad canal hosts an array of pleasant outdoor cafes, and students often gather for late-night drinks of wine or espresso.

During longer visits we learned to use the multiple-day public transportation passes available at the ticket offices. Not inexpensive, once they are purchased they make traveling around the city much easier. Even buses to and from the mainland are included in the price, so those booking hotels in Mestre, Marghera, or nearby mainland areas can slip easily into Venice and step directly onto a *vaporetto*.

We took advantage of the boats for late dining, cruising home on the Grand Canal past the famous Venetian *palazzi*. Once homes of prosperous merchants, these homes line perhaps half of the waterway, wedged between hotels, churches, markets, and even the town's famous casino. So spacious that a number have been converted into hotels, each *palazzo* was built so that merchandise could be stored on the ground floor, or *pianterreno*. Large doors opened directly to the vessels bearing the riches of trade, while the merchants and their families occupied the third level suites of the *piano superiore*. In between, the *piano nobile* was the site of the cooking and dining facilities, and was often replete with large salons capable of hosting parties for dining and dancing.

We explored more famous museums, including both the boggling litany of Renaissance religious paintings at the Accademia, the modern and sometimes bizarre works collected from artistic friends by American ex-patriot Peggy Guggenheim, and the civic museum of the Correr, located in a quiet upper level next to the Campanile di San Marco. There we were delighted to discover a marvelous museum of the history of the city, complete with dioramas, thousands of fascinating artifacts, and a portion of a preserved galley. Once teams of men propelled hundreds of these sleek vessels in battle, and heavy metal prows were used for ramming and sinking enemy vessels. Venice was a dangerous foe.

We shopped for art of our own among the dozens of booths crowded along the *riva*, or waterfront, near Piazza San Marco. Other artists preferred to paint in the quieter university area of San Polo. Artists practiced their trade and chatted with customers, pausing to wrap the occasional purchase. We chose a beautiful pair of paintings from a man who professed to have taught art to university students for thirty years. They hang framed upon our dining room wall.

For many visitors, a trip to Venice would be incomplete without a voyage on a *gondola*. We were no exception. At several points around the city we encountered *gondolieri*, dressed in their traditional black-and-white striped shirts and flat-topped boater hats, usually decorated by a red or blue ribbon. Gondoliers offered their services with repeated chants of "*gondole, gondole*" at passers-by. Everything about these men speaks of tradition, and admission into the limited ranks is not easily achieved. It was only in recent years that the first woman was accepted into their guild.

Gondole are the best-known of the several forms of boats developed uniquely for life in Venice. The boats themselves fascinated us. Built with a noticeable curve to the right, we learned that the unique design offsets the use of only one oar, always on the right. In the Dorsoduro, it is possible to visit the last remaining workshop where gondole are built and repaired.

The weight of the *gondoliero* standing at the stern required a counter-weight, which came in the form of *ferro*, or iron, at the prow. The uniquely distinctive shape of the *ferro* has evolved to represent both the past and present of Venice. Six forward-pointing and comb-like bars represent the six divisions of the city. The lone bar pointing the opposite direction represents the neighboring Giudecca island. Above, a curved form echoes the shape of the traditional head-piece worn by the Doge. It leaves a small arch shape below, which represents the beloved *Ponte Rialto*.

We spoke to a kindly-looking *gondoliero* standing near a quiet canal, and were soon gliding through narrow waters where he seemed to use his foot as much as the oar to turn tight corners, pushing away from walls as we navigated through oncoming motorized traffic. Once on the Grand Canal we glided slowly beneath the graceful arch of the Rialto bridge feeling like royalty.

Having evolved over the centuries, the *gondole* are used mostly by tourists today, with the sole exception of the long and useful tradition of the *traghetto*. We watched Venetians gather quietly at the secluded landings of the *traghetti*, places where slightly over-sized *gondole* have ferried the locals across the Grand Canal since long before there were any bridges.

The boatmen quickly carried each small group to the opposite shore, deftly cutting through the maze of boat traffic to deposit them closer to their schools, homes, or offices. In keeping with tradition, most of the passengers remained standing during the brief crossing. Within moments the boatman had collected a new group for the return trip, saving each passenger several minutes of walking to the nearest bridge.

Even the open waters of the lagoon offer a busy scene, as small boats follow the deeper channels back and forth between the islands. Occasionally we saw traditional boats rowed by teams of men standing, facing forward at the long oars, their gracefully rhythmic movements as traditional as the boats themselves.

Aqua Alta

Because of its proximity to the sea, Venice finds itself in an especially vulnerable position today. For years, heavy pumping of fresh water from aquifers below the city caused the land to slowly subside. Now, it is the rising seas that add the greater threat. It's a problem that becomes more serious during the autumn and winter.

Each December, at the time of the winter solstice, the sun approaches its apparent southern-most point in our sky. At the same time, the moon, principal ruler of the tides, reaches its apparent northern maximum. At the full moon and new moon, the tidal pull of those celestial bodies coincide. During those few weeks around the solstice the highest tides, sometimes known as 'king tides,' become even more significant. Those are coincidentally the months during which winter storms come to Europe. On those occasions that there may be a south wind, the sea rushes in with a vengeance.

Known to the Venetians as *aqua alta*, or high water, the tidal flooding is normally anticipated well in advance, and sandbags become the order of the day. Long before the event, city workers stack many hundreds of folding platforms along vulnerable walks. As the moon waxes toward full, they erect long cat-walks of elevated staging, allowing pedestrians to access areas that would otherwise be knee-deep in water.

Each tide reaches higher until it spills into the city, pouring out of storm drains to fill streets and flood shops. For a few hours flood conditions persist, and then retreat, only to reappear ten or twelve hours later. After three or four days of this the cycle is over, only to repeat itself at the new moon. The only question, always on the minds of residents, is 'how high will it reach this time.'

The floods sweep the streets of detritus, even as fish are sometimes seem swimming along them, yet they also leave behind their flotsam. Water damage to the palazzi, the stone-paved streets, and the public spaces is evident. Water marks can be seen on many buildings, and eroded stucco exposes the stone skeletons of some. Although built upon the seas, Venice was never intended to be submerged in them.

Over the years as the world has warmed the flooding has grown worse, and each new high-water mark is just temporary, until the next record is set. In response, the Italian government is constructing a massive public works project, a series of floating gates that will rise from the sea bed to block the advance of the tides at *aqua alta*. With more than a billion dollars already invested, it can only be hoped that the system will succeed.

•

We took our time exploring, saving some of the anticipated highlights for later. We began our tour of Venice's famous art at *La Scuola Grande di San Rocco*, a 'school' adjacent to the eponymous church, which today serves as an enormous gallery and concert hall. We had few expectations, but found ourselves gaping at the massive paintings by the famed Venetian artist known as Tintoretto. Born Jacopo Robusti about 1519, he earned the nickname of Tintoretto, or the tinted one, honestly, because his father, Giovanni Battista, was a silk-dyer. One can easily imagine little Jacopo splashing the dyes, and wearing the colors like a human bird of paradise.

Tintoretto grew up to become a legendary painter of portraits and allegorical topics, as well as enormous landscapes, often depicting dramatic events of the Bible. He became a *Fratello*, or brother, and spent virtually his entire life painting for *La Scuola*. He left a monumental body of work that still dazzles today, and inspires hundreds of street artists.

We passed back into the bright light of the day, following a *fondamenta*, or canal-side walk, as reflected sunlight sparkled across flowered balconies and windows, sometimes shuttered for an afternoon nap. We ambled slowly through the Santa Croce district and into the Dorsoduro, past Ca' Foscari university and through a quiet, shaded residential area. History seemed to ooze from the cracked and flaking stucco of the walls and rise from the well-worn stones beneath our feet. The city dozed in the warm afternoon in a sort of peaceful repose, and we felt a strange, relaxing peace settle over us as well, as if we, too, were back in the 15ᵗʰ century.

Wandering near Rialto we were approached by a man speaking English and wearing a plastic-covered license and photo ID, who described the beautiful *fabbrica di vetro*, or glass factory, to which he would transport us free of charge. Obviously spotted as tourists despite our best efforts, we accepted the ride in a sleek wooden boat, such as are the pride and joy of the city. The long, narrow boats, all polished teak and varnish, serve as the water taxis, and for a hefty fee bear well-heeled Venetians and wealthy visitors to all points of interest within the lagoon.

Feeling like royalty, we enjoyed the changing views as our boat threaded its way through narrow canals and emerged on the landward side of the lagoon into open waters, yet keeping to the marked channels that assured safe passage through the shallow tidal basin.

Several times we took advantage of the offers of free transport on the sleek powerboats to the *fabbriche* of the glass makers in the nearby island town of Murano. We learned that simply standing in Piazzale Roma or Piazza San Marco and unfolding a map was often enough to draw the attention of one of the people who recruited customers for these one-way rides.

The entire journey to Murano is little more than a mile, but there is a special reward at the end. Our boat soon approached a private dock and were assisted off at one of the half-dozen large brick *fabbriche* that stand on the waterfront of the island. These factories employ teams of highly-skilled craftsmen who fabricate spectacular art works in glass, *il vetro*, which is visible everywhere in shop windows throughout the city.

We knew that melting glass requires lots of heat. Those artisans ply their trade while working with molten glass at temperatures about 1,000° Celsius, or around 1,800° Fahrenheit. We stood at the entrance, and expected to feel the heat. Ushered inside, we were surprised to find that the room was cool, despite the fiery orange-red glow coming from multiple openings in an enormous *fornace*, or furnace, which is not extinguished until, after a year or more, the heat requires it to be rebuilt.

Treated to a show we have since revisited many times, we watched as the artist, known as *il vetraio*, deftly used metal tools and occasionally his breath to make simple art glass. The blowing of the hollow shapes for vases and other objects was fascinating to watch. Each artist showed his own flair for style, deftly heating and inflating their molten media with expert timing before pulling the taffy-like glass. We watched as they crafted their works of art, expertly shaping the glowing medium into figurines and vases.

Several men were working with small cast-iron bins in which had been melted the unique blend of minerals to create the rainbow of colors they employ: cobalt oxide for blue glass, titanium oxide for yellow, and gold oxide for the beautiful reds that show so dramatically. After each tour, guests are ushered into the vastness of the showrooms, where far more complex works, some requiring teams of men to complete, are displayed for sale.

Glass making has been concentrated on the island of Murano since the Doge ordered them out of Venezia in 1291 for fear that the furnaces would cause fire that might threaten the entire city. In more than 700 years, they have refined the process considerably.

It was on that small island that artists had developed the technique of creating fantastic confections in glass, including the *murine,* multicolored chips of glass with their layers of circles and stars. They had kept the secret of the *millefiori,* or 'thousand flowers,' their own for centuries, and those trained in the technique were forbidden from leaving, lest they be tempted to sell their knowledge. Used to make the famous *millefiori* patterns, they are made in long rods or *cane* which are then chipped into short pieces and re-melted. They take time to complete, and became a favorite ornamentation in the homes of wealthy Europeans, giving glass-blowing a cachet that has persisted today.

Famous families like Toso and Seguso passed their knowledge from generation to generation, and brought the old techniques to new and greater fame in the 20th century. Now, however, mass production, principally in China, produces imitations that flood small shops even in mainland Venice, and too often leave visitors owning inexpensive knock-off pieces. Small glass candies and figurines are sold for pennies, and make great souvenirs of Asia. For Venetian authenticity, it is best to visit an active workshop, and look for the local seal.

We surveyed the little island community, filled with glass shops large and small, offering the works of scores of talented artisans. Susan chose a spectacular lamp, and with a minimum of fuss had it shipped directly to our home, packaged and insured by the *fabbriche*. It arrived in perfect condition, marking an afternoon well spent.

Near the heart of Murano the web of canals form a bustling nautical crossroads. Boats of every shape and description converge, dodging the lumbering *vaporetti* en route to their stops. Nearby lies the Campo Santo Stefano with its tall Medieval clock-tower. In the shadow of that landmark we found a smiling, rotund and bearded man presiding over busy waiters serving his expanse of outdoor seating. In the process of requesting a table we struck up a conversation and learned his name was "Lele," and that he had a bit of a love affair with America.

"Come inside," he told us. "Let me show you my friends!"

In the cool recesses of the sprawling restaurant, he pointed out photo after photo of members of the Fire Department of New York. There, amid the groups, we inevitably picked out the smiling face of Lele.

"I go there every year, to New York, to parade with them!" he told us. Photos of many of the same faces gathered in the Campo Santo Stefano gave evidence that the visits were reciprocated. We had found the unofficial FDNY headquarters in Italy.

Lele was a gracious host, and although we could claim not the slightest shred of connection to the FDNY, we were well treated, and enjoyed the delicious local and regional favorites at his tables on several occasions.

We returned often to Murano, and during one January visit, when the tourists were scarce, we stayed in a four-room *albergo* on the island. After the shops and factories closed and the few tourists left for the evening we seemed to have the islands virtually to ourselves. We walked a few blocks to a local restaurant and enjoyed a delightful dinner, during which an evening thunderstorm swept the streets.

After the storm had passed we strolled back toward our hotel on shining damp stone pavement. The moon back-lit fluffy clouds, and stars peeked from a deep blue-black sky. Distant lightning occasionally flickered, reversing the lighting, and creating an enchanting effect.

We paused on a bridge, the only sound the tide lapping at the stones below, reflecting multiple moons on the rippling waters. As we soaked in the moment, we noticed a cat approaching along the *fondamenta*. It stopped and sat at the foot of the bridge and gazed upward at us, as if awaiting permission to cross.

Susan, always a fan of cats, gave a soft and friendly 'meow.' That was all the encouragement needed. The cat promptly rose and crossed the bridge, passing us with a glance that almost seemed like a smile. It quickly disappeared in the distance, apparently a feline on a mission. Murano was indeed another magical stop on our journey.

Passing back and forth from Venice to Murano, each *vaporetto* typically pauses at a stop called *Cimitero* on the fully-developed island of San Michele. This small, squarish island lies protected behind high seawalls, the better to defend it from the *aqua alta*. After all, it bears precious memories in the form of the graves of many thousands of Venetians. Originally lying alongside a monastery, the small cemetery grew to encompass all. The original church still dominates the setting. Many well-known people lie there, including Ezra Pound, Igor Stravinsky, and Horatio Brown.

Venice itself has little room for a cemetery, and even open spaces are limited. The principal park is that of the *Giardini Publici*, the public gardens. There along the waterfront a good distance from the heart of the town is the expanse of waterfront greenery that helps to dilute the concentrated humanity of the city.

The park is enhanced during odd-numbered years by the *Bienniale*, when artists chosen from around the world install their works to the delight of the public. Established in 1895, it now draws hundreds of thousands of visitors during its run of more than six months, and includes elements of art, architecture, cinema, dance, music, and theatre.

On a couple of occasions during long excursions on a *vaporetto* we stopped at the Lido, the long strip of barrier island that separates the lagoon from the waters of the Adriatic. There lie the famous beaches lined with hotels that had formed a magnet for visitors in the 1950's and 60's. We found it looking a bit subdued, having been largely cast aside by the "glitterati" in favor of the trendier Italian Riviera, Corsica, and other destinations. Still the beaches of the Lido remain popular in the summertime, and thousands of Venetians flock to bask in the sunshine and warm waters. Bars and restaurants abound, scattered among the plentiful, mostly aging, hotels. The Venice International Film Festival, a fixture for more than six decades, is held on the Lido. Like Venice itself, but lagging just a few centuries behind, the Lido seems charmingly out of date.

While Venetian hotels are uniformly expensive, most offer small rooms, some with wonderful views, others with none at all. The demand for hospitality on the crowded islands is partly relieved by mainland hotels in Mestre and Marghera. While some guide-books I have read slam the mainland towns as dirty and industrial, the writers had obviously not spent time wandering the leafy town centers, exploring the broad piazzas, or dining at the popular restaurants.

As part of a Delta Air Lines crew, Susan enjoyed many long lay-overs in a modern hotel on a main street in Mestre. From there it was a short ride on a city bus to Piazzale Roma in Venice, just across the causeway, or a pleasant walk to the *centro vecchio*, the old center of Mestre, where we dined at sidewalk cafes and watched throngs of locals enjoy the evening *passegiata*. Beautiful girls strolled arm-in-arm, still competing for the attention of handsome young men. Bicyclists wove between pedestrians and mothers pushed their *bambini* in strollers while grandfatherly men walked with their jackets draped across their shoulders in Italian fashion.

At the center of the town stands a historic clock-tower, and a small fee allowed us to climb the steps to see the ancient, hand-crafted clock-works, and peer out the windows at the roof-tops and busy walkways below. The museum on the lower levels tells some of the interesting history of the town.

We happened to be in Mestre in 2006 during the climactic game of the quadrennial World Cup. The Italians, like most of the world, are passionate about 'football,' which they call *calcio*, and Americans call soccer. The Italian squad is known as *Gli Azzurri*, or The Azure, because of the royal blue colors they wear in honor of the Savoy kings of Italy. They had made it to the championship game, but were facing the favored French squad in a game being played in Germany.

The streets were deserted and every television was tuned to the game that evening as the airline crew dined in the hotel restaurant. Even the waiters seemed understandably distracted as the game began, and we could imagine the chef in the kitchen riveted to every expert pass as our dinners smoked on the stove. Yet the food came out fine, and we enjoyed our meal in an otherwise empty dining room while the rest of the hotel's guests crowded into a conference room upstairs that contained a large-screen television. We joined them as soon as we had completed our dinner.

To say Italians are passionate about *calcio* fails to express the reality. When France scored first, Italia seemed to groan as if everyone had taken a direct blow. The pain was only relived by an answering goal by the *Azzurri*. When the game ended as a tie, it came down to the five penalty kicks, which each team took in alternating turns. The tension could be cut with a knife until a shot by the French bounced off the cross-bar, and Italy moved ahead. A second miss had hearts thumping.

When the final shot by the Azzurri hit home, and the game was won 5-3, the entire city seemed to erupt. Within minutes the previously-empty streets were gridlocked with honking cars, fans leaning from every window. Flags flew from every balcony, and more were carried by the exuberant people who ran through the streets and chanted on the sidewalks. Our hotel proprietor brought forth an entire case of bubbly prosecco, and even the waiters joined in toasting the victors. It was an over-whelming outpouring of joy. We joined in the fun, realizing that at that moment the scene was being repeated in every city and village across the country.

•

Venice and the Veneto *regione* continued to impress us at every turn. On a couple of other visits, we bought tickets for the *vaporetto* and took the long ride to the island of Burano, making a tour of stops throughout the northern lagoon in the process. The town of Burano is famous as a center of lace tatting, and we watched skilled hands swiftly working in silk and linen threads, and bought samples of their quality work.

We walked around the low island, which also features quiet canals serving as streets, and small wooden boats as the preferred form of transportation. We had lunch in a pizzeria, a bustling place obviously popular with the local residents, who stopped to chat with one another. Oddly, it was decorated with Confederate flags. I asked the owner about the peculiar décor.

"I am a fan of Southern Rock," he told me, and pulled out samples of his music collection, heavy with such American bands as the Allman Brothers Band and Lynyrd Skynyrd. "It's not political," he added, raising an eyebrow to emphasize the point. "Just for fun." Even he had an inkling of the dark American history.

Similar to Venice with its canals and boats, Burano is yet a world apart by nature of its modest-sized houses and distinct small-town feel. Here, away from the cruise ship crowds, tourists are fewer and the atmosphere more relaxed. Each dwelling on the island glows with a vibrant primary or pastel color that gives the entire village an otherworldly, remote feel. Bright blues, soft greens, and vibrant reds stand side by side. When I take up painting, this is where I will come to begin.

•

In our exploration of Venice we wanted to go far beyond the curious surface beauty that makes the city so unusual, and understand how things had come to be as they were. The magnificent public buildings and churches were augmented with things that seemed a bit out of place. We soon realized that many of them were from other, far older, civilizations. Our curiosity tweaked, we put on our sleuth hats, and began to research the 'whys' of what we were seeing.

Understanding Venice today requires understanding her history. It's not a dry story. The great wealth that made Venice the most important city on earth came from her command of the seas.

Venezia grew from a tiny fishing settlement built upon tidal mud flats before 400 C.E. Newer arrivals to the growing town were refugees from invading Goths and Germanic tribes that flooded into Italy during the Middle Ages, after the collapse of the Roman Empire. One can easily imagine that living on the soggy flats of the tidal islands gave the refugees a natural defense as many older cities were sacked and looted by invaders.

The growing population needed space, however, and they soon began to dredge up soil from the bottom of the lagoon, adding small amounts of earth to raise and enlarge their holdings, incidentally digging the canals in the process. *Venezia* slowly evolved into numerous higher islands and deeper canals.

Originally too soft to support permanent structures, the silty clay soils were fortified by cutting alder trees, (preferred for their dense, water resistant wood), removing the branches, and driving the trunks upside down into the mud to depths of as much as six or eight meters. Venetians foraged widely upon the adjacent mainland, cutting and pulling the trees back to their islands. More trees were wedged into any gaps until the entire mass became a tightly-packed bundle. Then the pilings were cut off level, and covered with more earth and, later, stone foundations.

Locked in an anaerobic environment, the trees petrified rather than decayed. Upon those foundations rose the remarkable assemblage of palaces, churches, and monuments that make Venice a world treasure today.

Born and bred on the water, Venetians grew to be expert boatmen and creative naval engineers. Their skills and craftsmanship allowed them to assemble a powerful navy that grew to dominate the Mediterranean for centuries.

Long galleys were powered with a combination of sails and oars, and featured powerful metal rams at the prows, encouraging the navies of other realms toward calm consideration of differing views, and leading to significant trade concessions. Those who opposed Venetian fleets quickly regretted their error.

Venice came to control trade with the far eastern world of silks and spices that had been opened by her native son, Marco Polo, in his explorations. Her monopoly grew as the city became the clearing house of trade for all points from China to Britain.

Venice became a republic, and leading citizens participated in a council that elected the 'Doges,' or dukes, who had varying levels of authority over the centuries. It was an age of enlightenment and prosperity that made wealthy men of thousands involved in the shipping trade as captains, merchants, ship builders, or shipping owners.

Now designated as a UNESCO World Heritage site, Venice features the art and creativity not only of its own cultural talents, but those assembled from the known world during its centuries of hegemony. As their thousands of ships visited far-flung ports, good captains and crews sought out the great treasures of those places, and, by skillful negotiation or skullduggery, shipped them back to Venice, where they ornament homes, churches, and palaces.

The monuments of Egypt, Byzantium, and the Levant found their way to Italy, to the glorification of the 'Most Serene Republic.' Each artifact has at least two stories: that of its origin, and that of its transport to Venezia.

Among the most enigmatic and controversial legends of Venice is the tomb of St. Mark which, some researchers aver, actually holds the remains of none other than Alexander the Great, missing for centuries. Alexander, who conquered most of the known world before his death at age 32, was widely revered as a 'god,' emulated and invoked by countless subsequent rulers through the ages. After his death, his body was stolen by Ptolemy and buried in Alexandria, Egypt, one of the cities he had founded. His elaborate tomb was eventually destroyed by war and a massive Mediterranean tsunami.

The relics in the tomb lying under the *Basilica di San Marco* were smuggled from Alexandria to Venice in 828 by two merchants convinced that the bones were those of Saint Mark, who had preached and died in Alexandria.

Secreted away by the Doge Giustiniano Participazio in his personal *palazzo* in Venice, the body was nowhere to be found when he ordered the construction of a Basilica to house it. The searching began in 1063 during the reconstruction of the Basilica. The bones were 'relocated' thirty-one years later.

Adding fuel to the theories are the stone images kept in the courtyard of the *Museo Diocesano d'Arte Sacra*, or the Diocesan Museum of Sacred Art, immediate behind the Basilica of Saint Mark. There one can stare wonderingly at the fragments of a relief, reported also from Alexandria, that depict what is certainly a shield of the type used by Alexander's Macedonian armies, as well as another with a portion of an arm raising a long Macedonian spear, which some speculate was a fragment of a relief of Alexander himself.

The Coptic Christian church, which descended from Mark's evangelizing, claims that it, in fact, retains most of the relics of the saint, who was reportedly burned. The convoluted and conflicting history gives the imagination free rein to speculate. It is a story that gives church leaders a bit of angst.

•

As a city of enormous wealth, Venetian architects designed and constructed works that rival the finest on earth. Not only the palace and the magnificent churches, but public buildings and private residences became part of their story. Among the most stunning is the gold-gilt La Fenice, the last surviving opera house in Venice. Destroyed in a fire in 1996. it was meticulously rebuilt and restored to its former glory. The stunning tiers of boxes that surround the stage are a sight worth seeing, even lacking a performance.

For another close-up glimpse of the ornately-lavish architecture and luxurious fixtures that have long marked the city, we paid a visit to the Danieli, typical of the luxury hotels that have broad reputations. There we walked on fantastically-colored marble floors under the incredibly-detailed plaster-work ceiling. Gleaming urns full of fresh flowers filled the corners of the lobby, and an elegant marble staircase wound its way skyward. Above, tiers of colonnades marked each floor within the tall atrium. Formal dining rooms offer lavish meals at stiff prices, and cocktails are served, weather permitting, on a roof-top terrace. A dozen such hotels are among the most memorable places to witness a Venice sunset.

Literary Venice

Gazing upon the canals of Venice today, lined as they are with the edifices of another age, one's imagination may run swiftly to bear the viewer back to another time long forgotten. These waters, these walls and bridges, appear much today as they did when the famous German author Johann Wolfgang von Goethe earned his first impression of the city and her realm, the sea, and told of them in his journal, Italian Journey.

Venice has survived both its trials and tribulations, and remains one of the most romantic and inspiring cities on earth, still enchanting millions. Teetering upon its buried wooden stilts, it retains the unique beauty that has captured the imaginations of writers through the centuries.

Modern Venice seems awash in a restless flow of visitors, a living tide that crests in the warmth of summer. The autumn and winter is given over to the waters of the Adriatic, which flood into the streets at the times of 'aqua alta,' scouring the soiled and worn pavement stones of the detritus of the invaders. It is then that Venice slips wraith-like into the past and assumes its proper form.

Sounds echo hollowly in deserted *viali* at night, and long shadows drape themselves around the shoulders of the *palazzi* in the cold winter afternoons. This is the way that Goethe found the city when he arrived on his long pilgrimage across the Alps from Germany: subdued, already stripped of much of its economic power and military might, awaiting only the final humiliation of falling to the armies of Napoleon nine years later.

On the last day of September, 1786, Goethe climbed to the top of the *campanile* of San Marco to behold, for the first time in his life, the broad expanse of salty seas beyond the lagoon. Those were the empowering waters that connected the city to the broader world.

Understanding Venice as Goethe did was to know that Venice had for centuries been a dominant force in world trade. Benefiting from her defeat of Constantinople, the 'Most Serene Republic' had controlled trade in the Mediterranean, and as far away as China. Her native son Marco Polo had opened the routes though which had flowed the silks and spices of the Orient. Her fleets of ships, once numbering over 3,000, had brought the wealth of the world to ornament her churches and public places.

Despite its already weakened state, Venice of the 18th century was the vessel that held the flowers of European art, literature, and architecture. It was a city both rich and enriching, and so it remains today.

Goethe rhapsodized at length about the mood of the city and its people, the architecture of Palladio, the humor of the operas, and the regal bearing of the Doge and the nobles of the city in their ceremonies. He praised the works of Titian, and Veronese. "The Venetian artists," he wrote, "must see the world in a clearer and brighter light than other men," an advantage he ascribed to the watery world in which it dwelt.

Venice, of course, has a magnetism that has long drawn the ferrous metal that seems to lie in the hearts of great writers. Goethe's countryman, the Nobel laureate Thomas Mann, arrived for a holiday more than 200 years later, and was inspired to compose his classic work, <u>Death in Venice</u>. Ezra Pound, Ernest Hemingway, and Proust all walked these narrow passages and strode upon the broad Piazza di San Marco. An inquisitive visitor may find himself standing before the hotel or palazzo that hosted their literary genius.

Standing just to the east of the arch of *Ponte Accademia*, The Palazzo Barbaro was for many years the center of life for expatriate artists, and hosted such luminaries as Elizabeth Wharton, Claude Monet, and Robert Browning, as well as Mann. In more recent years it was detailed, along with the complexities of Venetian society, in John Berendt's excellent work, <u>The City of Falling Angels</u>, which relates the story of the tragic fire at *La Fenice* opera house. There, too, Tiziano Scarpa crafted his beautiful tribute to the living qualities of the city in <u>Venice is a Fish</u>. This unique city continues to inspire those with poetry in their soul, and the ability to use language to show their greater insights to the world.

•

Venice is a place much different from the rest of Italy, as befits a city which was once the commercial center of the world. Yet tourists on their whirlwind tours often miss not only the subtle, but the dramatic differences. Learning to understand a place takes time.

During the warmer months, bloated cruise ships, often two or three a day, dump hordes of eager, guide-book wielding passengers to clog the streets for five hours at a time, running frantically from landmark to landmark, trying to take in all in, but in the end learning nothing but what they already knew. Without time to slow their pace, to see, to listen, to taste, to absorb, their experience is little more than 3-D television. Guided tour groups, led by umbrella-wielding guides, pass like herds of multi-color, language-coded sheep, listening to interpretive comments in Russian, Mandarin, English, Arabic, or Japanese. They descend upon the guides' favored shops with reminders to make their purchases quickly, as they will meet again in ten minutes for the boat ride to a glass factory.

To Venetians, like residents in other busy tourist destinations, the tourists fade into the background, blur to match the cobble-stones and walls so effectively that they disappear, chameleon-like, against the *terracotta* and mustard-colored stucco backdrops. It's not that Venetians aren't helpful. They are, particularly those whose livelihood depends upon a steady stream of customers to fill their shops and souvenir stalls, purchasing countless tokens they hope can somehow bring to mind the sheer wonder of the wizardry and light that combine in the strange and incomprehensible stimuli they have encountered.

"Look, look at the color of that building, isn't that amazing?" you may hear them exclaim. "Can you hear that gondolier singing? What's that tune? It sounds so familiar…"

Highly adapted to their environment, Venetians learn to avoid walking about at peak tourist times, or which back alleys to use to avoid the snaking queues of tour groups. Venetians, of course, see primarily each other. They know the faces and names of hundreds or thousands of other residents, people who will still be here next week, and next year. They congregate in their bars to debate politics or sports, and swallow hot cupfuls of potent espresso from tiny *tazzine*, or thimble-sized shots of *grappa*, the ubiquitous and fiery distillation of grape must.

Afternoon warmth led to the tradition of working men gathering to *prendere un'umbra*, literally 'take the shade,' but translated as a glass of wine, preferably sipped in the cool shadow of a *campanile*. Many of these bell-towers loom above the scores of churches marking the various parishes of the city. The melodious pealing of the *campane* have become as much a marker of the starts and stops of workdays and lunch breaks as a command to express religious devotion.

Standing in the shop of our friend Olivo as he prepared to close for a twenty-minute break to take a mid-afternoon glass of *prosecco* with us, we were overheard using both English and Italian. "Oh, do you know the city?" the pleasant American tourists inquired. "What would you suggest as the most important things to see?"

"After the Duomo and the Doge's Palace, which are first on everyone's list, it seems," we replied, "you should visit the Scuola San Rocco, or the Museo Correr. It's also a real experience to walk through the quiet northern residential districts along Fondamenta San Lorenzo or Castello district, and be sure to stop in the Museo Archeologico in Piazza San Marco with its excellent displays of Venetian history. We can also recommend some restaurants, such as…"

"We have to be back on the ship by 4:30," they sadly interrupted.

"Oh, that's too bad. Not enough time to see much, is it? Perhaps another trip, then. Enjoy your visit!"

•

The nighttime view of Venice is every bit as striking as that of the brighter hours. Glimpsed through open shutters and rich draperies from the deck of a *vaporetto*, fantasy images of gold-gilt rooms, brocaded furnishings, and enormous Murano glass chandeliers appear. Although today most are the homes of wealthy buyers from around the world, it is easy to imagine the lifestyle enjoyed by the burghers of Venice that inspired such writers as Shakespeare even from afar.

Many evenings we wove our way through darkened alleys and quiet *campi* back to Piazza San Marco. There we nursed glasses of wine while enjoying the competing, but happily alternating, restaurant orchestras, which played under broad canopies to patrons dining *al fresco,* in the fresh, cool of the evening. On other romantic nights, we watched the moon rise over the Giudecca, and the lights of the *Redentore* church reflecting as little sparkles in the wakes of passing boats. We tossed coins into the guitar, accordion, and violin cases of street buskers adding their musical spice to the magical elixir of a Venetian evening.

We strolled one evening along the nearly-deserted *Zatteri,* the waterfront *fondamenta* along the broad *Giudecca* ship channel at the seaward edge of the city. A constant parade of boats enlivened the surface, and the lights of the *Isola di Giudecca* in the distance illuminated the water as the sky darkened. A departing cruise ship glided slowly past, ablaze with its own lights, competing with the full moon hanging low in the eastern sky. We stopped to lean against the balustrade to watch the scene, listening to the water lapping gently at the stone breakwater. Susan turned to me and smiled, and her face seemed lighted with a mysterious inner glow. I knew, at that moment, that we were exactly where we should be.

The Roots of Romance

Today we speak of 'romance' only because of the Romans. The five 'Romance languages' are so called not because of their sounds, but because they descend directly from the Latin spoken by them 2,000 years ago. We apply the word, though, to affairs of the heart for good reason.

Romance is not just a thing of hearts and flowers. It includes a sense of wonder, and if we are fortunate, a sense of both the depth and brevity of our lives. Part of each of us senses the romance of 'time immemorial.' We are each participating in a short piece of a very long story, and should always keep in mind that our time is limited. We speak of our own love in terms of permanence, but what does it really mean when we offer 'forever love'?

Today we speak of 'romance' only because of the Romans. The five 'Romance languages' are so called not because of their sounds, but because they descend directly from the Latin spoken by them 2,000 years ago. We apply the word, though, to affairs of the heart for good reason.

Romance is not just a thing of hearts and flowers. It includes a sense of wonder, and if we are fortunate, a sense of both the depth and brevity of our lives. Part of each of us senses the romance of 'time immemorial.' We are each participating in a short piece of a very long story, and should always keep in mind that our time is limited. We speak of our own love in terms of permanence, but what does it really mean when we offer 'forever love'?

We gain perspective when we examine the things of the ancient past. The voices of others long ago seem to speak to us through their personal effects, the every-day objects they used, the houses and temples they stood beneath. Their lives, if fully imagined, bring a deeper perspective to our own.

Near Napoli lies the excavated remains of the Roman town of Herculaneum, which was buried by waves of scorching mud in the 79 C.E. eruption of Mount *Vesuvio*. The long-forgotten city was only rediscovered when men digging a well in 1709 found voids in the soft stone, and began to explore. Today the *scavi*, or excavations, are about four blocks across. Tunnels run deeper into the hillside under Ercolano above, the name an echo of the old Roman name of Herculaneum.

We walked quietly, as though in a cemetery, for that is how it struck us. The ruins contained impressive works of art, including colorful murals and floors created from thousands of tiles. It was hard to imagine that more than 1,900 years had passed since a Roman craftsman had knelt, hefted hammer and chisel, and chipped the edges of these vibrantly-shaded ceramics to fit into these intricate and marvelous patterns.

Roman architects had designed highly-livable houses, with comfortable rooms arranged around central courtyards. Most contained a feature known as an *impluvium*, a square pool which filled with rainwater flowing from a *compluvium*, a square hole in the inward-sloping roof. It was a useful asset in water-poor southern regions, assuring handy fresh water for basic needs, while pipes drained away the overflow and waste. The hole also allowed light into the center of the home, which was often ornamented with plants and statuary.

The ruins of the old city center include fast food restaurants, opulent palaces, and tiny apartments. Deep ruts cut into the paving stones by the wheels of passing chariots stand in testimony to the vibrant life that had existed here. Cut well below the sidewalks, the streets also served to carry away the rain and the wastes of the horses. To avoid stepping in the mire, citizens used the four, foot-high stepping stones, cleverly placed so that the horse and the wheels of the chariots passed between them, and the axles passed above them. Chariots had to be built to fit the streets, which were apparently all one-way. Such precise standardization was another hallmark of the Roman civilization.

Pliny the Elder, perhaps the world's first front-line news reporter, had bravely documented the eruption of Vesuvio in vivid terms, but died in the process. An admiral of the Roman fleet, he left the relative safety of his home in Napoli and commanded his ship to sail to Herculaneum in an attempt to save survivors of the initial eruption. The violence of that eruption is hard to grasp. Paintings of the mountain from Roman times depicted a single sharp pyramid that may have soared a full mile higher than the current profile. It was that massive mountain which was blown many miles into the air before it fell back and buried the surrounding countryside.

Through a steady rain of flaming stones and clouds of choking ash, Pliny navigated close to the shoreline where refugees were desperate for rescue. Although his battered ship survived, his own constitution, perhaps made frail by age, was no match for the conditions, and he collapsed on the deck, dictating his final reports as he lay dying, choking on the volcanic ash.

We contemplated Pliny's fate, and that of the thousands who had died in that eruption. At a row of cut-stone warehouses that had marked the original waterfront of Pompeii, excavations had discovered strange hollow spaces in the hardened ash and mud. By filling them with plaster and then excavating around them, they were revealed to be the voids left by the remains of more than 300 persons who had huddled there, hoping to escape to the sea. They had remained entombed within the hardened mud for nearly 2,000 years.

We toured the ruins of Pompeii as well, located a few kilometers farther south. There, a group of archeologists invited us to enter their excavation to see the delicate work they were performing. Using small trowels and soft brushes, they were removing the dirt and dust of centuries to bring to the light the vivid colors of mosaic tile floors and frescoed walls, or buried treasures. The beautiful art and jewelry they left behind speaks to us across the ages. The broad lawns, luxury homes and arena of Pompeii are evidence of the opulent lifestyles enjoyed by wealthy Romans.

Most of the art of the dead towns has been moved to the *Museo Archeologico Nazionale di Napoli*, safe from the effects of weather, but also out of context. We wandered through the vast halls of the museum with an interpretive booklet, and attempted to picture the often-enormous works of art in their former settings, surrounded by the rattle of passing chariots, the bustle of young mothers with children, open-air markets, and workmen with their animals.

Gazing out across the broad bay to the distant islands of Procida and Ischia, and the long curve of the Sorrentino peninsula embracing the bay to the south, we enjoyed the same view that those Romans had, and found the dark magic of that place palpable. The crater of *Vesuvio* loomed silently above us, as though considering when next it might like to remind the bay of its dominance. The thin plume of smoke seeping from it reminded us that all fate is unpredictable.

Seeing the destruction wreaked by the volcano made us determined to see the monster from a closer vantage point. A ten-euro ticket for the bus ride, and another ten euros for the passes into the *Parco Nazionale di Vesuvio* were worth the money spent.

Although today the mountain appears to have two distinct peaks, they are actually two halves of the mountain that existed before the 79 AD eruption. A large flow of hardened grey lava was visible halfway up the crater, the remains of an eruption in 1944 that burst from a vent between the two halves, killed almost a hundred residents, and completely eradicated two villages. It partially filled in the gap before spilling out to the north, toward Napoli. Most of the deaths resulted from heavy stones and ash raining down upon houses, and eventually collapsing roofs upon the occupants.

We scrambled from the bus to begin a climb up a steep path of loose stone and gravel toward the rim. It's a challenging hike for anyone not in good shape, and good shoes are needed to resist the sharp pumice stones. Looking toward the *Golfo di Napoli* to the east, I could barely make out the distant location of Pompeii, far below and several kilometers to the south. Herculaneum is closer to the foot of the mountain.

The steaming chasm, viewed from the top, is a sheer funnel that reaches about 300 meters into the interior of the mountain. Escaping steam pours from vents and small stones cascade down the sheer throat of the volcano, especially when small temblors shake the mountain. The magma chamber beneath still grows.

About 800,000 people live within the thirteen-kilometer 'danger zone' specified by the government. They will all have to be evacuated the next time the mountain erupts, which is only a matter of time. It is believed that the entire population could be brought out in three days. Just across the imaginary line of safety lies the city of Napoli, home to another million.

We were glad Vesuvio was relatively quiet that day. Our search for the traces of ancient love would go on.

•

With Susan helpfully reading tips from a guidebook and making vain attempts at navigating the confusing array of road signs, we headed south in our rental car from Salerno. The coastal road traverses a broad flat plain filled with farms bisected by irrigation canals. We passed through nondescript beach towns with only an occasional sighting of the sea. Signs pointed towards resort hotels and beach parking, but we were aiming for something we had not seen before: the temples of ancient Greeks.

Some 2,600 years before our arrival, when southern portions of Italy were part of *Magna Graecia*, or Greater Greece, they had come to Italy for the rich farm lands, good fishing, and broad beaches. At Paestum they built a town they called Poseidonia in honor of Poseidon, god of the sea. They also built two enormous temples dedicated to Poseidon and Hera, whom they loved. No doubt they also loved the setting, because the Greeks hung around for about three hundred years, at which time the city leaders managed to choose the wrong side in a war between Rome and Pyrrhus.

The city became a Roman possession, was renamed Paestum, and thrived for another 700 years, until the time of the decline of the Empire. Eventually it was abandoned and forgotten, somehow escaping notice by anyone other than local farmers until the 1700's, when the older Temple of Hera was thought to be a Roman basilica. Actual Roman ruins have since been discovered nearby, including a small arena, a basilica, and the foundations of another temple. The sprawling city was surrounded by an expansive wall with guard towers, most of which remain.

We found the two best-preserved temples still standing side by side, basking in the suddenly warm April weather. Rows of monumental columns reached into the sky calling into question the construction techniques used by the creative builders. We pondered the age-old question that has generated many theories, but no certain answers. How did they manage to stack the enormous stones, each a meter thick and several high and weighing many tons, atop one another in columns seven stones high, in rows in rows sixty-five meters long by twenty-five wide, and then top those rows of columns with even more massive stone beams bearing a high peaked roof? Obviously, they didn't use stepladders. We were awe-struck, as visitors to such places usually are.

We walked in silence studying the structures as if the stones could speak, but the chirping of emerging grasshoppers provided the only narration. Wildflowers blooming between the ancient stones were as fresh and new as the temples were old, as if uncaring nature wanted to make it clear that she paused not a moment for the follies of humans.

Once again, Italy had managed to impress us, and we loved it. We determined that, along our way, we would learn more about those ancient lovers who had stood where we stood, and looked upon the same view.

Leaving the ancient Greek temples of Paestum and the pleasant seashore behind, and without an idea where we would end up, we headed eastward, deeper into the Campania countryside. Here, where twisting mountain roads have imposed centuries of isolation, the cultures are steeped deeply in old traditions and superstitions.

The land of southern Italy is a difficult master, and it is only through an intimate relationship with the seasons and the earth that people can survive. A year of drought in an already arid region can bring hardship, hunger, and disaster, but ownership of land is deeply prized in a place where the only known alternative is poverty, and families have been bound to their most critical possession for many generations.

Towns sit above steep slopes, the better to be protected from hostile neighbors, whether from across the sea or across the valley. Sometimes the people of these fiefdoms would rebel against the imposition of taxes too steep to bear, or ducal masters too prone to cruelty and abuse of power. It was this land, unused to welcoming visitors, that we intended to see for ourselves.

The road east from the temples of ancient Paestum climbs slowly at first, then more rapidly, into the rugged country around Roccadaspide. We passed wordlessly through the town, soaking in the views of the steep slopes covered with stunted, scrubby trees. The winter snows were gone from the mountains, and a green freshness had replaced it. A tractor crept along the mountain road, and we followed until it was safe to pass.

Despite traveling beneath high peaks, we crossed few streams, evidence of the dry climate. Vineyards with a flush of spring growth appeared, and flocks of white sheep clung to mountainsides blushing with spring grasses. An old man led a donkey and cart toward a newly-plowed field. Ancient olive trees clung to a few of the slopes.

We passed along the margins of, and then finally into, the *Parco Nazionale dello Cilento* and *Vallo di Diano*. Italy is blessed with several spectacular national parks, and this one did not disappoint. We climbed over high passes and around steep slopes on a patched two-lane asphalt road. Directional signs were few and scattered, but by studying our map, we managed to track our aimless progress.

An hour of driving brought us to the village of Castel San Lorenzo, which featured a cluster of buildings huddled around a small piazza that provided room to park perhaps a dozen vehicles. Half the unmarked spaces were empty. A tractor and a three-wheeled *ape* occupied two of them.

We exited our rental car and set out on foot to see what we could of the village. It seemed to consist of about four good blocks filled with terracotta roofed houses, set on sharply swerving streets that circled above and below each other on a carousel of a mountainside. It was just the sort of place to lose oneself for a day or two. Only two commercial establishments appeared to be open on the tiny piazza.

Stepping into the small grocery, we noticed the shelves held only a sparse selection of commercial canned goods, but there were bins filled with tantalizing fresh vegetables and local cheeses. We walked over to the tiny stand-up bar with its ever-present espresso machine, and asked the elderly *barrista* where we might find a hotel, "*un' albergo.*"

"*Come?*" came the response from the grandmotherly figure, obviously a widow, clad in her black dress and a shawl. Such mourning dress is expected of widows in the socially conservative south of Italy, and must be maintained for long periods, as much as ten years, during which time the surviving spouse is expected to forgo celebrations aside from baptisms and weddings, and even avoid such comforts as television and radio.

"*Un' albergo??*" she repeated my question.

"*Si,*" we replied, we would like to get a room.

The two or three other occupants of the store and bar stared at each other as if we had just told them the Pope was coming for a visit. I had the distinct feeling that the arrival of foreign visitors in the isolated hill town was little more than an annual event, and overnight stays perhaps less frequent.

"*C'e un' albergo qui vicino?*" I tried again, hesitatingly. 'Is there a hotel near here?'

"*Si, si,*" I was assured. "*Proprio qui.*"

"This is a hotel?"

"*Si, abbiamo le camere, sopra.*"

I turned to Susan. "They have rooms, Susan. Here. Upstairs. Above the store."

"Ohhkaay," she replied tentatively, offering a little smile that said, 'let's see about that.'

I turned back to the barrista and pulled out a credit card and my passport. "*Possiamo vedere la camera?*" May we see the room?

"*Certo,*" certainly, she replied at first, but then changed her tune. "*Ma, ah, no,*" she told me, upon seeing my credit card. "*Me dispiace, non possiamo accettare le carte di credito,*" she said.

I turned back to Susan. "She's sorry, but they don't take credit cards."

I knew I had depleted most of my cash buying ceramic art in Positano, and Susan had purchased a beautiful set of replica Greek pottery in Paestum. "I don't have much cash left," she whispered.

I turned slowly back to the woman, who watched closely, as if I might suddenly spring over the counter to rob her. The local one-window bank office was, she explained, closed for the day. It had already been open from 10 a.m. until noon, after all, and what more could one expect?

"*C'e una bankomat qui vicino?*" 'Is there a bank machine nearby?' I asked.

"*Si, ma non qui, c'e a Roccadaspide,*" she replied. Yes, there was, just not in Castel San Lorenzo, but nearly an hour back the way we had come.

"*Grazie, mille grazie,*" I told her, and received a broad smile in return. We headed back to the car. "I'm not going back that way," I said to Susan, unhappy at the prospect of retracing our path not once, but twice more. After all, I reasoned, we still had a couple of hours of daylight left, and could just push on to the next, hopefully bankomat-equipped, town.

We followed the snaking road through the national park, following our progress on the map, careful not to take any wrong turns at the few intersections. We headed on through a couple of small villages, determined to find either a bankomat, or a substantial hotel that would accept our plastic...or, if not, at least a bottle of wine, and a good view.

The sun drew low behind us, beginning to dip behind the peaks. We had crossed the highest passes of the mountains and begun a slow, winding decent through scattered woods, vineyards, hamlets and high pastures when we noticed a small orange sign with an image of a bed at the side of the road, the sort that typically indicate an '*agriturismo.*' We quickly braked, and glanced up the gravel, tree-lined drive at an inviting stone-and-stucco house. "Want to give it a try?" I asked, and Susan was game.

We crunched our way noisily up the driveway, our tires churning the granite pebbles. I parked and I rang a bell which hung from a post near the door. A surprised, pleasant-looking woman responded, perhaps expecting to shoo away a salesman and surprised to see guests in this off-season, arriving without a reservation.

Asking if a room was available, we were assured with a smile that, yes, there was. She welcomed us into a beautiful great room and led us up the stairs to show us a marvelous and reasonably-priced room on the top level of the spacious home. It opened onto a broad, rooftop terrace offering spectacular views of the broad valley of the Tanagro River to the east. Beyond the surrounding groves of olive trees, a landscape of irrigated farms spread across the land like an enormous patch-work quilt.

Enthusiastically we accepted, but were reminded that we had no cash. Yes, she assured us, there was a bankomat in the village nearby, and gave us detailed directions.

Leaving our luggage in the foyer as a guarantee of our return, we scrambled back to our car, and drove the four or five kilometers through deepening dusk to the town of San Rufo. The town was ablaze with lights, the streets filled with people out for an evening *passegiata* before dinner. Strands of lights were strung across the main street at intervals, creating an enchanting tunnel effect along its length through the town. There we found our bankomat.

Stopping at a *groceria*, we bought crusty *panini*, fresh *mozzarella*, tomatoes, *basilico*, and a promising-looking bottle of local wine, adding to our conserved bag of fresh fruit, olive oil, balsamic vinegar, and other condiments. We were, at last, set for the night.

We hurried back to our rooftop and had a casual dinner *al fresco*. Then, enthralled by the beauty of the evening, we quietly pulled a light mattress from our room and stretched out under the the moonless pinwheel of stars above, watching the twinkling lights that marked the scattered farms below and the far distant villages that climbed the heights beyond, some mere whispers of existence dimmed even by the glow of the celestial lights above. It was purely magical.

Beautiful Basilicata

The southern lands of Italy are wide-open spaces where few tourists go. There on the shore of the Ionian Sea, Greeks had built colonies long before the rise of Rome. We wanted to learn more about this isolated region, so we found an apartment in Policoro Lido, and settled in for a month's visit.

Among our first priorities was stocking our refrigerator. The directions our hosts had written down seemed simple enough, but didn't lead us to a supermarket. They must have omitted a turn somewhere, we decided. We wandered aimlessly reading signs, trying to find ourselves on the map, and at least learn our way around. At last we stumbled upon a post office. Surely someone there could direct us to a supermarket.

I had just opened my car door to go in and ask when a silver and blue car pulled in. *Polizia Municipale* was stenciled in large white letters down the side of the blue car. Maybe that was an option... I waved at the officers, and they greeted me pleasantly. Asking directions to *un supermercado*, I was surprised when they suggested that I simply follow them, and they would lead us there.

For the next several minutes we trailed closely behind our police escort, threading a complex route back across the town to a suitable supermarket. They apparently led us past another market simply because the parking lot was full. We stopped the car, thanking them profusely.

"*Non c'e di che. Buona vacanza!*" one replied. "Don't mention it. Have a good vacation!"

It was a great welcome, and apparently typical of the attitude of the locals. A helpful clerk in a camera store closed her shop to drive across town to get us a battery for our television remote, and spent most of her time telling us about all the wonderful features of Policoro.

The arcaded sidewalks of the *centro* shelter old men who sit playing cards or watching the passers-by. A few bars, grocery markets, and a fair number of stores line the '*Corso*,' the central boulevard of the town. Shady passageways flank the central piazza, which fronts a simple, spare church. The surrounding rugged hills nestle peach and olive orchards that give the town much of its purpose.

The beach of Policoro Lido, a mixture of coarse grey sands and smooth stones, seemed almost vacated in its weekday slumber. Waves broke listlessly upon the steep, stony face of a low bluff. Rows of umbrellas remained folded in the summer warmth for lack of all but a handful of visitors. Very few birds even bothered to patrol the transparent, pale green waters, which seemed all but devoid of fish. It was far different than the broad, sandy Atlantic beaches of Florida.

For us, familiar with the bustling wildlife of Florida's beaches, the lack of the usual sand crabs and gulls, terns, dolphins, and pelicans gave the lido an almost haunted feel on that week-day. Yet on a hot and sunny Sunday afternoon in late June we found the same area clogged with parked cars stretching for blocks from the shore as thousands of Italians flocked from inland towns to escape the heat.

We spent several quiet evenings sitting on the terrace of a sea-front restaurant watching the moon rise. The light dancing upon the roiling waters of the sea and the sands of the beach cast a soft glow against the forests that crowded close to the shore. It was a lovely setting.

Policoro's marvelous story is well documented in the town's excellent museum, known as *Metapontum*, and the adjacent *scavi*, where archaeologists continue to excavate the buried layers of civilization.

In Paleolithic times people had left their record in the form of their arrowheads, stone tools, and other artifacts. Over the last seven thousand years a series of agricultural and fishing towns have stood in that place under a variety of names and rulers. The sequential towns of Siritide, Herakleia, and Metapontum rose and fell as the region was conquered and annexed by more powerful neighboring civilizations over the millennia.

Cultures known as the Enotri and Lucani thrived there, and it became one of the most important cities of the eastern region of *Magna Grecia*. There, "between two rivers," fled Nestor of Pilo, fugitive from Troy, seven hundred years before Christ. The remains of the simple stone houses of the Greek settlement have surrendered a wealth of ancient coins, bronze art, and virtually intact ceramic vases and urns.

There the armies of Republican Rome fought the Lucani in 280 BCE. Here Hannibal's forces swept through after crushing the Roman Legions at Lake Trasimeno during the Second Punic War only sixty-three years later. Spartacus then controlled the region for two years as he led his slave rebellion against the Roman Empire, falling in 71 BCE.

Each of the cultures and events were represented to a degree in the contents of that museum. To call it impressive would be an understatement. The museum was amazing, a resource almost overlooked in a country filled with such wealth. We walked alone through the large, echoing halls, marveling at cases filled with dazzling ancient jewelry, pottery, figurines and busts. Some cases were filled with helmets, spears, armor, and other evidence of war. All had been unearthed in the immediate area, bringing layers of history to light.

Near the museum, the foundations of the Greek temples and theatre that once stood upon the acropolis, or high city, can still be easily traced. Knee-high walls and mosaic floors, piping for wash water and sewers mark the buildings aligned along the narrow streets. A few small areas were in the process of being excavated by archaeologists, as mapping was still proceeding.

We walked there alone in the cool of the evening, finding the ground virtually paved with fragments of broken pottery and ceramics. There were thousands upon thousand of pieces too small to be useful to the researchers, and we finally chose one to keep, as a souvenir of our time in ancient Greece.

For lovers with an understanding of their place in time, and the capacity to grasp the randomness of their coincidental existence, places like Policoro evoke the deepest of emotions, and add value to the treasures they hold dear. It is worthwhile to go, see, and feel the timelessness that only a place such as this can give.

•

We explored neighboring towns both along the coast and inland, befriending locals. The long Spanish rule of southern Italy as part of the Kingdom of the Two Sicilies is reflected in numerous Spanish words and place names. Locals refer to the Ionian coast as the *Jonico*, even though the Italian alphabet contains no J.

We visited the mountainous heart of Basilicata known as the Dolomiti Lucane, and climbed to the improbable village of Pietrapertosa, perched upon a peak, more than a thousand meters up. Stunning views were our reward for slipping past a stretch of road reduced to one lane, because the other had disappeared into the canyon below. Friendly elderly men chatted happily with Susan as I hiked the steep streets to retrieve our car, apparently delighted with their American visitor.

In the town of Montalbano Jonico, a few miles inland, we stopped to view the famous *calanchi*, mountainsides eroded by millions of years of scant rainfall into a landscape of pinnacles, ridges, and deep canyons. For the town they provided more effective defenses than any walls they could raise. Pausing to photograph an ancient bronze plaque mounted on a building, I was questioned by an elderly man sitting on a stoop nearby.

"Why are you interested in that?" he asked me. I explained that I was an American, and that I was learning about the history of the area.

"Come with me," he said. Susan and I followed him through the doorway and found ourselves in what appeared to be a private club, filled exclusively with men. Some looked up questioningly from their card game as we were escorted through the room and into a walled courtyard behind the building. There, a few workmen were busy erecting a set for a theatrical production. We stepped around their equipment to approach a low wall. Below us we took in an incomparable view into the canyons. "This is a special view that we keep to ourselves," we were told, "but we are happy to share it with you."

•

Our stay in Policoro was enhanced when we discovered that only a scant few kilometers north along the coast at Scanzano Jonica one could find the *Via Lido Torre*, a road which led to superior beaches at the *Lido di Scanzano*.

We passed the namesake tower, a squat square lighthouse now standing a kilometer from the shoreline due to the constant accretion of sand.

We found the beach just beyond a broad swath of vegetated land. Soft white sand was everywhere, and the waves broke gently over a clear sandy bottom. The beach-front featured a line-up of casual outdoor dining terraces. Shaded by large parasols and colorful awnings, they offered specialties that ran from barbecue to plates of fried seafood. Calamari was served in cups from seemingly temporary kitchen shacks. Cold beer, wine and cocktails were the order of the day for many. There we spent lazy days basking in the sun and sea.

One such beach bar caught our attention, as it poured forth a mix of afternoon jazz and evening Reggae tunes. 'Peter Pam' offered an inviting wooden deck shaded by broad strips of cloth, but it was the furniture that gave it a very-unique vibe. Each low table and chair was made, at least in part, from the enormous Canary Island date palms that were once a symbol of the coast. Chair backs were carved with whimsical figures, and strange, smiling wooden faces watched from every corner. The tattooed owners of 'Peter Pam,' Pam and Valerio, explained to us that they had been made by a friend after an infestation of insects had spread through the area. The bugs had killed virtually every one of the magnificent palms.

The results of the blight were obvious all around the area, as many of the palm trunks, up to a meter thick and ten meters tall, still stood next to houses and streets throughout the area. Almost without exception, they ended in a thin spray of dead fronds. The few healthy survivors often featured a seven-meter spread of spiky green leaves. A similar insect-borne disease has begun attacking Italy's iconic olive trees, and has spread across the south, and on to Sardinia and Corsica. The same disease, known as Xylella, can reportedly kill more than three hundred other species of plant life, including grape vines and citrus trees.

We compared notes on a separate infestation that is now killing many of Italy's famous *castagne*, or chestnut trees, pointing out that a similar outbreak had wiped out those towering giants of North America's forests more than fifty years earlier. As went the Dutch Elms, so now new diseases are killing off the hemlocks of the Appalachian Mountains, the citrus of Florida and Brasil, the coconuts of the Caribbean, and the spruce and pines across North America. Although we each mourned the loss, solutions to the global crisis were difficult to imagine.

Calabria's Coast

Exploring southern Italy is an assurance of adventure, and best done by auto. The Jonico coast of the *Mare Ionio*, from Basilicata southward into Calabria, features a succession of small towns and villages lying close to the idyllic blue waters of the sea.

Along the route we passed by the foothills of the mountains of the Pollino, and could see Albidona perched upon its lofty peak. Other towns, viewed close-up, were sometimes rustic, but at other times featured boulevards lined with expensive palms, broad promenades of colorful new paving stones, and bright awnings. Each town seemed to have its own spin on what it meant to be a beach town, and many seemed to attract their own cadres of vacationing fans. Beach-goers in rubber sandals and shorts browsed road-side shops stocked with vividly-hued floats, umbrellas, and beach chairs.

We passed a few ancient-looking castles and fortifications, designed to protect the old ports from attackers. In many of these small towns, signs directed visitors to local museums, each helping to explain the complex histories of the coast, which has been subject to so many rulers over the millennia. It was helpful to note a couple of places to visit upon our return northward.

Within a few hours we arrived at our destination, the seaside town of

Isola di Capo Rizzuto, and pulled into an open space at the side of the tight urban street. It was time to call for keys and directions to the temporary lodgings we had arranged through our home exchange site. Our apartment was to be found on the point of Capo Rizzuto itself, another ten minutes south along a narrow two-lane road.

After phoning and meeting our delightful hosts, Eugenia and Gino, and the apartment manager, Peter, we followed the trio to the modern, two-story building which would be our base for a few days. All three of them spoke English, and we were surprised to learn that Eugenia and Gino had lived for years in Massachusetts, where Gino studied and received his degree. He now taught both English and French in a local university.

Our apartment stood only a few meters from an impressive round structure called simply the *torre vecchio*, or old tower. Gino explained that it had been built by the Aragon knights to keep the Saracens at bay. Centuries later the tower and a related series of fortifications along the coast were used to defend the shoreline against the Turks.

Arabs and Turks each had short periods of dominance over the region, thereby joining the dozen or more diverse cultures that are blended into the bloodlines of the local inhabitants. Phoenicians, Greeks, Celts, Macedonians, and Normans, each left their indelible marks upon Calabria.

Today, Isola di Capo Rizzuto is a peaceful tourist town, with a popular beach and white-washed apartments that draw visitors and owners for seasonal holidays. Reaching the center of town from our apartment involved negotiating a 'traffic circle' that was nothing more than a two-meter-wide painted disc in the middle of converging roadways. Surviving that unpredictable thrill, we found the modest main street of the town. An ancient stone wall with an improbably modern clock holds the remains of large wooden doors that might once have offered slight protection to a body of citizens huddled behind them. That small, treeless *campo*, protected on the opposite side by a cliff, was further defended only by the rear of the town church, and some adjacent buildings. It would have been a difficult refuge in a siege.

The high point of the cape itself, just behind our apartment, stood twenty meters above the sea. We walked onto the narrow, grassy spit of eroding land that supports the *torre vecchio* and took in the broad sweep of marine-blue waters surrounding it.

To the north we could see flat, sandy beaches filled with people enjoying the sun and water. Here the scene was much different. Signs and barricades warned of the dangers of the crumbling cliffs. Ignoring them, as did others, I walked around the *torre* to look down upon the scenic cove on the southern side, where rough *scale*, or steps cut into the crumbling stone, led down to the clear blue waters. Enormous slabs of earth and stone had broken away and were clinging to the cliff face several meters below. Other enormous boulders had tumbled into the waters below our feet, where they were washed by crashing waves. It was obvious that the slowly-eroding point will one day carry the tower into the sea.

Glancing around, I spied a man plucking what appeared to be small berries. He chose each carefully from a tangle of vines which displayed complex white flowers. I approached to see if I could identify the fruit.

"Buon giorno," he said, noticing my curiosity. *"Sa quale sono questi?"* 'Do you know what these are?' He asked

"No," I replied.

"Loro sono capperi, buoni per cucinare," he told me. "They are capers, good for cooking."

I looked closer at the small green buds he was picking, and I realized that they were indeed capers, which I had only seen brought forth from a jar in their pungent pickled form. They are most often added to sauces, olive oil, or used in many other dishes, including one of my favorites, *pasta puttanesca,* or as a powerful pizza topping, sometimes in conjunction with anchovies. I thought perhaps we could try them on a dish I might create in our apartment kitchen.

My new acquaintance, who identified himself as Franco, handed me a plastic bag, and I spent the next twenty minutes gathering some to bring home. He patiently explained to me that you need only pick the tiny flower buds from the vine before they open, then soak them in water for a few hours to remove the bitterness.

Franco was curious about where I was from, and why I spoke Italian. I explained our travels, adding that I had never seen wild capers before. He told me that they might grow in Florida, because they thrive in warm places.

"Give me your telephone number, please, I want you to meet my daughter and son-in-law," he told me, and always ready to increase my cultural contacts, I complied. "Call me!" he insisted, and I promised to do so.

That evening, dining with our new friends Peter, Eugenia, and Gino at a seafood restaurant called "*L'ancora*," the Anchor, at the tip of the point, we told Gino about my encounter. He explained that, fifty years earlier, before development had changed Capo Rizzuto into a working-class beach resort, the entire point had been covered with wild caper vines, and people had come from far and wide to pick them.

We dined in southern style and chatted for hours. Local culinary specialties lean heavily to seafood, and we enjoyed six courses, including platters of steamed mussels, mixed grilled seafood, pasta, and *Calamari Fritti*, or fried squid. Everything was washed down with pitchers of water and bottles of the flavorful local white wine called *Aglianico*.

 The dinner was finished off with small glasses of *lemoncello*, while on a nearby television locals were watching Germany demolish Brazil in a semi-final match of the World Cup. It was a full-bore Italian experience. Eugenia, apparently home-sick for Boston and her American friends there, cried when we said our good-byes a few days later. It was a touching reminder of how quickly friendships can form.

The next morning, eager to explore the area, we walked to the small local bar facing the *torre vecchio*, where we struck up a conversation with the matronly proprietor. She offered us the popular *cornetti*, flaky hollow horns typically stuffed with a delicious filling of *crema, frutta,* or *cioccolato*. While we munched our breakfast and sipped our *cappucini* in the shadow of *le torre*, we watched small neighborhood children kick their soccer ball around. The sound of waves washing lazily upon the long strand of beach below the bluff mixed with their shouts. The morning sun painted the distant houses a dazzling array of colors, like so many dots in a pointillist painting.

The coast is marked by numerous towers and other ruins, but none are so impressive as the stunning waterfront castle known as *Le Castella*. The castle and town lie just south and west down the coast, and we set off to see it. A breeze from the water stirred the air under a cloudless sky that promised afternoon heat, but was momentarily benign. We parked in a shaded lot near the center of a busy strip of restaurants and shops to walk the last few blocks down to the waterfront. There, just across a narrow isthmus built of sand and stone, the fairy-tale castle looms larger than life. It stands on its own tiny island, once connected to the mainland by a short bridge. The surrounding waters lap close to the bottom of the walls, and a tall crenelated turret overlooks the waterfront and the sea. It is one of the most uniquely scenic castles we found in our explorations of Italy, given its unusual setting, yet it remains unmentioned in many travel guides.

We crossed and paid a small admission to learn more about this picturesque place, entering through huge wooden doors. Standing in the small courtyard, it is easy to see that an attacker would be exposed to the fire of defenders above. A narrow street leads into the interior of the castle, and a staircase of stone allows access to the upper levels.

We climbed to enjoy the views of the town and the sea, and walked along the weathered stone battlements to gaze down into what was once the center of a village, bracketed by long extensions of the castle walls. The inner wall of the pair still stands, sheltering a tiny harbor on its landward side. Much of the outer wall had apparently been collapsing over the centuries because of the actions of the sea, and their remains had been pulled down to stop them from falling upon tourists. The rubble of broken stone was explained by artists' conceptions on large sign-boards, allowing visitors to understand the original layout.

I scrambled through a low doorway, then climbed in hunch-back style around three turns of spiral steps to reach the top of the turret. Long views down the coastline and far to sea would have allowed defenders some time to prepare for an attack from that direction. Surf crashed upon the rocks below. The middle level of the turret was a simple round room that probably served as a barracks for the watchmen. Openings without frame or glass allowed the warm summer breeze to filter through, and would have done as much with harsh winter winds.

Inside on the main level a transparent floor allows visitors to walk above the excavated, multilevel space below. With sheer stone walls, the dungeon would assure that a prisoner dropped into its hole wouldn't easily escape. Peering down into that depth, we could see hundreds of coins tossed by those who had come before us. I pulled a coin from my pocket, we made a wish, and I tossed it over my shoulder, turning quickly to see it land. It dashed off the opposite wall and shot downward. To our surprise, it struck, and remained standing on edge, perhaps captured by sand or gravel at the bottom. It is very likely still there today.

We explored the area around Capo Rizzuto for a couple of days, but were soon off on another adventure, heading farther south into new and unexplored parts of Calabria. A mostly mountainous *regione*, in many places the heights reach the sea, creating engineering challenges, but some very memorable drives. Roads snake over high passes to confront the sea a hundred meters below. Not unlike parts of the Amalfi coast, they offer spectacular views. The road to the southern resort town of Tropea is one of those.

We drove over the spine of Calabria through the mountains known as the Sila, which are partially protected within the *Parco Nazionale della Sila*. There, endangered wildlife finds refuge, including the light-grey Apennine wolf. The road passed mountainsides topped with the enormous wind-generators that power much of southern Italy. They had become very familiar to us in our travels, and here they again numbered in the scores. From the heights the deep blue of the Tyrrhenian Sea offers a dramatic sight.

Our destination lay on a broad prominence that appears on a map like an enormous bunion on Italy's big toe. The two-lane coastal highway was both challenging and delightful, clinging tightly to the cliffs of the *Mare Tyrrhenia*. Reminiscent in places of California's Highway One, the road dipped and climbed, passing over a spectacular bridge standing upon stilts more than fifty meters in the air, then retreating to near the sea before scaling the cliffs once again.

The sharp contrasts that mark southern Italy were evident. Passing by abandoned houses with shutters ajar, we stopped to explore. Partially collapsed rearward walls permitted views of the blue of the *mare* below. We made time to photograph the sea framed by the scenic ruins. Nearby stood modern and expensive resort-style homes, their balconies filled with colorful blooming geraniums. The palette of their colors ran to the warm tones, and houses of sunny yellow and rich *terracotta* competed with the rough stone and unpainted stucco facades of the homes of working people.

Isolated from the urban crush, Tropea has nevertheless become a resort for the wealthy, and a popular destination for tourists. Perched upon a bluff high above the sea, the town features a shady piazza, where we made a picnic from bags of fresh breads, cheeses, and other local delights purchased from the abundant small shops. As we relaxed the *campane* of the nearby church clanged out the hours, and locals went about their business weaving through the camera-wielding tourists.

The town was lovely and well-tended, with the air of exclusiveness that seems to attract some. One could sense that here was a re-creation of the old French Riviera of the 1950's, as yet not completely spoiled by over-priced resorts.

We lingered for hours, browsing through shops, reading the menus of a few high-end restaurants, and exploring the old church. We sipped glasses of local white wine, priced at more than double what we had paid in Basilicata. The main *corso* ran decidedly downhill, and we strolled along window-shopping at stores filled with ceramics, clothing, and jewelry made of pink and red coral. The street ended abruptly at a low iron fence. Just beyond it the earth seemed to end as well.

We clung fiercely to the cliff-edge railing in a sharp wind to take photographs of the beach, which lay more than fifty meters directly below us. It was enough to set butterflies loose in my stomach. On the long stretch of sand below us and to our right, hundreds of bathers seemed content to stay on the shore, preferring the sun to the frothy water, but a few adventurous souls were willing to challenge the rough breakers.

Huge waves rolled in from the west, crashing dramatically upon the rocks of a long, treacherous-looking point, and throwing spray eight meters into the air. Susan spotted a lone figure sitting on the jagged, wave-swept boulders at the end of the point. The crashing surf repeatedly sent its wind-whipped spray over him, but he seemed unaffected. Then, as we watched, he stood, perhaps pondering the sea, and then leaped into the surf. He quickly disappeared, and whether swept around the tip of the point, or simply indiscernible from our distance amid the giant waves, we couldn't tell. We stood for several minutes watching for him, wondering.

La Chitarra battente

After our exploration of southern Calabria, we returned to our base at Capo Rizzuto. As we had agreed, we called the gentleman I had encountered picking capers at the *torre*. Franco was apparently delighted to hear from us, and insisted that we come that very evening for dinner at his home. Italian hospitality seemed to have no bounds!

Enticed by the opportunity to spend time in the home of a Calabrian family, we naturally agreed. There we were introduced to his charming wife, Elena, his daughter, Alina, and his son-in-law, Pasquale Ciacco. The women's names were cause for just a little bit of confusion at first.

The younger couple's English was as good as our Italian, so we sometimes turned to it in conversation, but spoke mostly Italian for the benefit of Elena and Franco. Although Alina and Pasquale lived and worked in Rome, they often made time to visit family in this southern retreat. With this hospitable family, we enjoyed a delicious dinner which included fresh seafood, pasta, and Franco's fresh *capperi*. Surprising us both, they were very mild, tasting a bit like peas or beans cooked with herbs. It was yet another minor revelation, and we decided that we would have to try growing some in Florida.

After dining *al fresco* and glasses of delightfully-crisp white wine, we relaxed in the sitting room, and noted the beautiful collection of guitars, including one in a form we had never seen. Pasquale explained that it was called a *chitarra battente*, and was a traditional instrument of southern Italy.

As the birthplace of the classical and modern guitars, Europe has a long relationship with the instrument in its many forms. An older cousin of the modern Spanish guitar, the *chitarra battente* is strikingly handsome, and produces a haunting, ethereal sound. It is traditionally built by hand in alternating layers of light and dark woods, which endow a striped finish. The back of the instrument is deeply bowled, to a depth of thirty centimeters or more, giving it a peculiar resonance. It features intricate layers of rosettes cut from parchment paper that partially cover the sound hole, offering an intriguing three-dimensional effect that is very pleasing to the eye.

Pasquale was a man passionate about preserving the ancient form, sound, and playing style of the unique *chitarra battente*. He was eager to demonstrate the unique tonal qualities of the guitar, and rewarded us with an impromptu concert as he described its features. The sound of the strings was similar to that of a harpsichord as he played several traditional folk tunes.

"The guitar's name is actually an adjective, in that *battente* means beaten," he told us. Using five, or five pairs, of steel strings of equal thickness, mounted very low, the instrument is traditionally used to play traditional southern Italian music like the *tarantella, pizzica, stornelli,* and *serenata*.

He demonstrated the rhythmic circular motion he employs to allow the strings to resonate continuously. This, he explained, was similar to that used in Flamenco guitar. Along with being a favorite of Medieval troubadours, it served a more serious civic duty: the courtship of young ladies by their suitors.

In the strict society of southern Italy, where marriages might even be arranged by parents, dating was not an option. It was only through elaborate courtship rituals that a young man could make his fondness for a girl known to her. The *chitarra battente* was most often used by a single musician, but sometimes accompanied by accordion or mandolin. To avoid embarrassing the object of the young man's fervor during the serenade in the village street, he traditionally used a pseudonym, most popularly 'Carmela,' to mask her identity.

The *chitarra battente* was also used to perform one of Italy's best-known folk songs, the *Riturnella*. In the dialect of southern Italy, *riturnella* refers to the swallow, the small bird that was the symbol of arrivals and departures. For the impoverished people of the region, emigration in search of work was a hardship, because it often separated families and lovers, usually forever. The sweet, poignant strains of the music are an allegory to recall the pain of those separations.

Pasquale explained that the advent of modern music from radios and recordings had made the unique live performances of the *sunaturi* and *battente* obsolete. Happily, a few young people have conspired to keep alive the old traditions before they were lost forever.

"It's impossible to be taught a tradition," Pasquale insisted. "It's only possible to acquire it by living within the emotional context. The magic synchronization between vocals, right hand position, chords and notes, and above all the interpretation of lyrics, create a unique and unrepeatable performance."

Today the *chitarra battente* is rarely found outside the remote towns and villages of the southern mountains and coasts, but Italy's long musical tradition has produced not only poignant folk music, but some of the world's most beautiful operas and symphonies. Italians remain proud of both their classical and traditional musical heritage.

We chatted for a while, and the conversation almost inevitably turned toward the differences between the *Settentrionale*, northern Italy, and the *Meridionale*, southern Italy. Here they considered themselves *Napolitani*, Neopolitans, as much as Italians. I surprised them by singing the unofficial anthem of the south, 'Return to Sorrento,' in dialect, having learned it some years earlier. They declared that I certainly had an Italian soul! Our evening ended with warm embraces and promises of our early return. It was start of great new friendships.

Lost in Puglia

Ready to delve into the mysteries of Puglia, the heel of the Italian boot, we drove eastward along the *Mare Ionio* on the *Strada Littorale*. Getting lost in Italy, we found, is not really very difficult, and perhaps easier in the southern regions where traffic engineers seemed to assume that everyone knew what road to follow.

We passed onto the tangle of highways that thread through the industrial port city of Taranto. Our immediate goal was to get through the city as efficiently as possible. Thanks to poor signage at a major *rotunda*, or traffic circle, we soon found ourselves off north-bound instead of south-east bound.

We reversed course, re-navigating the confusing series of roundabouts, and got on the right road, only to miss the subsequent and immediate exit because, once again, there was a lack of signage. Our goal, Lecce, is a significant city, but it was a case of "you can't get there from here, you have to go somewhere else first." The highway system engineers were apparently determined that one could only go to Lecce by going first through Brindisi, a good distance farther northeast.

We decided to press on, hoping to cut across to our correct road at the next opportunity. Call that opportunity missed, because, once again, the sign gave references to other towns, some back along our track, but none of Lecce. As the highway headed still farther from our goal, we finally took the plunge, and the next exit.

There were no signs to any place that we recognized. The flat countryside offered no overviews that might provide any encouragement, but we aimed our car southeast. The road narrowed, eventually reaching the width of a single car, although still paved. We pressed on past remote farms and a few larger estates, hoping that we would not run out of asphalt. After about twenty kilometers we found a road which clearly turned south, but lacked signage of any sort.

The midday sun washed out the colors, leaving the countryside of Puglia as sere and brown as that of coastal Basilicata we had left behind. But here we crossed no rivers to offer cool refreshment to the eye as we passed, nor were there mountains to sweep the clouds of their moisture, to pull their liquid bounty down upon the baking earth below. Only sparse scrub oaks, a few cypresses, and the silver-leaved olives seemed to thrive in the harsher climate and baking sun.

After more than an hour of driving in the general direction of our destination, a large sign indicating the exit to Lecce led instead to a local road through the town of Campi Salentina. Still lost, we stopped to study our map in the shade of ancient trees flanking a heavy iron gate. Two rows of cypresses flanked the straight entrance drive of the seemingly-abandoned estate beyond. The gate stood invitingly ajar, and the weathered facade of the enormous house looked like a setting for a Gothic novel. We were tempted to explore, but thought better of it, satisfying ourselves with pictures of the imposing entryway.

We pressed on and at last found the main road, and soon passed into the city of Lecce. Instinct had triumphed, and we drove a victory lap around the *centro storico*, the old city within the modern.

We had reserved a quiet and inexpensive apartment just inside the high stone walls, and were delighted to see the high arched ceiling of *tufa* stone over each room, and the delightful, awning-shaded terrace on the roof, with a breakfast table set amid large pots full of flowering shrubbery and palms.

"The building is fairly new, only two hundred years old," said Karin, our kind, English-speaking hostess. "The city is much older." Indeed, the walls that encircled us were built in the 13th century.

We walked into the pedestrian city center of Lecce, which features narrow streets festooned with more balconies than a New Orleans dream. Here the Baroque of the late Renaissance surmounts the ancient architecture of the Roman Empire. It was only in the 1600's that the prosperous city received that makeover. The fronts of most of the private buildings echo the city's love affair with the enormously popular style, which sought to depict movement. Richly-decorated churches and the venerable Duomo drip Baroque decorative motifs. Gargoyles leer from high walls, and elaborate details dazzle and delight the eye.

A tram pulled by a tractor offered tours of the old town, complete with multi-lingual narration from ear-buds worn by the passengers, for a fee of ten euros. We preferred to walk and rely upon our own guide maps, and the wealth of information we could readily access on the Internet. The churches and the impressive *Duomo* offered interpretive signs as well.

We eventually reached the Roman Amphitheatre, at the heart of the city. Rediscovered in 1901 during a construction project, subsequent excavation revealed the horseshoe-shaped amphitheater, which originally might have seated 15,000. Here, playwrights from Lecce, Rome, and elsewhere across the empire once staged their dramas and comedies, and today's audiences expect no less. Although the tall galleries that once surrounded it are now reduced to low arches and fallen stones, the well of the theatre is still the scene of many productions. Workmen busily load and unload the scaffolding, lights, and sets for each, offering a romantic setting for a relatively small number of guests for an evening's entertainment.

Lecce has a long history, having fallen to the Romans, who had relocated the town, and added a network of straight roads to the coasts, making it an important center for the Puglian peninsula. It was later ruled by Byzantium, followed by the Normans of France, and eventually the Kingdom of the Two Sicilies.

We discovered the old stone *Castello Carlo V*, once the home of the Orsini del Balzo family. Legend tells us that they kept a white bear in the dry

235

moat of the castle, to discourage thieves intent on stealing their silver or jewels. Today the castle is used by the *commune* as a cultural center, hosting meetings and conferences, as well as theatrical showings.

Away from the busy *corso* of *Via Giuseppe Libertini* we found a small *piazza*, also named after the popular King Carlo the Fifth, with an eponymous *pizzeria*. The small space was quiet, but still busy enough to enjoy people-watching as we sampled excellent wood-oven *pizze* and local red wine. The southern varieties of Primitivo Salentino and Pinot Nero are rich and delicious, with flavors concentrated by the warm Puglian sun.

As we lingered, we studied the doorways and facades of the buildings facing the small *piazza*. The unique and strangely-formed entries that decorate thousands of Italian homes and buildings are normally remarkable, but I was especially struck by one that instantly became my favorite. Off-centered above the peculiar doors, a lop-sided pediment carried a small balcony. The window above was also misaligned. The facade of the building appeared to have been twisted and distorted, as though designed by some mad architect.

Overhead, hundreds of *rondini* swirled and whistled in the evening light to play their mysterious circle games of aerial tag, dipping low into the tiny *piazzale* to skim the cobblestone streets. We were charmed.

•

From Lecce a fast *superstrada* leads to the seaside town of Gallipoli. Although not to be confused with the city and peninsula of the same name on Turkey's Straits of Dardanelle, Italy's Gallipoli shares the same name origin, that of 'Beautiful city,' and a similar record of violent conflict. The long history of contention over the possession of this strategic point of land has left its evidence today.

Built upon a former island and an adjacent cape extending into the sea, the two are now joined by both a bridge and a causeway. The 12th century waterfront castle of the Angevins was expanded and modified several times over the centuries, and the surrounding city walls date primarily to the 13th century. It is both scenic and interesting, and features a small, protected beach on the seaward side below the castle walls, offering a sea view with a broad spectrum of dazzling blues that shame the sky above. The beach is popular with the *nonne* of the area, who bring their grandchildren to bathe in the clear water and learn to swim.

We walked along the waterfront in the summer sun, sticking to the shade when possible. More than a dozen restaurants offered views of the *Mare Ionio*, and featured fish, freshly-caught in the surrounding waters. Fishermen sat in the shade at noon, repairing their nets or rigging the long-lines which they would carry to sea at their next excursion.

A colorful and somewhat noisy trolley, dubbed the "Ciu cuif train," (pronounced 'choo choof') carried tourists on the short circuit of the former island, departing from before the castle. The castle itself, we were disappointed to learn, wasn't open to visitors.

We had lunch at an outdoor *ristorante-pizzeria* facing the castle's obviously-new marketplace annex. The terrace offered both shady tables and exposure to the refreshing summer breeze. We watched in amusement as a shop owner came out to argue with a truck driver who had blocked her windows on the narrow street, and noted the accompanying emphatic gesturing. A police officer soon arrived, quickly flushing a queue of parked vehicles away. It was typical of the chaos of Italian street parking.

We turned our attention back to lunch, and sampled a few offerings from the menu. The food, including the shellfish, was excellent, the service inattentive, and the bill in error. Although we were the only diners, the two bumbling waiters debated each move as though in a scene from an Italian comedy. We overlooked the fiasco to focus on the beauty, romance, and history that surrounded us.

Like many coastal cities of southern Italy, the history of Gallipoli is rich and convoluted, and helps explain the different world view developed in the southern culture. The writings of the Roman historian, Pliny the Elder, suggest that the primitive roots of the town go back far into the past. Its' ideal position makes that very likely.

According to the mythology of ancient Greece, Gallipoli was founded by Idomeneus, who had been exiled from Crete for sacrificing his own son, to keep a pledge to Poseidon, god of the sea. He had sworn to sacrifice the first living thing he saw if he would be saved from a storm. The other gods were reportedly not happy with the excuse, and sent a plague upon the Cretans, who sent Idomeneus away to Italy, where he founded Gallipoli.

The bitter roots of the city suggested by the legend may perhaps be blamed for the later plagues of war that have repeatedly descended upon this picturesque fishing town. Waves of invaders followed.

It was conquered by Senones Gauls, a Celtic tribe that had invaded Etruria and eventually sacked the young city of Rome. They dominated much of the Italian peninsula until the Romans finally drove them out after a hundred years. The expulsion of the Gauls more than 2,300 years ago led to the adsorption of the city into 'Magna Grecia,' the league of Greek colonial city-states.

Eventually the Romans decided that they should have control, and when Gallipoli sided with sister colonies Pyrrus and Taranto against the Romans, it lost its independence in the defeat.

It was later sacked by Goths and Vandals after the fall of Rome, and rebuilt by the Byzantines, only to fall under the dominion of the Papal States, who were warring with rebellious Greek religious orders.

Gallipoli was then conquered by the Normans in the 11th century, besieged in the 13th by Norman Charles of Anjou, and assaulted by the Venetians in the 15th. It eventually became part of the Kingdom of the Two Sicilies under King Carlo V, before being incorporated into the Italian Republic during the Risorgimento. A lot of blood was spilled over control of this scenic spot.

•

We returned to Lecce and lingered, basking in the classic beauty. Even amid the qualities of Italy, it was a standout. Each morning we enjoyed a basket of fresh fruit and pastries in our roof-top retreat, compliments of Karin, and each evening we sampled a different restaurant from the choices along the *corso*. A beautiful, sunny June morning, though, found us reluctantly northbound. We followed the fast *superstrada* that clings to the coastline past the city of Brindisi, aiming instead for the northern Puglian city of Alberobello.

Famous for its unique ancient architectural form, the *trulli* houses, Alberobello was reached by leaving the *superstrada* once again and climbing steep hills on two-lane country roads. It is probably only this fact, and its relative southern isolation, that has prevented it from becoming another tourist magnet, overrun with visitors.

We turned westward near the town of Fasano and climbed the steep hills that lie just to the west. Passing over the ridge, we began a slight descent into the high valley beyond, where we found the *Contrada di Pirro*, a tiny crossroads hamlet outside the village of Cocolicchio. There we stopped at a small *frutti-vendolo*, where a friendly vendor provided a beautiful *languria*, a watermelon, for only two euro. Lacking the exact change, the young vendor explained that he couldn't break our ten-euro note. We got change by buying *cornetti di gelato*, crisp cones filled with *ciocolatto* and *crema*, at a small cafe across the steeply-sloping road, before returning to the vendor to pay for our luscious purchase. Our friendly vendor then handed us a small cantaloupe as a gift, as thanks for purchasing his watermelon. Life in Italy was getting pretty easy to deal with.

Looking around that tiny crossroads we found ourselves in the midst of several of the very *trulli* houses we had been en-route to find. They were scattered in the heights, now standing amid newer, more conventional homes. Not the relics and ruins of our imaginations, they seemed inhabited and well-maintained.

Across the region we were rewarded by clusters of the conical, stone-roofed farmhouses, now looking more like we had pictured them. These traditional structures employed prehistoric techniques, as farmers built homes and barns using only rough-cut limestone boulders gathered from their fields. Without the use of mortar to bind the stones, they built round, double-thick walls, filling the hollow core with rubble. Roofs were likewise built of the plentiful stone, steep cones that rise directly from the walls, leaning only gradually inward. Clever drains built around the foundations were typically used to collect rainwater, precious in the arid region, and funnel it into underground cisterns.

Lonely and iconic, the structures were sometimes surrounded by weeds or broad pastures filled with sheep and bright yellow wildflowers. One or two may have been used as tool sheds. Others seemed abandoned, although no doubt protected. Their tall, pointed roofs reminded us of so many hats, perhaps left behind by a race of gigantic wizards. This was scenic rural Italy at its best, a photographer's dream.

The long-settled, rolling lands seemed to doze in a dream-like state of eternal summer. We passed a dozen large farms with their inevitable gnarled, centuries-old olive trees, and fields of corn, wheat, or rye, ripening in the June sun. Incongruous modern cars and tractors shared farmyards with sheep and wooden-wheeled wagons, while cattle and horses eyed us dolefully from their fenced pastures. Yet we knew that the peaceful appearances were deceiving. Here, where there are no fortified hills to help repel invaders, a hundred generations have endured the trespasses and looting of rebelling slaves, and powerful generals. The armies of Hannibal, Spartacus, Caesar, and Hitler had marched and fought over these lands.

While we found the trulli houses fascinating, one of the most telling features of Alberobello was a large cemetery that stood upon a prominent hill. Overlooking the town and guarded by rows of tall cypress trees and an impressive faux-Roman entrance, the cemetery was filled with several acres of large family crypts, monumental structures better-built, perhaps, than any home inhabited during life by their current occupants. Marble and bronze, thick glass doors, and masses of flowers fronted the individual drawers within, which contained the remains of former residents of the city. A few older, original crypts were built on the ground in horizontal positions, with the names of the deceased deeply engraved in stone, or molded into bronze plaques.

Over the years the need for new tombs grew, but the cemetery didn't expand. Instead, around the old graves rose veritable condominiums of crypts, modern structures with steel staircases, allowing families to visit their ancestors even on the third and fourth levels, six meters above the ground. It was a typical solution in a land where the living are valued above the dead. Italians are survivors, and episodes of hunger many generations ago taught them lessons. Many Italian cities huddle in confined areas, in order to conserve prime farmland.

Santa Severina

Exploring the Calabrian toe of Italy's boot led to some interesting experiences. South along the Ionian coast lies the valley of the *Fiume Neto*. The river winds a stony path through barren-looking hills that offered thin forests, but irrigated fields of grain all along the river proved that there was value in the soils. On either side, occasional stony outcroppings exposed by erosion marked the landscape, bordered by two mountainous ridges.

A short drive brought us to the junction that led to Santa Severina, which we had learned hosted an old castle and a museum. As the road climbed to the south we passed through the outskirts of the town, but then a curve revealed the old city, high atop the bluff ahead. The road passed almost underneath the castle, its ramparts clearly dominating the valley below.

Passing behind the mountain, the road approached from the rear. The drive became steep, once again challenging the gearbox of our Fiat. We arrived at a broad piazza that formed the heart of the town, and could see the castle itself at the far leftward end about a long block away. Palm trees improbably stood around a small formal garden. To our right we could see an ancient church that begged to be explored. The castle came first.

Il Castello di Santa Severina is a squarely-built 11th century Norman structure that perches precariously on the edge of a sheer bluff, the better to limit possible routes of attack. We entered across a solid bridge that spanned a drop of perhaps ten meters. Today there is a street running under the bridge, but once it may have harbored spikes and other defenses.

We were greeted by a friendly young staff, who answered questions and seemed very dedicated to sharing the history. Paying a scant few Euro for admission at the museum bookstore, we entered a courtyard. Partly grass and partly stone-paved walkways, it allowed easy access to the battlements that faced the east and south sides, where an attacker would most likely appear. Peering between the blocks of completely-restored crenelation, it was easy to take an archer's quick view of the clear space outside the walls, now filled with a beautiful, geometric park. From atop the walls the graceful Romanesque church was visible beyond the broad *piazza*.

Inside the large castle, high ceilings bore evidence of the smoky torches that one lighted the spaces. Arranged in a square formation around a large flag-stone courtyard, the rooms are reached in sequence, each separated from its neighbors by heavy doors. Most of the rooms had only tiny openings in the walls as windows. Thick stone walls offered little warmth. but some rooms included large fireplaces, which would have been useful in the chill winters.

In the most secure corner of the castle, high above the valley below, is what was probably a dining room, where elaborate frescoes decorated a ceiling with geometric designs and human figures. One can easily imagine a succession of minor dukes and lords holding sway there over the centuries.

In the foundation of the castle lies a sort of basement, where once fires were maintained, which may have served to heat the castle, even as they were used to melt iron. There, cut carefully into the earth, is the shape of a bell, where molten metal was once poured for casting.

As Susan continued to explore the castle, I walked back to the museum store and purchased a book about the castle, and spent a few minutes speaking to the enthusiastic staff, who expressed their hopes that I would include their castle in my book. I then walked across the piazza with thoughts of an *espresso* or perhaps a *gelato* from one of the two small bars I had noticed. As I walked, the previously calm, sunny afternoon suddenly erupted in a violent whirl of wind that sent tables tumbling and large parasols flying. I found myself evading zooming chairs like an elementary school game of dodge-ball. The wind disappeared as quickly as it had sprung up, and I joined the proprietor in carrying the chairs back toward the bar, forty meters away.

When Susan joined me a few moments later we walked to the opposite end of the *piazza* to visit the town's old church. As we passed near our car, one of only two remaining in the piazza, I noticed two men standing near it. One, a bearded, middle-aged fellow, seemed to be looking into the car. I was immediately suspicious. As Susan and I entered the interesting architecture of the church, I glanced back, still concerned about our borrowed car.

Eventually my concern grew too strong, and I left her to walk back to the car. "Is there a problem here?" I boldly asked in Italian as I approached.

"Is this your car?" the bearded man asked me.

"Yes, at least it belongs to a friend."

"I am a police officer," he said, as his companion gave me an evil look. "Do you have a parking permit for this car?"

I was flummoxed. A parking permit? The area was clearly marked for parking. "I don't know, perhaps not?" I answered. "I am a visitor, from Florida."

The second man, obviously agitated, began to speak loudly, demanding to know if I would be permitted to park in the middle of town in Florida. Before I could reply that, yes, of course I would, the self-identified police officer told him to be quiet, and informed me that there was a *multo severo*, a severe fine, for parking there without a permit. "Hadn't I seen the sign?" he demanded to know. Somewhere below, he insisted, we had passed a sign that had explained the limitations. He seemed skeptical that I was really from Florida. Perhaps my Italian was proving a bit too good. I began to apologize, still a bit incredulous that parking was forbidden in the forty or more marked spaces, all of which were by then empty.

It was only when I turned and called to Susan in English, to inform her that we had to leave immediately, that the police officer's attitude suddenly changed. He brought out his badge and papers, told me he was sorry that we had to move, and seemed to regret his original approach. We had seen enough, however, and were quickly headed back down the mountain with our book, our photographs, and our somewhat tarnished memories of a beautiful place.

The Mystery of Mysteries

From Santa Severina we drove back to the Ionian Sea, and then northward along the Strada Littorale, eventually reaching the coastal town of Rossano, which overlooks the water. There we turned west and headed once again into the mountains, high above the bustling town. Following the scattered signs and our instincts, we began a steep and winding climb into a verdant wilderness. Our goal was the isolated monastery called the Pathirion, which has stood atop the mountain since the 12th century. We had read that a group of monks still lived there, and we were told that at least some of them kept vows of silence.

We climbed relentlessly until the engine of our aging Fiat once again began to show signs of overheating. Since the weather seven hundred meters above the town was cooler and much windier, we turned off the air conditioning, turned on the heater, and opened the windows. The cool breeze quickly dispelled the warmth, and the car's temperature gauge responded by beginning to fall away from the red zone. The increasingly-spectacular views back to the deep blue waters of the sea far below kept our minds off the potential car problems. We resumed our climb.

We eventually reached a zone of alpine forest without passing another vehicle, and the swaying of tall evergreens emphasized the power of the strengthening winds. The road, never wide, narrowed to a sliver of asphalt, the last house apparently left far below. There were no further directional signs indicating the presence of a monastery, but we pressed on into the wild beauty, mindless of our destination.

After ten more minutes of driving we arrived at a fork in the road, where a small sign indicated the unlikely presence of a *pizzeria*. Perhaps that would be a good place to rest for a few minutes, and ask directions. We followed the signs, but when a kilometer or two down that track produced no further evidence of any sort of human habitation, we realized that the desired pizza could be at the other foot of the mountain. We turned back, climbed to the intersection, and pressed onward. We didn't want to admit to ourselves that we were lost again, but according to our maps the road we were on simply didn't exist.

As we continued to ascend through dense green forest, a layer of dark clouds suddenly appeared from the north, riding the gusting winds. A few sprinkles of rain dampened the windshield, rinsing away the dust of the kilometers of road behind us. We paused to let the engine cool again at a small level area. There a stream of water poured forth from an ancient spigot set in a stone wall, splashed upon the boards below, and ran in a rivulet down the steep slope. I filled a cup and poured it into the small overflow reservoir of our radiator. The melodious sounds of water and wind seemed the only things worthy of disturbing the sylvan silence.

Pressing on, we rounded a curve where the trees parted enough to offer a view. There, far below us, we saw the sea and the coastal towns laid out as though a scale model. We stopped to admire the striking view, knowing that the drive was already worth our time. It was so peaceful we were no longer concerned that there was still no sign of the monastery.,

We continued winding along the mountaintop until we came to yet another fork, the rightward one of which seemed to lead downward and to the north, the direction we would eventually need to go. Putting the car in low gear to save the brakes, we began our descent, passing an arched stone shelter, perhaps once a shrine, but now apparently empty. At each leftward curve of the road, it seemed to lean over empty space, the distant bottom of the chasm clearly visible. We proceeded cautiously.

After a few more minutes, to our surprise, we found a small sign indicating the presence of a *sanctuario*. We turned and saw before us the unlikely bulk of a large, yet virtually windowless, Romanesque church. To its right stood an arched wall, behind which we could see a solid, two-story building, which we guessed housed the silent monks.

We parked quietly and walked into the grounds. The monks who built and maintain the property were nowhere to be seen, as we expected. Their vows require them to remain cloistered, away from direct contact with the outside world. Immersed in prayer, they remain in contemplation, working quietly in their large *orto*, or vegetable garden, wood-working, or performing other productive tasks.

Susan chose to return to the car, so I walked alone around the grounds, and the stress of driving the twisting mountain roads seemed to melt away. The beautiful arcaded courtyard next to the church, and the remains of an ancient *campanile*, seemed to fit into the landscape. Peacefulness permeated the scene. As I walked I encountered a large, flowering oleander that almost blocked the ancient stone walkway. I stopped, and the brilliant colors filled my vision. The wind caused a flower to brush against my face, and the sensation seemed profoundly purposeful, like a caress from nature. I stood transfixed.

At that instant, a thought crossed my mind, seemingly from nowhere. How short is a lifetime? A century? A thousand years? How rare that we can share our lives with a partner, that we love and walk the earth with another at the same point in that endless stream of time? Suddenly time seemed to shift, to melt away. I was there for a thousand years. Time, it was clear to me in that moment, was all we had, and yet it was unimportant, an ephemeral phenomenon. A moment had become a month, or a millennium. For those passing seconds it was all very clear. Time is transient. Love stands eternal. Perhaps I had stumbled upon the purpose of that special mountainside.

Peering into the Soul of Italy

Tourists often travel to see things: scenery, art, architecture, the cities themselves. We had come to the realization that the essence of Italy is measured in none of those, but rather in people. Nowhere do the foundations of this diverse nation become so apparent as in the small towns and villages, where the old ways are still adhered to.

Off the well-worn paths one may begin to encounter those living, not in the busy, caffeine-fueled buzz of modern Italian cities, but in the ancient rural ways of the farmer, the tradesman, and the merchant. The source of Italian culture lies in its lore, in the tales and superstitions, the beliefs and traditions that have bound people to their neighbors for millennia. To find such deep roots, one must look beneath the mountain.

People are tied closely to their ownership of land. Standing among the *agricoltori*, the farmers who still sharpen the hoes to tend their crops, a visitor may begin to sense the depth of these traditional sources of strength.

Rows of olive trees, hundreds of years old, are the blessings bestowed by great-great-great grandparents, or generations before them. Fields of yellow rape-seed flowers, tomatoes ripening on their vines, pears, apples, lemons, peaches, plums: every sort of fruit imaginable is brought forth in abundance from seemingly barren, rocky hillsides. Plots of lusciously-sweet *l'angurie*, watermelons, ripen in the late summer sun alongside fields of golden wheat, while flocks of sheep decorate green pastures. Wine grapes are picked, crushed, and fermented almost as if a religious act.

We stopped on rural roadsides to watch the *agricoltori* harvest olives from the gnarled trees, carefully spreading broad nets over the ground before beating them from the branches with long wooden poles. Some of the rich fruit would be cured in brine and spices for the table, but most would be brought to presses where the golden-green oil would be extracted by modern centrifuges in thick streams of what is called *extra-virgine*, the first extraction. The fruit might be heated and re-processed to extract the remaining, lower-quality oil. While farmers may once have fed the *sansa*, the left-overs, to pigs, today most is burned as fuel for electrical co-generators. Some is composted and used to re-nourish the soil.

The rural cultures of Italy are complex, but some features are obvious early on, if one is determined to escape from the tourist-oriented agenda of travel companies. One of the striking differences between Italy and the United States, for example, is her wealth of farmers' markets. Cooperative stores are also common. Many are owned and operated by the municipal government, known as the *commune*. They typically offer seafood, flowers, meat, cheeses, preserves, and more. In rural Italy, it is not unusual to see the shops of shoemakers, blacksmiths, and bakers filled with neighbors dependent upon them for their needs.

Traveling markets are another fixture of Italian life, and they move from town to village on a regular and rotating schedule. Residents look forward to the market day to find a wealth of products that may not be available in local stores. Rather than drive long distances to shop, they wait for the shops to come to them. In large cities, markets appear in specific neighborhoods, rotating around on a fixed schedule.

Markets are entertaining events. Often featuring a hundred or more vendors, they stretch for blocks, with mounds of fresh, fragrant peaches and plums, rosy apples, barrels of olives from Italy and Greece soaking in their brine or oil, and whole roasted hogs displayed to lure customers. Great wheels of hard cheeses stand on their own tables, while fist-sized lumps of the morning's fresh mozzarella are displayed near booths wafting the aroma of their natural partners, round crusty loaves of fresh-baked *pane rustico*. Banks of fragrant herbs, tied in neat bundles, struggle to overcome the distinctive odor of fresh fish on ice. Nearby, lobsters and *scampi,* like over-sized crayfish, make repeated efforts to climb out of their glass tanks.

At some stalls knock-off sunglasses and purses can be found piled high next to banks of colorful cheap tee-shirts and attractive shoes, including those *tacchi alti,* the high-heels that Italian women flaunt so very well. Everywhere merchants cut, trim, count change, or package products for the locals, who swarm five or six deep around their preferred vendors.

Other days are reserved for antique markets, which also bring out vast numbers of vendors and customers alike. Much of the merchandise offered may be labeled simply *occasione,* meaning 'bargain.' Murano glass, silver tableware, and old wooden cabinets tempt the buyers. Tables piled high with tools compete with others laden with fine china and stemware. Copper pots are always high-demand items, and bring top price. No Italian kitchen is complete without a variety of them hung overhead.

The markets are more than merchandising fairs. They are social events that help to define the society itself. The craftsman quietly explaining his skills in trade to a visitor is sharing the accumulated knowledge of many generations of his family. Farmers may bring their produce to their own market stalls for weekly sales, while in the next stall a farrier makes a new lead for their donkey. They trade stories, tips, and jokes, and commiserate over failed crops, pests, or untimely rains. Like tending the grapes and olives, building and rebuilding the fortifications of their city, or deepening the well after 500 years of use, these things tend to lie deep in the Italian psyche.

Food remains very much at the center of Italian daily life, understandably so, given the record of famine and hardships that Italians have endured for millennia. Among the staples, of course, is pasta, and it comes in hundreds of forms. Each *Regione* has its favored shapes, and many offer humorously-descriptive names. From large tubes called *cannelloni*, or big pipes, ideal for stuffing with rich cheeses, to short tube-like pieces called *ditalini*, or little thimbles, perfect for adding to *pasta e fagioli*, or pasta and bean soup, there is an artistic shape for every purpose.

In southern Pulia, flat hand-pinched ovals are known as *orecchietti*, or little ears, which they resemble. Florence offers us *gigli*, a folded pasta named after the lily that is the symbol of the city, while Rome proffers *bucatini*, a sort of thick *spaghetti* with a hole through the center. Perhaps Italy's prettiest pasta is something Americans refer to as 'bow ties' but the Italians call *farfalle*. The name means 'butterflies.' *Gnocchi*, or pasta 'knuckles,' twisted *fusilli*, or little fuses, and *capellini degli angeli*, or little angel hairs, are known around the world.

As the seat of the first Christian church, Italy is theoretically among the most religious nations on earth, but the irreverence of Italians is legendary. In Emilia Romagna, the favored pasta is a twisted shape known as *strozzapreti*. The name means "Priest strangler," because it was said that if it was offered to the village priest, he might choke wolfing down a plate of the delicious meal. A rare event is referred to as something that occurs "*ogni morte di Papa*," or every death of a Pope. The Pope's skullcap is a *zucchetto*, or 'little pumpkin.' Housewives in Campania created the popular pasta called *penne*, which carries the same name as a certain part of human anatomy. Among their favorite fruits is a small, sweet, heart-shaped plum known as a *Coscia di Monaca*, or Nun's Thigh.

Fanciful names extend to other interesting foods as well. Especially in southern Italy it is a peasant tradition to serve rich red sauces stewed from tomatoes and other garden products, and those are the flavors that have captivated palates around the world. Creating those sauces, however, is an all-day process, involving stewing the tomatoes and herbs for hours. It kept women busy while their men worked on farms or fishing boats. Yet there also arose a curious alternative: a delicious sauce that could be made in minutes, using a few pungent ingredients such as cured capers, anchovies, and garlic. It attracted the interesting name of *puttanesca*. The name was a reflection of the rumors about how those long hours may have been otherwise spent. It means "of the whore."

•

Italians are proud, very proud, of their history. Yet, there were times, a thousand years ago, when the already ancient relics of the Roman Empire were scavenged, stripped of marble cladding, and disassembled for new uses. The properties of the church were protected, but the old monuments and temples, even the Coliseum, were picked over and pillaged. Times have been hard many times before.

For a thousand years after the fall of the Empire, trade and communication were reduced, education was the dominion of scattered abbeys, and those who could assemble land-holdings, through marriage or battle, rose to become powerful rulers. Wars followed invasions, and death would quickly overtake the unwary. Walls were necessary, even essential for survival.

During that long millennia, Italian cities and towns were swept up in a perpetual swirl of espionage and changing alliances. Allies became enemies, virtually overnight. No stranger could be trusted. Cities and towns were isolated, independent civilizations, enjoying only a modicum of the cross-pollinating of outside cultures. The once-unifying force of ancient Latin devolved into dozens of dialects, thousands of new words, and expressions used only among remote populations.

Italy wasn't a single nation again until the *Risorgimento*, the 'reorganization' that brought on the establishment of the Kingdom of Italy in 1861. America was fighting a civil war of division while Italian kingdoms, duchies, and Papal states were being overthrown and stitched together in a war of patriotic unification.

Italy is today a land of strange contrasts. On one hand, it is among the most Internet-connected nation on earth, with one of the world's highest rates of cell-phone usage. On the other hand, it is often rigidly provincial and divided. Criticism of other regions, and their customs or habits, is an ingrained trait. The nation shares a deep pride in being the curator of a rich heritage of art and historical relics, including those of earlier Greek, Etruscan, and Roman civilizations, yet the urban streets of the modern Republic are too often treated as receptacles for all sorts of refuse. The problem is especially apparent in Napoli, which once was considered the crown of the Mediterranean, and now houses a wealth of, seemingly, uncaring citizens.

The north is the industrial heartland of Italy, and some there campaign to leave the rest of the nation, to create an independent state which would ultimately be forced to depend on others for its security and economy. Some of the southerners in return consider themselves victims of the wealthy north, one telling me that Napoli was the wealthiest city in Italy, until their young king was swindled out of the royal treasury's vast horde of silver during the Risorgimento. It was carried off to Milano, she claimed, leaving the region in poverty. The southerners who resisted were labeled *brigante*, or brigands. Today that obscure history is used to justify the constant machinations of the five family branches that constitute the Mafia.

Some *Napolitani* believe that they are still treated less-than-equally by a government dominated by powerful northern financial interests. A larger tax base and greater investment in public infrastructure in the north has resulted in better airports, highways, seaports, and rail service. Less populated and lacking the industrial infrastructure and moister agricultural climate, the south of the peninsula depends partly on tourism from northern residents to sustain its economy.

Some in northern Italy, especially those with right-wing politics, regard southerners as less than Italian. "They are North Africans," one neo-Fascist said mockingly of anyone from south of Rome. His friend, a dedicated Communist, had a very different opinion. The fact that they remained friends was a testament to hope.

Aside from such obvious north-south differences, each *regione* has subtle characteristics, preferences, and even what might be described as quirks. Many are the result of customs, dialects, and dietary traditions. It might take a lifetime to sort them all out, but they begin to emerge after even casual visits.

As in many other nations around the globe, multiculturalism and foreign influences are resisted. "Today Italy has a great problem," one gentleman told me, referring to a tide of immigration, particularly from the Middle East. With different religions, customs, and social mores, he saw 'them' as a threat to the culture of the nation. Yet Italy is already an amalgam of foreign influences brought by Phoenicians and Greeks, Turks and Libyans, Mongols, Celts, and Germanic invaders, as well as all the regions Rome once ruled. Like all our over-crowded world, today the nation is slowly changing, absorbing, and molding itself into a new form.

Chaos at Cassino

Through all the years of our travels in Italy, we kept in mind the extraordinary emotions we had experienced during our first visit to Monghidoro with our friend George DeLuca. His tales of the war, the Alpini troops, and the battles they had fought together gave us a different perspective of many places we visited. Day-long drives along the length of Italy made us ever more cognizant of the fact that our friend had walked most of the way, on an indirect path, often under the threat of enemy fire. We continued to seek out details of his story.

Eventually we decided it was time to head south to one of the promised destinations on our list. Moving along at posted *autostrada* speeds, and struggling to match the furious pace of traffic, we headed down the Tyrrhenian coast toward our rendezvous with historic Cassino.

The road we traversed was relatively flat, but that simply added to the drama of the ancient and decaying volcanic cones we passed, and the brooding heights of the *Appenini* to our left. The sun beat down upon their dark folds, revealing villages teetering high above the thin threads of roadways that rose toward them.

By afternoon, we were driving into Cassino, following a broad, divided boulevard that passed a couple of modern hotels. We drove into the shadow of the sheer bulk of Monte Cassino far above, and entered the narrow streets of a bustling city abuzz with life, moving with the familiar flow of city buses, private cars, motorcycles and scooters toward the *centro storico*.

After driving around several one-way city blocks without finding a hotel, making convenient right turns when in doubt, we decided to return to one of the establishments we had passed entering town. It was a fortunate choice, and led to one of the most poignant moments of our trip.

While walking to our elevator for the ride to our fourth-floor room, we passed an expanse of wall that was covered with photographs, many obviously very old. Prominently featured were several of the landmark abbey on the mountain that was the pride of the city. Among the military insignia displayed was the familiar blue emblem of George DeLuca's own Blue Devils. His stories of war experiences were about to come to life in a way we didn't anticipate.

Italy had become embroiled in the war due to the maniacal visions of *Il Duce*, Benito Mussolini. In a sharply-divided nation, Mussolini's far-right Fascist movement had crushed his Italian opposition. His pact with Hitler had brought Italy into the Axis fight for control of Europe. The U.S. Army was tasked with helping conquer the mountainous peninsula, fighting alongside an international force that included those of Great Britain, New Zealand, Brasil, India, free Polish troops, and others.

The experiences of young men pulled from their occupations and thrust into the American war effort were sometimes challenging, sometimes boring. George and the men of the 88th comprised the first new division created within the U.S. Army as the threat of war grew in 1940. They landed quite 'green' in Casablanca, Morocco, in December of 1943. The hard fighting in North Africa was already over, but months of hard training in the desert helped prepare them for what was to come.

When the Allies conquered Sicily in September, 1943, with little resistance, Italy's government rebelled, arrested Mussolini, and signed an Armistice. Only a few weeks later the new liberal Italian government declared war on Germany, but Germany reinforced its troops already there, and Italy became yet another German-occupied nation. Thousands of Italian soldiers, including most of the Alpini, took up the fight against them, joining a Partisan resistance.

After a year of service in the heat of the desert, George's 351st Regiment moved at last to Napoli, arriving on the frigid 6th of February, 1944. The D-day invasion of Normandy was still four months in the future. Only in Italy were Allied armies facing the might of Germany's feared legions.

After a few nervous weeks of waiting George's regiment was moved forward to join the line before Monte Cassino. The mountain was the rock that anchored the western end of the Germans' Gustav Line, heavy fortifications intended to keep the Allies contained in southern Italy. Posted to Hill 706 at the foot of Monte Cassino, they were close to the German defenders above.

The mountain appears from the city of Cassino as an almost monolithic upthrust, with extremely steep slopes. Only by following a narrow, snaking road can one normally reach the summit, which stands some four hundred eighty meters above the town. During the war, it was only by crawling that a man could approach it without being killed. The day they arrived George's unit took their first combat casualties.

The artillery unit assigned to their battle group was directed to shell the southeast corner of the mountain. It was believed that German artillery spotters had taken positions there. Heavy artillery rained down upon them daily from the heights, and German snipers took their toll. The Allies made several unsuccessful frontal attacks against the steep flanks of the mountain, but only slowly was ground gained. The battle had been long and bloody, and the Germans had successfully stalled the Allies' northward march.

It was there at Cassino that George lost several of the men he'd been serving with for more than a year. Good friends. Despite the training, it was a tough adjustment for many formerly peaceful men, accepting that now it was kill or be killed. They became true soldiers.

"We served alongside a British company," he had told me once, when he was in mood to share stories. "They relied upon tradition. Every afternoon, no matter how bad the shelling and the snipers, they would stop to make tea. They built fires, which gave away their position with the smoke. We told them not to, but they insisted on taking tea." He shook his head sadly.

"The next day they came to us with sad tales. 'Did you hear about Tommy? Poor Tommy bought it yesterday, right after tea. A sniper got him...'"

At the top of the mountain above them was the Abbey of Monte

Cassino. With its large complex of buildings, some dating back 2,000 years, it was a national treasure. Full of priceless religious works and golden artifacts, it housed a population of Benedictine monks. Generals had long argued about the famed abbey, high above the battle ground. Were the Germans using it for an observation post to watch Allied movements? Could it, should it be, a target? Or was it too important, a world treasure that should be spared?

Lieutenant-General Sir Bernard Freyberg, commanding British forces, had a dark reputation, having ordered a last-minute charge on the hour of the Armistice that ended the First World War, thereby sending his men to useless deaths. Freyberg wanted the abbey destroyed, and eventually he won the debate. On February 15, 1944, waves of Allied bombers had reduced the history and riches to rubble and dust. George had watched the destruction from below.

Ironically, after the bombing of the abbey, the Germans had mounted a stubborn resistance from the rubble, which provided an outstanding defensive position. It was only the fierce and sustained attack of the Free Polish Army that had finally liberated the Abbey at a heavy cost. Their hatred for the Nazis who had crushed their homeland was said to strike terror in the hearts of the defenders.

Cassino held a wealth of history that we were eager to explore. After settling into our room and freshening up, I returned to the lobby, where Susan had agreed to meet me before dinner. I stood and studied the wall of photos, including those showing the magnificence of the abbey before the war and the rubble that remained afterward. As I stood there, a solidly-built but elderly Italian man approached, and commented on the photos.

"*Lei piace*? Do you like them?" he asked, and I told him I did, although many of the photos also showed the ravages of war, the destruction wrought by Allied bombs, the months of combat, shells and grenades.

He told me he had lived in Cassino all his life, and his family owned the hotel. Gazing at the photos, he began to describe the events of the war, which he had experienced as a child. He spoke of how many city residents, including his two brothers and much of his family, had fled the tanks and guns to take refuge in the abbey. Everyone believed it was "sanctuary," a church which would never be attacked.

Tears swelled in his eyes as the memories came vividly to life for him, recalling the day the planes flew over. Clouds of heavy bombers with blockbuster weapons had reduced the Abbey, and all inside, to dust and gore. For him it all seemed to come crashing back. It was only yesterday...

There were no Germans there, he assured me, only monks and refugees. "*L'Inglese*," he said, the English, did this, and he still blamed them for the act. He was correct in that a British commander had argued in favor of the bombing, but I knew that our United States Army Air Forces had dropped many of the bombs, and shared responsibility.

We stood there together for a long moment in silence, contemplating the horrors depicted in the photos. Something needed to be said. Something completely inadequate, I knew, but something... meaningful. Words sometimes fail to express what we are thinking.

"*Sono solo un' Americano,*" "I am only one American," I said, "but I am very, very sorry."

He looked at me a moment, as if in recognition. His eyes were still wet with tears, but he nodded, shook my hand, offered a faint smile, and slowly walked away.

My thoughts that night were of both the wonder and majesties of life, and the tragedies which we too often bring upon ourselves.

•

Early the following morning we made our pilgrimage, like so many before us, to the *Abbaye di Monte Cassino*. We followed the narrow, serpentine road that wove steeply upward through forested slopes, then suddenly turned sharply upon itself to climb higher still.

The view changed quickly from pretty, to commanding. It was easy to envision the military advantage of controlling these heights, and watching every move made by an enemy on the plain below.

The road abruptly reached a crest and emerged onto a rolling mesa, still forested, but with what appeared to be open meadows interspersed. Then around a curve we saw the impressive abbey, not a single building as I had imagined it, but a huge cloister of four or five stories stretching several blocks in length, and a complex arrangement of smaller buildings. As we entered we saw that all were gathered around lush gardens and walkways paved with broad stones. A fountain and statuary marked the principal paths. A staircase of more than fifty steps ascended to the heart of the edifice.

It was far grander than I expected, with massively thick stone walls, rows of windows, and broad *terracotta* tile roofs. High on that mountain, it seemed an odd juxtaposition of place and purpose.

The Christian abbey had originated in the 6th Century, when St. Benedict of Nursia came upon this place and its Roman Temple of Apollo. Benedict struck immediately, smashing the sculpture of the god of light, along with the altar and its offerings. The local population may have been a bit nonplussed, but Benedict never left his new stronghold, and began to gather followers to defend it.

We entered the abbey grounds and were impressed by the beauty of the restored buildings. Displays of photographs from the war made the scene even more impressive. The destruction had been nearly total. Massive piles of broken stone and concrete, smashed sculpture and fountains were all that remained. There was very little that could be salvaged after the 'block-buster' bombs had done their work.

After the war, the Allies and the new Italian government had funded the reconstruction, perhaps as a form of penance. The work was magnificently done, each stone in its place, and the monastic residences were completely restored as well. The architectural details of Corinthian columns and rows of graceful arches lent the grounds a quieting solemnity. Balustrades line the edges of walkways that flow onto rooftops to look down into a central courtyard with an octagonal *pozzo*, or well, and balconies extend from above. Interior rooms feature colorful marble mosaic floors.

Despite the beauty, the monastic life here must have been difficult, with rugged isolation and daunting slopes discouraging all but the most ambitious visitors. Enduring brutal winters of ice and snow, only the lofty and compelling views of life below provided a humanistic touch to the ascetic discipline of religious contemplation and undoubtedly-demanding physical labor.

We perused the *museo*, admiring the preserved fragments of earlier iterations of the abbey that had survived repeated sacking and looting, first by French Lombard invaders in 584, and then by the Saracens in 883.

An earthquake in 1349 caused major damage, but again the majesty was restored, only to be sacked again by Napoleon's forces in 1799. It was a history that boggled the imagination. Yet there, preserved from the original Roman temple, were relics of its ancient past, including votive motifs from the 4th Century BCE, Roman coins, and a mosaic greyhound, one of a pair that had originally decorated the floor.

The entrance to the Basilica, which we saved for last, was marked by an impressive sight as well. We stood in awe before an enormous bronze door with more than forty panels, each bearing Latin inscriptions with silver Damask lettering. A gift from a pious admirer, it had survived the earthquake, sackings, and the Allied bombing. The restored panels pictorially documented the origin of the doors, and the state of affairs of the monastery and its dependent churches at the time of their construction in Constantinople in 1066.

We entered the Basilica and gasped. Nothing had prepared us for the gold-gilt splendor of the interior of the cavernous structure. The space seemed to glow with an ethereal light, which no doubt was the intent of the designers.

Banks of candles lit by visitors gleamed brightly, and cast their warm glow across the walls, and sunlight through stained glass added to the atmosphere. Frescoes and inscriptions ornamented the arches, and an incredible Baroque pipe organ, featuring more than 5,000 individual pipes and three keyboards, redefined the category completely in our minds. The massive columns of the Basilica soared upward to the vast golden ceiling accented with magnificent paintings of religious scenes. Four allegorical figures surrounded the central dome, representing Chastity, Poverty, Stability, and Obedience.

Beneath the main altar we discovered a chapel, its heavy marble columns and ceiling bearing the weight of the church above. A golden altar-piece seemed to glow in its place of repose. It was hard to imagine that this incredible beauty had been repeatedly reduced to rubble and restored, an architectural rebirth to rival the legend of the Phoenix.

From the Abbey grounds, one can look down and out across the surrounding lands. There were the meadows: several cemeteries laid out in neat rows atop the mountain. Before we would depart, we spent an hour viewing those of American, Italian, British, Polish, and yes, even German troops. Each are clearly marked and well maintained. After the horrors of the terrible fight, it was here, in the peaceful shadow of the Abbey, that the remains of those victims of war were brought to be laid to rest with reverence. Among them were many of the compatriots of our friend George, killed in the battles around the foot of the mountain.

It is said that war is the result of the failure of diplomacy, but I would beg to differ. That war had been caused by the failure of good men to stand in opposition to the rise of madmen, who manipulated people through fear and blame. The specter of war will always lurk beneath a thin veneer of nationalism, and those who would wage it will always be ready to step through any gap we leave them. May such horror never again stalk the face of the earth.

The Deepest Connections

Through all the years of our travels we kept the memory of our friend, George, close at hand. We looked for, and frequently found, the connections between his life and the places we went. We sometimes recognized his features shared by some of the people we met. We also remembered his kindness, his creativity, and his caring for others.

Our friendship with George had been relatively brief, cut short as it was by his passing. Our entire time had been scarcely a handful of his eighty-five-plus years. We felt that we had missed so many stories that he never had time to tell. Yet the memories of what he had done, and the way he had influenced so many people, motivated us to do something more in his honor, something that would serve to recognize and remember him.

At the approach of the twentieth anniversary of our original visit, and that of the seventieth anniversary of the Liberation, we knew that we must return at last to Monghidoro. We knew it would bring back many memories, both sweet and sorrowful. Perhaps most of all we wanted to thank the people of that town for the kindness they had shown George, and by extension ourselves. We also wanted to recognize and thank them for the careful way they continued to preserve and honor the memory of what others had once done for them.

Hoping to locate at least some of the individuals who had been so gracious to us, I found the new website of the Alpini of Monghidoro. I wrote an email telling them of our wish to return and find our former hosts. The response we received was overwhelming. Not only would they assist us in our quest, they would welcome us as guests.

Signor Giovanni Gitti, who served as the contact point for the group, had reached out to his fellows, and to the *commune* of Monghidoro. It was his pleasure, he assured us, to welcome us to Monghidoro.

With high hopes of learning a bit more about our friend and what had happened, we set out to reach the town, perched high upon its mountains. Even today, more than seventy years after the war, Monghidoro is far from the beaten path. It is a refuge from the urban jungle reachable only by steep, twisting roads. To avoid the challenge of navigating through urban traffic en route from Venezia, we bypassed Bologna to follow the *A1 Autostrada* into the Apennines That brought us to the closest exit, which in turn led us onto different mountain roads.

We navigated the switchbacks and curves, basking anew in the beauty of the ever-changing views. After half-an-hour's drive, we turned onto the route marked on our map, only to find that the road was closed. No, not just closed, it was completely gone, carried away down the mountain in a collapse. We back-tracked and tried a different approach, beginning to regret not suffering through Bologna city traffic to take the old road between Bologna and Firenze, known as the *Futa*, which passes through Monghidoro.

We stopped to asked directions, and were assured that once we reached the next valley and crossed the river, we would reach the *Futa* road to the south, which would take us where we needed to go. The washed-out road, they told us, had been closed for about three years. "They have fixed it, but it just falls again. Now they gave up." We were just glad not to have been driving on it when it chose to head downhill.

After another hour of beautiful scenery and twisting navigation we at last sighted a small sign that read "Monghidoro." Underneath, smaller type read "*gia Scaricalasino.*" I didn't remember seeing that before, and couldn't translate it. The sign marked the limits of the *commune.* Just ahead we could see the familiar spire of the new church, a post-war replacement for the shattered original. Once located in the center of the town, George and his compatriots had re-roofed it with army canvas for Christmas services seventy years earlier. Its ruins were later demolished, leaving a trace of the foundations marked in the pavement.

Monghidoro is a tidy collection of upright stone buildings, the tallest only a few stories, and much was still as we had remembered it, but we had little idea how to find *Antica Frontiera*, our reserved bed-and-breakfast. Monghidoro still had a few laughs in store for us. We circled through the main streets twice, stopping to ask directions.

"Turn right, and drive straight ahead, *sempre dritto*, for two kilometers," we were told. "*Guarda per la fontana su la destra*," they added. "Watch for the fountain on the right. Turn there and go down the hill."

"*Guarda per la fontana*." It sounded simple enough until, five or six kilometers from town, we knew we had gone too far. Turning around, we retraced our course, twice. No sign of a fountain. We stopped and asked again, and were again reassured, yes, it's right by the fountain. Back and forth we went. No sign of a fountain, or the turn toward our B&B.

Eventually we spotted a woman placing her recycling into a set of bins near the road.

"*Scusi, Siamo perduti*," I told her. "We're lost. *Puo dirme come trovare l'Antica Frontiera, una B-and-B?*

"*Signor Connors?*" she asked me.

"*Uh, si?*" I replied, flummoxed. How did she know my name based upon that question?

"*Sono Silvana*," she said.

"I'm Robert. I'm pleased to meet you, Silvana," I answered, not yet realizing how pleased.

"Go back that way one hundred meters and turn by the fountain," she told us in Italian, pointing back to a place we had just passed six times. "Turn right and go down the hill to Via Penelope, my husband will be waiting for you."

"Oh! You are the owner of *Antica Frontiera*!" I stammered. A bit of serendipity. "We were just looking for the fountain, and can't find one anywhere!" I told her.

"It's in a little piazza, and there's a phone booth there, too. Go slowly, and turn into the *piazzetta*, then back to the right, a narrow drive between the buildings, and go down the hill."

It sounded so simple! We obediently followed her instructions, having spotted the phone booth, an increasingly rare object in modern Italy. There, next to the phone, was a meter's length of chest-high stone wall, upon which was mounted a small garden spigot. *Eccola!* The fountain!

Minutes later, we discovered that Silvana's smiling husband, Claudio, also spoke English, helping get around the sometimes-confusing details. Explaining our confusion in their pleasant company, we all shared a laugh about the 'fountain.'

"Not exactly like the Trevi fountain, is it?" Claudio observed wryly.

We asked him about the sign we had passed.

"Scaricalasino is the antique name of the town, from hundreds of years ago," he explained, trying to hide a sly grin. "It was then a tiny village on the border, naturally at the top of the pass. People came here to trade, but by the time their heavily-loaded donkeys made it up the mountain, they were exhausted, so they put up a sign that said *Scarica l'asino*. It means 'Unload the ass.'"

Whoever said that history was a dry subject hadn't spent much time with it.

They had named their B&B *Antica Frontiera* from the same history. It means 'antique frontier,' and refers to the fact that Monghidoro had stood on that old border between Firenze and Bologna long before Italy was united as a single country. Goods were taxed, often on both sides of the border. Today that line is marked by the division between the *Regione di Toscana* and that of *Emilia Romagna*. Only a pleasant walk separated our temporary residence from Tuscany, just over the rise.

Silvana and Claudio, we learned, were dedicated history buffs. Claudio is also a philatelist, and maintains a vast store of historic postage stamps online. He was a fountain of information. We talked about our reasons for returning to Monghidoro, and what we knew about our friend George and his unit. Claudio proved enormously helpful, and offered to show us where to find information about the Blue Devils.

He kindly drove the four of us on a twisting, scenic route across some of the region's most unique geology to the town of Castel del Rio. There we found significant surprises. The first was the *Ponte Alidoso*, a graceful forty-two-meter-long arch of stone that rises nineteen meters high above the *Fiume Santerno*, another scene of heavy fighting on the Gothic Line. The old stone bridge remained standing through the battle, and carries pedestrians over the waters of the Santerno on its high arch. At one time, it served traders and their mules and ox carts, and locals sometimes refer to the elegant arch at the *schiena d'asino*, or the donkey's back.

Like the rest of Italy, Castel del Rio was in the midst of remembering and celebrating the Liberation seventy years earlier. The residents of the area were very supportive of the partisans during the war, and are proud of the wonderful museum that marks the center of the village. It fills the squarish bulk of the namesake castle that the Alidosi family once called home, having derived their revenue in part from tolls on the bridge traffic.

Today the museum is marked by a WWII American fighter plane parked on the lawn, and an excellent assemblage of war memorabilia, uniforms, and weapons. A large relief map of the mountains makes it possible to trace the routes of battle through the rugged terrain, and a video tells the story of the battles that occurred in the area during that brutal winter of 1944-45.

We took particular interest in one room of the museum. There above the door was the familiar blue clover-leaf device of the 88th Infantry, and a sign that proclaimed it to be the "Blue Devils Inn." The room is a cornucopia of artifacts from George's division, and brought to life still more of the events that his unit endured. Battered helmets, tattered uniforms, and well-used rifles were among the items displayed. In the main room of the museum's second level we found an original U.S. Army jeep with the Blue Devils' insignia still wired to the grill.

We lingered in the town to have a late lunch, chatting with some of the locals, and were welcomed, both as visitors, and especially as Americans. It was a day when the service of the liberators was on many minds. Our return journey to Monghidoro carried us through deep canyons while terrific thunderstorms raged, the flash of lightning and the crash of thunder like echoes of that long-ago war. It was an altogether memorable day.

To show us still more history of the war, Silvana and Claudio invited us to travel with them on another day to a private museum a few dozen kilometers north. We followed the twisting, legendary road known as the *Futa* through hamlets and villages. It was the *Futa*, then a narrow mud and gravel road, that had carried most of the traffic for both the retreating German army and the advancing American one. Once little more than a mule trail, the Germans had used it heavily in fortifying their positions. Since the war, it has become a paved but still twisting thoroughfare.

We traveled through steep forests past several small towns, arriving at last in Livergnano. Here the rugged countryside was dominated by enormous teeth of bare rock that the earth had flung skyward, reaching upwards a hundred meters or so. Perhaps they were the result of some prehistoric upheaval, or perhaps only the bare bones of ancient mountains. This was the backstop of the Germans' second "Winter Line."

As their last hope of stopping Allied tanks and trucks before they could swarm into the broad Po Valley, the Germans had equipped the rocks, peaks, and passes with snipers, machine guns, Panzerfaust tank killers, mortar teams, and artillery. The rocks were so vertical as to provide an almost insuperable obstacle before an attacking army, which would find itself funneled into the narrow gaps where the German guns were trained.

Although other American forces were already fighting on German soil as the Third Reich collapsed, the battle for northern Italy would be decided in Italy in these waning days of the war. Mark Clark and other Allied commanders were determined to share in the victory they knew was fast approaching. The 88th was holding the center of the Allied line, which stretched across the peninsula. The line had to move forward. There would be no respite.

The hardened survivors of the long drive up the peninsula would have to sacrifice much to overcome this final barrier. Beyond these last obstacles, they would drive the German army from the mountains, and have the supreme advantage in the plains beyond. Bologna lay only twenty-three kilometers away. Beyond, the cities of Padova, Venezia, Milano and Torino would lie defenseless, with sympathetic populations waiting to throw off the yoke of Fascist terror and oppression. The German Army would have to flee the industrial heartland, and attempt to escape northward toward their homeland. The Blue Devils and all the Allied forces knew what was at stake: beat the Nazis to the northern passes, close the bottle necks, and they could trap them all. But first, they had to break their final defensive line.

In that evocative place today stands The Winter Line Museum. At Claudio's request, the owner of that private establishment had consented to open it on a Sunday so that we, his American guests, could view it. We met Umberto Magnani at the door. The artifacts we would see, he explained, were his personal collection of war memorabilia. During hikes in the woods as a youth in the years following the war, he had begun finding and collecting thousands of objects, cast aside or lost by the soldiers of both sides. There were even whole tanks, he told us, but those had been removed by the government. He never bought anything, he added, but people often came to give him things. Many were donated by American veterans, who returned to the scene of the fighting years later to honor their lost friends, and try to absorb the enormity of what they had done.

Two cave-like rooms penetrated the rock of the mountain itself, and were filled with every imaginable artifact. Several uniforms were displayed, some equipped with belts, canteens, shell pouches, the tiny details of daily life for the troops. Personal notes and letters were displayed among ammunition boxes and shell casings, pistols, mortar stands and helmets, portable radios and bayonets. Spools of telephone cable and boxes once containing hand-grenades (with printed warnings not to store over 120°F.) bore stacks of American military posters, along with 'safe conduct' fliers once dropped from planes upon the German positions. The latter featured phonetic pronunciations of English phrases: "Ei Sorrender!" one read. The effect was to bring the war, and the events that had occurred just outside the door, to vivid reality.

Scattered photos of the gun emplacements, the burned buildings, and the bodies of fallen soldiers hung between large, heavily-creased maps used by the military forces. A table full of books, in Italian, English, Polish, French, and German, recounted the stories and events, and contained many thousands more photographs. They showed men loaded with weaponry, crouched behind walls and buildings, dashing across streets past the burned shells of houses. We recognized many of the settings, including the vertical cliff just above our heads, and the enormous monolithic rock that dominated the town. Each detail helped us more clearly fathom the hardships endured by the soldiers and citizens in these hard mountain towns, on this, the "Forgotten Front."

One display brought to life the humanity and dark humor of troops during their rare breaks from the front lines. There stood a tent with a tattered door of canvas strips tacked between two wooden posts. Upon it was painted, in clear block letters, "my room." The other half of the door read "Hotel Atoll," perhaps in recognition of the word newly-familiar, due to the concurrent war in the far Pacific islands. Below the name itself, the soldier had painted a list of the comforts of his "Hotel Atoll: No beer - Atoll, No women - Atoll, No nothin' - Atoll."

Our education about the war in Italy had expanded, and we grew steadily more impressed at what George DeLuca's 88th Division and 351st Regiment had accomplished. They had been in the thick of much of the fighting, spending 344 days in combat. In the process, George's unit earned 3,784 Bronze Stars, 522 Silver Stars, sixty-six Legions of Merit, two Distinguished Service medals, forty Distinguished Service Crosses, and three Medals of Honor, along with two Unit Citations for action at Mt. Battaglia and Mt. Cappello. We had walked with a hero.

We returned with Claudio and Silvana to our B&B, and Susan and I were soon back in our own car, our determination to learn more whetted. We began driving slowly along the quiet road back to the town, looking for the vaguely-familiar locations where we had walked, stood, and prayed so many years before. We were back on sacred ground.

Less than a kilometer up the road from our apartment we recognized the large furniture store with the name, Montanari, emblazoned across the front. It was there, twenty years earlier, that we had spent our first rainy night in Monghidoro, thanks to the hospitality of the master of the house. We didn't even recall his first name, but we spotted an elderly man sitting in a chair in front of the building.

"That's him!" I said to Susan.

"Are you sure?" she asked, and I admitted that I wasn't, but was going to find out. I quickly turned into the parking lot of the building, exited our car, and approached. He was sitting with a young boy, perhaps a grandchild, or even a great-grandchild.

"*Signor Montanari?*" I asked.

"*Si?*"

"*Sono Robert Connors, un amico di George Fortunata DeLuca,*" I said. "We stayed here in your home, twenty years ago."

He smiled as I continued, explaining that we had returned, in part, to thank him for his kindness to us so many years before.

"*Era niente,*" he said. It was nothing. He paused a long moment, then turned back to me. "He's dead now, isn't he?"

"Yes, I'm sorry, he passed away a few years ago. He was a good man. I'm glad he was here to help so many people."

"So few of them left now, seventy years after..." he said.

Another silent moment passed, both of us lost in very different memories. But there was something more I wanted to tell him.

"*Signore,*" I continued, "When I ask people why George was considered a hero, why they made him an honorary citizen, why they called him "The Mayor," I get lots of different answers. Everyone seems to know a bit about something he did. But when I asked George years ago, he told me a story about how a father had asked for his help to save his son, a small boy, sick, starving, and freezing in a mountain cave, and how he bent the rules to get him food and medicine from Army sources..."

"I was that boy," he replied slowly, turning to look at me. "He saved my life."

"I thought it was you, but I was never certain," I said.

"He eventually arranged for me to be moved to the field hospital near Firenze. When I got well I was sent to live with relatives. I didn't come back to Monghidoro for two years. He was gone."

We regarded each other solemnly for a long moment. At last he broke a hint of a smile. "I have something to give you," he said. "Come inside please." He stood, his large frame considerably leaner than I had remembered him.

We walked into the vaguely familiar expanse of his furniture store.

Memories came flooding back of that rainy night twenty years earlier. Our party had been scattered among friends, and Susan and I had spent the night here. I remembered George speaking animatedly to Signor Montanari as we unloaded our luggage.

We walked across to an office, where he reached up to a shelf and withdrew a copy of a large book. The title, "*Voci e Volti,*" was printed across the bottom of the dust jacket. "Voices and Faces," it said. The remainder of the cover featured small reproductions of a pair of creased and faded photographs: a man in uniform, a woman in a peasant shirt. Scattered between the photos were a collage of stamps and signatures reproduced from passports and official documents, and the words of social division: *Antifascisti; Partigiano; Socialisti.* Anti-fascists, partisan, socialists. These were the words used by Nazi SS officers to condemn men and women to prison, or death.

Then he opened the book and leafed through a series of photos and the stories of more than a hundred people, recollections of the events of the war, the hardships, the pain, the loss of family and friends. He turned a few pages and there appeared his own photo. There was his face, his eyes exhibiting the same far-away look I had seen a few moments earlier. Next to the photo was his story, told in detail. His were only a few of many hard memories shared by survivors of those rough, dark years.

"*Questo e per te,*" he said, holding the book toward me. This is for you.

"But this is yours!" I protested.

"I can get another. Please keep it. Will you join us for dinner tomorrow night?"

"We would be honored, I'm sure. Yes, thank you very much."

We exchanged phone numbers, and promised to call. "Goodnight, then, Signore. *A domani.*" Until tomorrow.

•

During the many long conversations that marked our time in Monghidoro we learned just how difficult life under Nazi-Fascists had been. The day before the arrival of the Americans, as the Nazis prepared to fall back to yet another line of prepared fortifications farther north, they performed their darkest deeds around Monghidoro.

Arriving in the night, soldiers led by Fascist collaborators had rounded up groups of men for brutal interrogations. Families were terrorized, and many were forced from their burning homes into the freezing night without food, water, or clothing. On that first day of October, dozens of people were simply executed, led to their deaths by platoons of soldiers.

Fanatic Nazi SS troops had slaughtered entire villages in nearby Tuscany, simply rounding up the population in house-by-house sweeps before machine-gunning them. Bodies were left where they fell. Small monuments scattered across the district mark where they fell. It was only later that people arrived from neighboring villages to find and bury them.

It is hard to grasp the depth of emotion that still runs through the Italian people over the events of the war. They have not forgotten, and still strive to teach their children, to keep alive the memories of the horrors, and their joy and gratitude for their liberators. At one of the memorial services we stood in front of a low wall with a modest marker as moving speeches were made. There, it was said, four men had been executed by the Nazis.

"*Fucilata*," shot, one priest said.

"They weren't shot, actually," a friend told us afterward.

"No?" I questioned.

"No," he confirmed. "The Nazis didn't want to waste the ammunition. They used machetes and bayonets to slaughter them."

It was no wonder that the events of the war made such a deep, lingering impact on Italy. Yet I wondered: "How did these people remain so warm and open after such horrors were visited upon their society, their communities?

•

Arriving at the *municipio* on Friday afternoon, we were ushered into the offices of the gracious Mayor Alessandro Ronny Ferretti, where we were also introduced to the charming vice-mayor, Morena Baldini. They set aside their busy duties to spend a delightful half-hour with us. There we shared photos of our prior visit as they identified many of the participants.

We were saddened to learn that Mayor Arnaldo Naldi, who had greeted us in 1995, had passed away. We were presented with a copy of a beautiful biography entitled *"Arnaldo Naldi, Un Sindaco di Razza,"* written by Renato Tattini. Italian hospitality seemed to have no bounds. Then we were further surprised to be presented with a copy of an official poster created by the *Commune di Monghidoro* which announced several events in recognition of our return visit. It was then that we learned that Signor Gitti had arranged a program that included ceremonies at the *municipio*, or city hall, with the mayor on Saturday evening and further ceremonies on Sunday. They had rolled out an unexpected red carpet.

Afterwards a group of Alpini led us to a bar, where we shared local beers and poured over photographs. One showed an American tank parked at the door of the building we sat in.

Saturday afternoon we returned to the *municipio* and assembled with a small crowd to watch a display of projected photographs of the war presented by Signor Gitti, who was himself an Alpini war veteran. He shared and narrated a hundred photos clearly displaying the destruction that had been suffered in Monghidoro. The town had been reduced to rubble, and was described as a *macelleria*, a butcher's shop. The burned hulks of buildings lined the streets, deep snow piled about. American soldiers hunkered over flaming barrels for warmth, while Alpini troops led files of mules laden with ammunition through the town's main street. Children huddled, shell-shocked faces peering from the doorways of roofless houses. It was a sobering reminder of the horrors of war.

Afterwards, our hosts again surprised us. They called us from the audience and presented us with official gifts, including a dense book about Monghidoro's history, which Mayor Ferretti suggested, to much laughter, would be useful if I wished to continue my studies in Italian. I in turn gave him an official letter of greeting from Mayor Eugene Fultz of our own City of Lake Wales, along with letters of greeting and thanks from other Florida officials. Then they stunned us by presenting us with a beautifully-engraved, brushed-metal *targa*, or plaque, featuring the Medieval heraldry of the town.

Translated, the inscription reads:

"Plaque of remembrance presented to our American Friends
In Memory of our honorary citizen
George Fortunata DeLuca
Official of the American Forces of the ranks of the glorious 'Blue Devils,'
the 88th Division Infantry, for his shining example, military and civil,
in favor of the population of Monghidoro
during the events of war from 1944 to 1945."

It was set upon a blue velvet mount. Blue, the color of loyalty. The color of his division. It was a moving moment. Our thoughts flew to the many who served, those who perished, and those who persevered through the terrible carnage and conditions. It falls to us to remember their contributions, and honor their service.

Afterward, we stood on the roof of the building with Mayor Ferretti in the late afternoon chill as banks of clouds swept overhead, and shafts of sunlight played upon the surrounding mountains. He pointed out the jagged peaks we had visited across the valley to the north. There the German Army had fallen back to their formidable Winter Line, from which they continued to shell the slowly advancing Allied forces. Entrenched machine guns, fields of land mines, and many other dangers had stood before the advancing Blue Devils, yet they had doggedly pressed on, driving the Nazis farther from this town, and a thousand others.

We pondered the terrible price, the heavy casualties, suffered by the

American forces in assaulting that line in the spring of 1945. Few remained who could recall the events from their own memory, but they were forever chiseled onto the soul of this mountain town.

The sun glinted off far peaks, and dashed to illuminate the green slopes. We posed for photos, and sucked in great lungsful of the fresh mountain air, dispelling darker thoughts in favor of life renewed and sustained.

•

For two days we were hosted as ambassadors. We dined in the home of the mayor, which commanded a spectacular view of the mountain valley that formed a northern approach to the town, the sort of place the town must have long posted a watchman. Broad swaths of green meadows fell steeply toward a wooded stream. The following evening, we enjoyed yet another feast at a crowded church hall with our hosts, the Montanari family, Claudio and Silvana, and a number of other friends, both old and new. It was true Italian hospitality, and we were immersed in a sea of warmth.

As the dinner wound down, musicians began playing tunes in the courtyard outside the door, and soon dozens of friends and neighbors joined in the local tradition of round dances, which featured intricate steps that failed to baffle even the oldest citizens. Children, we were told, learned these steps in school. Another gentleman explained that the origins of the dances were from many cultures, learned as pilgrims had passed through the village in past centuries, on their way to Rome. "Some of them are Celtic," he told us, and from the rhythm and the flavor of the tunes, it was clear that both music and the dances were closely related to the jigs and reels of far-away Ireland. The world seemed to be shrinking.

•

The next morning at the *Municipio* we were greeted by a small crowd led by a dozen smiling Alpini in their smart, feathered caps. They bore flags and banners, and after a round of warm hugs and handshakes, they quickly organized a procession. Our thoughts went back to the similar events of 1995. Our parade was led by Mayor Ferretti, who insisted that we walk at his side. Susan was given the honor of bearing a large spray of flowers, and together we marched down the main street of the town. Traffic stopped and citizens watched our informal parade. We paused at a monument commemorating twenty-four individuals executed by the Nazis between the 11th of August and the 2nd of October, 1944 in Monghidoro and surrounding villages.

We passed down several blocks before arriving at *l'incrocio*, the principal intersection of the town. There at the entrance to the city stands the *cippo*, where an American flag is permanently displayed, alongside those of Italy and the European Union. An inscription on the large, rough-stone monument reads "To remember the Liberation which occurred October 2, 1944." Above, set into glazed tiles, were two photographs featuring American soldiers.

In the first a soldier in winter battle gear is seen unveiling a sign, posted upon that very spot, marking the area as "city limits, Los Angeles, Italian sector." An unidentified officer looks on, smiling.

In the second photograph is seen General Mark Clark, commander of the Fifth Army, sitting in a jeep accompanied by the American actress, Clair Luce Booth. Of Italian descent, she had come to the front to boost the morale of the soldiers fighting to liberate the nation. She was later to become the United States Ambassador to Italy.

The stone had been raised by the townspeople of Monghidoro in recognition of their liberators generations before, and remains a prominent reminder of the sacrifices of the U.S. Army. The cadre of Alpini veterans stood at attention as the national anthems of Italy and the United States were played, their lined faced evidence of the long service they had rendered, and the memories of those they had served with.

After brief remarks by Mayor Ferretti and a moment of silence in honor of the fallen, Susan placed the flowers at the foot of the monument. There they remained days later, still fresh in the chill and fog.

•

It is said that the creases of an old face are the work of the joy and pain that has passed over it and remain held in memory. If this is true, then I have seen upon the faces of others the deepest of both.

Memories are very personal things, and impossible to fully share. Most often they are of places or events which changed our lives. These things tend to make a deeper impression upon our psyches than the mundane, the ordinary ebb and flow of our days. We may spend a thousand days in a single schoolhouse, and recall only the days upon which we were bullied, or tested, or fell in love. Regrets of deeds done or left undone, love or loved ones lost, still have power years later. Important things leave deep impressions. Only by these can we know what, and who, we truly love.

My earliest memories, like those of many others, begin from infancy. I can recall the day when, yet unable to walk, I crawled into the dust of broken plaster to gape in awe at the hole which had resulted from the noisy banging of hammers upon the wall, which had formed the edge of my world. Until that moment I was sure that's what a wall represented: the solid, immovable surface of immensity, the edge of the universe. Wonder of wonders, it wasn't. It was but a thin barrier to new worlds. Swept away from danger and dust, I was left in my crib to ponder the new rules of the universe, and the shape and limits of my own secure room.

Throughout our lives, many memories are made of such events. They are times when walls fall, when the rules are bent, when limits are broken. They are times when our world, and ourselves, are somehow changed.

We remain malleable even in our adulthood, but often such moments of change are resisted by the increasing calcification of our attitudes, by the hardening of the flexible cartilage of our openness into the rigid bone of prejudice. It is only we who can prevent this ossification, to keep ourselves bendable, and not breakable. Our lives' experiences help us in this effort, keeping our souls and spirits from premature aging and death. It is up to each of us to seek out those things which challenge our beliefs, our norms, our prejudices, so that we can continue to grow, to learn, and to truly live. Each such change is a small victory, and most often leaves behind a memory of the event that created it.

Love grows not just from shared joys and similarities, but springs from deep roots and channels through the darkest days of shared challenges. Facing the world together, come what may, pulls us closer to each other. These are things known well to those who served, who survived, the terrors of war. The bonds between soldiers are stronger, perhaps, than any others.

•

We returned on Sunday afternoon with our hosts, Silvana and

Claudio, to the *Baita degli Alpini* for the final chapter of the official remembrance. There a crowd had gathered to participate in yet another ceremony, which to our satisfaction also included yet another delicious multi-course luncheon. Italians seemed intent on fattening us up, even though they never seemed to gain an ounce.

We wandered through the *museo* of war memorabilia that the Alpini had gathered on the lower level. There we spoke with Signor Raffale Rossetti, one of the last of the veterans who had served in the war, still vigorous at ninety-three years of age. He posed beside a photo showing him as a young *Alpino*, standing with two compatriots, looking serious in his long coat and feathered cap.

We spent time again touching the dusty uniforms, the old leather saddle which a mule had carried, the photographs of American patrols, soup kitchens, field hospitals, and the ruins of Monghidoro. Other photos of veterans were displayed around the room, often with the caption: *"Andata avanti."* Gone ahead.

After addresses by Mayor Ferretti and comments by a local historian, I had an opportunity to present letters of greeting from our hometown veterans of the American Legion and Veterans of Foreign Wars to the *Alpini di Monghidoro*. As Mayor Ferretti kindly held the microphone for me, I had an opportunity to share an American perspective.

After thanking them for all they had done for us, I turned to the memories they keep alive. "George DeLuca was a man who gave a great deal of himself to others," I said, "as a teacher, as a soldier, and as a friend. A life well-lived echoes like a bell through the following generations. We were honored to be here with him and the people of Monghidoro to celebrate the Liberation which he and his compatriots helped to bring about. The men of the Alpini of Sulmona, the men of the 88th Division, and millions of others were part of what we must call "the Greatest Generation. George had an ardent desire to liberate the land of his patrimony from the Nazi-Fascists."

How could I explain to these people that Americans have little grasp of the horrors they had endured? That people who have never experienced was can never share the emotions they attach to their liberation? I had to try...

"The men of the 88th Division, the Blue Devils, came from cities and towns where peace was all around," I told them. "Far from the war, their families were safe and secure. Yet they left them to come here, and to North Africa, and France, and the Philippines, and China, and to Germany itself, to liberate others that they did not know."

"They were changed in many ways; some good, others not. Yet their families did not share the same experiences, because they didn't see, with their own eyes, the horrors of war. The men who returned spoke little of what they had seen. They suffered in order that we, their children and grandchildren, could live in liberty.

"Today in America, far too few understand or remember what they did. It is good to know that here, nothing is forgotten. It is good also perhaps for you to know that, notwithstanding the passing of the American veterans, a few of us there also remember. For every kindness you have shown, and for everything you have done in their honor, we say thank you."

Afterword

We had spent twenty years in our explorations of Italy, crossing to and fro across the peninsula, visiting and revisiting both people and places. It would be impossible to include every adventure, beautiful place, or kind person we met. Sicily, Corsica, and the other islands of the Italian archipelago are not included in this volume. Such is the richness of Italy that they would require their own.

The world had changed since our first trip to Italy in 1995, and for our purposes perhaps the greatest change was the development of the Internet, which eased travel, and offered us a wealth of information. During my research for this volume, I read many of the accounts of the Alpini of Monghidoro, which are available, thanks primarily to the diligence of the late Signor Giovanni Gitti. I had been pleased to locate the website, and be able to explore their large library of photographs of the events of the war.

The stories posted there had been written by the Alpini, brave men who had served in those terrible years, and were willing to commit their memories to paper before they would be lost to the world. Each story was a glimpse into a time that has passed away, and some seemed to travel gingerly above the powerful currents that no doubt lay just beneath the surface. While some are filled with emotion, others are told with almost emotionless recall, as if from a life once dreamed. Cold and hunger, the sudden death of friends and family, terrible wounds, and a scarcity of hope rose vividly from their stories.

One story that particularly moved me recalled the surge of joy that had passed through the despairing people of Monghidoro on the day of their liberation. Weeks of shelling and frontal attacks by the Allied forces had finally driven the German Army back. Monghidoro was vacated.

As the first soldiers of the U.S. Army began to wind their way cautiously up the muddy track that led from the south, slogging on foot or in jeeps, it was the second day of October, 1944. Wearing the blue clover-leaf shoulder patches of their division, the Blue Devils who climbed that hill were themselves a haggard lot: muddy, unshaven, and exhausted. Our friend George had no doubt been among them. To the citizens of Monghidoro, the writer recalled, they were as beautiful as angels. It was then that they first heard the longed-for words spoken in Monghidoro. *"Arrivano gli Americani!"* The Americans are arriving!

The troops met the townspeople, and were soon passing out luxuries unseen in many months. Fresh fruit, chocolate, real coffee, and medicines appeared. It was liberation from hunger, liberation from war, liberation from fear. It was, for them and many others in Italy, the end of a long nightmare.

The story assured us that *"Ancora ai giorni nostri a Monghidoro, quando c'è un evento di una certa grandezza si dice..."* Translated, it says that "Still in our day, we of Monghidoro, whenever there is a great event, say: *"Sono arrivati gli americani."* 'The Americans have arrived.'

Life had changed for the better.

About the Author

Robert James Connors was born in Chicago, Illinois, eldest son of a bank auditor. He began work as a newspaper carrier at age eleven and joined his school newspaper in high school, where he displayed his passion for the written word. He was hired as a full-time news reporter before his graduation. An award-winning writer and journalist, he is author of more than 1,000 human-interest stories, features, and commentaries. He is a contributor to publications covering topics ranging from environment to politics, classical music to history. He is presently writing a novelized history of Florida, expected to publish in late 2018.

Connors is an experienced public speaker, a former Polk County, Florida, County Commissioner, and has served as an invited guest speaker (in both English and Italian) at military commemorative events in Italy, recognizing the service of American veterans of World War Two in the Liberation of Italy from the Nazi/Fascists.

When not traveling, he resides with his wife, Susan, in Lake Wales, Florida.